# THE
# *ROBIN WILLIAMS*
# SCRAPBOOK

Stephen J. Spignesi

A CITADEL PRESS BOOK
PUBLISHED BY CAROL PUBLISHING GROUP

A Citadel Press Book
Published by Carol Publishing Group
Citadel Press is a registered trademark of Carol Communica-
tions, Inc.

Editorial, sales and distribution, and rights and permissions
inquiries should be addressed to Carol Publishing Group, 120
Enterprise Avenue, Secaucus, N.J. 07094.

In Canada: Canadian Manda Group, One Atlantic Avenue,
Suite 105, Toronto, Ontario M6K 3E7

Carol Publishing Group books may be purchased in bulk at
special discounts for sales promotion, fund-raising, or educa-
tional purposes. Special editions can be created to specifica-
tions. For details, contact Special Sales Department, Carol
Publishing Group, 120 Enterprise Avenue, Secaucus, N.J.
07094.

Designed by Andrew B. Gardner

Manufactured in the United States of America

10 9 8 7 6 5 4 3 2 1

Library of Congress Cataloging-in-Publication Data

Spignesi, Stephen J.
    The Robin Williams scrapbook / Stephen Spignesi.
       p.    cm.
    "A Citadel Press book."
    Videography: p.
    ISBN 0-8065-1891-X
    1. Williams, Robin, 1952 July 21-   2. Comedians—United
States-
       -Biography.    I. Title.
    PN2287.W473S65   1997
791.43'028'092—dc21
[b]                                                  97-8682
                                                        CIP

*For Tom Schultheiss,*
*who could use a laugh*

# Acknowledgments

I would like to thank Jim Cole; Barry Friedman and Dan Holzman of the Raspyni Brothers; Ron Mandelbaum, Howard Mandelbaum, and the staff of Photofest; Mike Lewis; Steven Schragis; John White; George Beahm; Susan Sullivan; James Waite; Lee Mandato; Frank Mandato; the staff of the University of New Haven Library; and the staff of the Hagaman Library in East Haven, CT.

# Contents

# THE ROBIN WILLIAMS SCRAPBOOK

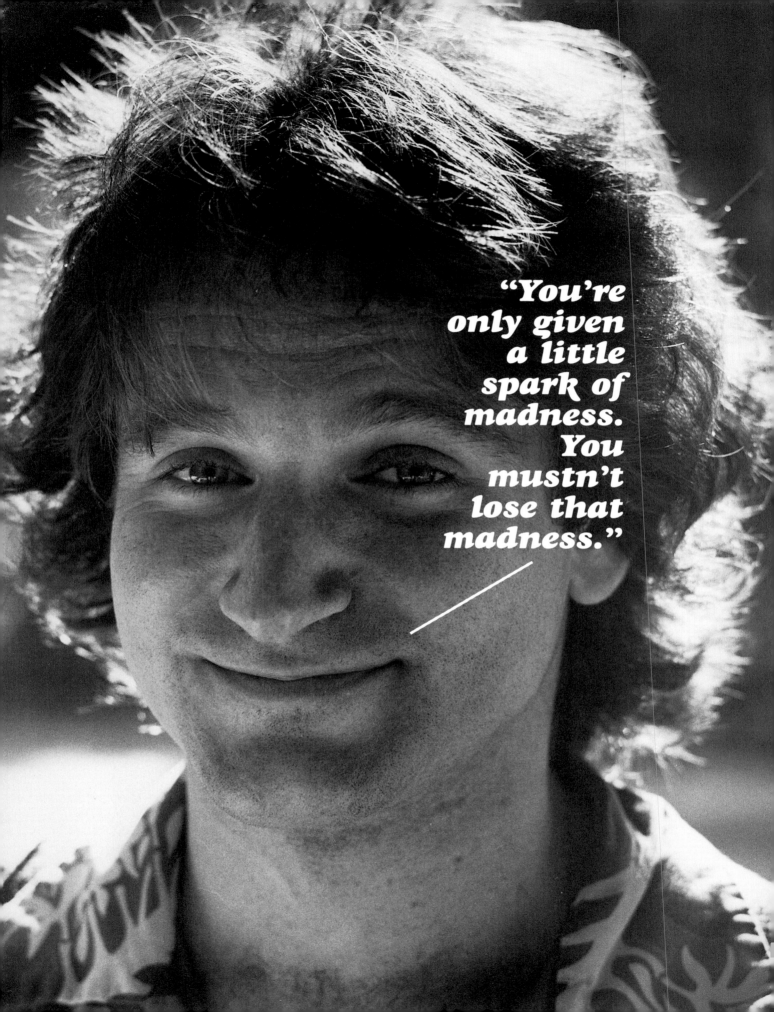

# Introduction:
# Legalized Insanity

*"Performing and acting? One is hang gliding, the other oil drilling. With live comedy, the total freedom you have, to go from the Ottoman Empire to Madonna, is incredible. With acting, you have certain constraints. What do I like more? Sure, I like performing full out."*

— *New York Times*, May 28, 1989

The title of this Introduction comes from Robin's oft-repeated use of the phrase "legalized insanity" (*most recently in an interview on E!'s "The Hot Spot" site on the Internet*) *to describe what he does for a living. After you read* The Robin Williams Scrapbook, *I think you'll agree he's got a point.*

I have always found the dry recounting of the biographical details of an artist's life boring.

I truly believe that we can most appreciate genius in all its forms through an artist's lifetime body of work.

The fact that a writer or an actor or a musician went to high school in some small burg in the Midwest is nowhere near as interesting as their first published work or first TV or movie appearance.

David Letterman went to high school in Indiana and worked as a grocery bagger in his teens. So what? Isn't it more interesting to learn that Letterman got fired from one of his early broadcasting jobs as a weatherman for telling his audience that they could expect "hail the size of canned hams"? *This* bit of information sheds a whole new light on Dave's ongoing passion for handing out canned hams every night to members of his *Late Show* studio audience. Once we know about the ham incident from the early days of his career, we can recognize the canned ham giveaway for what it really is: Dave thumbing his nose at his early bosses (and also *rubbing* their noses in his phenomenal success). This is revealing and, ultimately, more entertaining.

Therefore, I believe that the dry, biographical details of Robin Williams's life are not anywhere near as important as his body of work.

Robin's career choices (so far) reveal him as one of the twentieth century's funniest artistic geniuses (even though he cringes when people use the word "genius" to describe him). But to keep the purists happy, here is a brief biography of Robin (with a few pithy comments by Williams himself from his October 1982 interview in *Playboy*).

Robin Williams was born in Chicago on Monday, July 21, 1952. He went to elementary school in Lake Forest, Illinois, and to a private day school in Birmingham, Michigan. When his father retired from Ford Motor Company, the family moved to Tiburon, California, north of San Francisco. Robin graduated from Redwood High School in Marin County in 1969.

> All my friends were Jewish, which is why I know so much Yiddish. I went to 14 bar mitzvahs in less than a year, and it was great. My friends made me an honorary Jew and used to tell people I went to services at Temple Beth Dublin.

Robin briefly attended Claremont Men's College and College of Marin while trying out his licks in comedy clubs around Los Angeles and San Francisco.

> I played a lot of tiny clubs, like the Holy City Zoo in San Francisco—I met Valerie there [who became his wife]— and the Salamander in Berkeley.

*Mr. Happy himself. (Photofest)*

3

*Mork and Mindy share a weiner. That's all we'll say about this photo. (Photofest)*

This period served as a time of learning and comedy experimentation for Robin:

> In the beginning, you find yourself doing a lot of drug humor, and when you can't be funny, you can get some laughs by saying "motherfucker" a lot. One of the initial reviews I got tore me up, because it said I was a "scatological pubescent," and that was true. It hit me right on the nose! In the beginning, you're also imitating everybody you've ever seen—for me, it was touches of Winters and Pryor. But all of a sudden, you get to a point where you go, 'Ah, I can be me. I can develop my own stuff.

Robin eventually moved to New York:

> I got there in September of '73; one of the first things I learned was the Brooklyn alphabet: fuckin' A, fuckin' B, fuckin' C. . . . I was the walking epitome of furshirr meets yo' ass. . . . My first week there, I was in a bus going uptown to see an apartment when an old man

two seats in front of me suddenly collapsed and died. He slumped over against a woman sitting next to him, and she said, "Get off me!" and moved away. Somebody told the driver what had happened, so he stopped the bus and ordered everybody off, but I wanted to stay and help. The driver told me, "He's dead, motherfucker, now get off! You can't do shit for him, so take your raggedy California ass and get outta my bus!" I knew that living in New York was certainly going to be different.

Robin studied at the Julliard School of Music—a renowned New York institution that teaches budding performers all facets of the musical performing arts—for three years. At Julliard, John Houseman was one of Robin's instructors and Christopher Reeve one of his classmates:

> Me and Chris Reeve had come in together as advanced students—Chris had gone to Cornell—and we had to catch up to the other students who'd been at Julliard for a year. Chris lived

about five blocks away, and we used to go up to the roof of his apartment building and drink cheap wine and talk about present and lost loves. Except for my friendship with brother Reeve, that first year was rough, especially at Christmastime. . . . When I came back to Julliard . . . [the following] fall, Chris had left to do a soap opera.

Robin has remained very close with Christopher Reeve and provided emotional (and possibly monetary) support for him and his family after Reeve's tragic equestrian accident in 1995 that left him paralyzed from the neck down. In a scene that had to be reminiscent of the obstetric examination scene in *Nine Months*, Robin reportedly visited Chris at the rehab center where he was staying after the accident. Robin pretended to be a Russian doctor who presumably wanted to do unspeakable things to Reeve. Apparently, Reeve ended up in hysterics over this warmhearted, impromptu performance.

Shortly after Julliard, Robin auditioned for *Mork and Mindy* in 1977 and the rest is history.

As to Robin's personal life, he married Valerie Velardi on June 4, 1978 and they had one son, Zachary. They divorced ten years later and on April 30, 1989, Robin wed Marsha Garces, with whom he has two children, Zelda and Cody.

Here is a brief look at the many accolades that have been heaped upon Robin during his career:

■ Robin has appeared on the cover of *Rolling Stone* magazine seven times: once in 1979; twice in 1982; once in 1983; twice in 1988; and once in 1991.

Robin has received . . .

*Robin as Jack. (Photofest)*

- an Emmy nomination for his guest appearance in 1994 on *Homicide*
- a People's Choice Award for *Mork and Mindy*
- a Grammy Award for *Robin Williams: An Evening at the Met*
- a CableAce Award for hosting *Shakespeare: The Animated Tales* on HBO (Robin appeared as on-camera host for this series)

*Robin as Mrs. Doubtfire. (Photofest)*

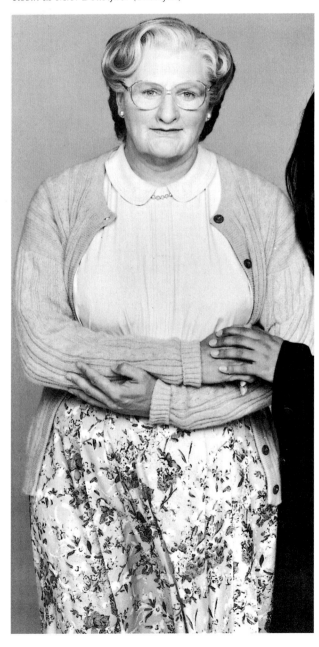

- a Golden Globe Award and an Academy Award nomination for Best Actor for *Good Morning, Vietnam*
- a Golden Globe nomination and an Academy Award nomination for Best Actor for *Dead Poets Society*
- a Golden Globe Award and an Academy Award nomination for Best Actor for *The Fisher King*
- a Special Achievement Award from the Hollywood Foreign Press, National Board of Review for his work in *Aladdin*
- a Golden Globe Award and a People's Choice Award for Best Actor for *Mrs. Doubtfire*
- a Grammy Award for his album, *Reality . . . What a Concept*
- an Emmy Award for *ABC Presents a Royal Gala*
- an Emmy Award for *Carol, Carl, Whoopi, and Robin* (This was a variety special starring Carol Burnett, Carl Reiner, Whoopi Goldberg, and Robin)
- a Golden Apple Award from the Hollywood Women's Press Club

Also, Robin was . . .

- voted *E! Entertainment Television's* "Entertainer of the Year" for 1996
- named Video Man of the Year at the Video Software Dealers Association's 1996 Home Entertainment Awards ceremony for being in more $100 million grossing films than any other actor
- ranked as the 33rd Most Powerful Person in Hollywood by *Entertainment Weekly* for 1996
- ranked as one of *Entertainment Weekly's* "100 Greatest Movie Stars of All Time" in 1996
- and perhaps his greatest honor, in 1997, Robin was ranked as The Funniest Person Alive by the editors of *Entertainment Weekly* magazine

Robin Williams truly loves his work. He has been very productive and very successful.

*The Robin Williams Scrapbook* will take you on

*He can always make us smile. Do you think the shirt helps? (Photofest)*

a guided tour—in words and pictures—through the many facets of Robin's life and career. Most of the important milestones—concert performances, TV appearances, and, of course, movies—are covered in detail.

So, na-noo, na-noo, and let the laughter begin!

**Playboy:**
What's the difference between a Michigan girl and a California girl?

**Robin Williams:**
A handgun.

**"When in doubt, go for the dick joke."**

—Robin Williams's
Philosophy of Humor

*How do you get to the Met? "Money." (Photofest)*

# Chapter 1

# Robin Williams Onstage

"God gives you a penis and a brain and only enough blood to run one at a time."
—(He makes it look easy, doesn't he?!)

We begin our journey through the whirlwind career of Robin Williams at the same place that he did: onstage.

This first section looks at some of Robin's most notable work *off* the silver screen, including his unexpected turn as a serious stage actor in *Waiting for Godot*.

We also talk about the one joke that might very well be Robin's favorite of all time, and we're provided with a fascinating glimpse of the behind-the-scenes Robin by someone who toured with him when he was still doing live comedy concerts.

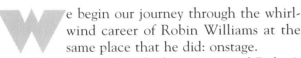

## Robin Williams's All-Time Favorite Joke

"Hello, I am a Guardian Comedian. Jokes are dangerous things. Don't use them at home unless you have a premise and a punch line. Remember: Two Jews do not walk into a bar without a reason. If you are heckled, prepare to deal with the heckler. If his heckle works and you have no response, you are dead."
—One of Robin Williams's stand-up comedy characters expounding on the dangers of performing live (*Playboy*, 1982).

Robin Williams has repeatedly used one joke throughout his career that is very funny and never fails to get a laugh.

During my research for *The Robin Williams Scrapbook*, I bumped into this gag several times, convincing me that it must, indeed, be the most beloved of witticisms residing in that strange land known as Robin's Brain. I counted Robin using this joke, or a variation of it, on the following occasions:

▧ During his 1982 San Francisco concert

▧ During a skit on the November 22, 1986 episode of *Saturday Night Live*

▧ During his 1989 interview with Barbara Walters

▧ Backstage at *Comic Relief* while rehearsing for a Seigfried and Roy sketch (recounted in the book *Comedians*, by Arthur Grace)

▧ In the movie *Shakes the Clown* during his scene as a mime instructor

▧ During his promotional interview for *Jack* on *The Tonight Show With Jay Leno*

▧ During his promotional interview for *Jumanji* on *The Tonight Show With Jay Leno*

During a ballet skit performed by him on one of the *Comic Relief*s (repeated on the *Comic Relief* 10th Anniversary Special on HBO in December of 1996)

And you may be asking, what, exactly, *is* the one joke that might very well be Robin's favorite? Here are a few versions of the gag:

"I found it very difficult being in tights. You're wearing tights and you're doing Shakespeare and they can tell what religion you are." —From the 1989 Barbara Walters interview.

"You know, they [luge athletes] wear those really skin-tight suits, and you can go, 'Oh, I can tell what religion you are!'"—From a 1996 appearance on *The Tonight Show With Jay Leno*

"Can you tell what religion I am?"—From the Betty and her Boys skit on *Comic Relief* (to Billy Crystal, while wearing a skin-tight leotard)

"I love them [Seigfreid and Roy] in those tight pants. You can tell what religion they are!"—From his 1995 appearance on *The Tonight Show With Jay Leno* to promote *Jumanji*

This joke, of course, finds its humor in the Jewish tradition of circumcising male babies, thus giving the penis a "distinctive" look easily recognizable through very tight trousers.

A runner-up favorite joke might be Robin's one-liner about having just had a "pina colonic," another gag he's repeatedly used and which always gets a laugh.

# An Evening With Robin Williams
## (1982)

*"Having Alexander Haig negotiate the peace is like having Charles Manson as a male nurse."*

This 1982 concert performance was one of the more elaborate productions of Robin Williams's body of stand-up work. It included a wrap-around story and character, props, and a couple of musical numbers.

But for all its ambitious attempts at scope, this performance is looser and somewhat less structured than Robin's later, more polished 1986 Metropolitan Opera appearance. Nonetheless, Robin's verbal and physical pyrotechnics, as well as his sheer unrestrained glee in performing makes this concert a milestone in his career.

The concert took place at the Great American Music Hall in Robin's home town of San Francisco. John Sebastian, formerly of the group The Lovin' Spoonful, was the opening act. Sebastian also did the theme music for the show's broadcast and video release.

*An Evening With Robin Williams* opens with scenes of the Golden Gate Bridge and San Francisco street life, accompanied by Robin's voice-over narration discussing his love for the City by the Bay.

We then meet Robin in character as a newspaper vendor who knew Robin Williams in the early days. Sprinkled throughout the newsstand guy's monologue are hilarious headlines from the tabloids he's shilling (specifically the fictitious, yet representative, *National Intruding Sun*):

**HITLER FOUND IN HOLLYWOOD! SIGNS 3-PICTURE DEAL**

**MAN MARRIES SISTER, FATHER OF OWN NEPHEW!**

**YASSER ARAFAT, RINGO STARR —SAME MAN!**

The news vendor then talks to "us" about not being able to get into Robin's show. This is a fascinating monologue because it gives Robin a chance to comment on and make fun of himself through the character of the news vendor:

*Robin in his role as Pops, the aging newsboy who helps us sneak in to enjoy "An Evening with Robin Williams." (Photofest)*

I used to see this guy in the beginning. Yeah, he'd play anywhere. Go to the opening of an envelope. Bug run, worm wrestle, he'd be there. And benefits! He was the benefit pig. I saw him do a benefit once—Save the Shrimp. Ain't that a bitch. Crazy guy, though. Grew up around here, yeah, he did. You know what I'm sayin'? Grew up in Marin County. Was sixteen before he had his first Porsche. Had to work all winter long just to go to Europe. Oh, ain't that a bitch there. . . . They're still going in there. Sneak in. Take a chance. That's what he's doing. He hasn't got an act. Come on. Let's improvise.

[Robin later used the "first Porsche" and "Europe" lines in his extensive January 1992 interview with *Playboy*. He cited them as an example of how he tried to be self-effacing about his privileged upbringing.]

The vendor then sneaks into the concert as a member of the press and watches the whole show from behind a curtain.

Robin was introduced, and the first thing he did when he came out was grab his penis and do his "Laugh Meter" routine, that visual bit he does when he pretends his other arm is a needle on a meter that is measuring the amount of laughter he's generating, à la the "Applause Meters" used on old TV game shows.

Then he was off and running. In the first minute or two of his performance, he described the garish ceiling of the concert hall as the "Sistine Chapel designed by Fredrick's of Hollywood" and the hall itself as "Wayne Newton's living room." He also imitated Slim Pickens singing *Aida* and called the balcony seating area the "severely medicated section." He said he was glad to be in San Francisco, "where God save the Queen has a *different* meaning."

Robin then left the stage to wander through the audience and this is when we get to witness his improvisational genius firsthand.

First he made a bandana joke and then made fun (in a yuppie voice) of a guy for wearing "a lovely shade of tweed," musing that the fellow must be in the Marin section of the audience. He then made another Arafat joke, saying into his microphone, "Arafat, party of six thousand." An earthquake joke was next: "If there is an earthquake in San Francisco, it's just God's way of saying, 'Get those condominiums off my back!'" He then played with a wine bottle, called a heckler Goofy, imitated an effeminate hairdresser, sang Hare Krishna with a woman's ponytail strategically placed, and, in the funniest moment of this impromptu audience participation routine, accidentally walked into a puff of exhaled cigarette smoke, and told the smoker, "Mmmmm, more smoke! I *want* to die!" He then picked up a drink that had a white head and said it was an Acne Pimple. He took a sip, and told the audience member not to be afraid of his open sores. After massaging a man's shoulders (while reminding him that men had nipples, too), he tried on a woman's raincoat and told the crowd that now he could go on the buses again. He finished this "tour" with a joke about the "Marquis De Suede" and then returned to the stage and a huge ovation.

Here are some highlights from the rest of this hilarious concert performance:

- Robin's mother, Laurie, was in the audience for this performance, and Robin made a point of introducing her and saying, "Oedipus, Shmedipus, I love you, momma!"

- In a very funny bit, Robin called rainbows over Marin County "ethnic detectors," and said that people in Marin are so damn wealthy "they don't get the crabs, they get the lobsters!" He also said later that Marinites don't buy Izod shirts, they actually staple a live alligator to their house, and that many of them wear little medical alert bracelets that say, "Please, a Perrier and a BMW. Quickly!"

- Robin's mocking of his hometown continued when he told the audience, "While you've been here, groups of gay men have broken into your home and redecorated it."

- Robin took a camera from someone in the audience and took a picture down his pants, describing the resulting photo as "an anaconda pressed against a plate glass window."

- Robin then riffed on a myriad of pop culture topics, including old water ballet movies, Amway, James Watt, California surfers, Polish people, Brooklyn accents, Julia Child on Valium, Ronald Reagan, nuclear war, Richard Simmons tormenting women in his exercise

class ("You call those tits? I've seen better lumps in oatmeal!"), and Richard Simmons's sexuality ("The man has a house of nothing but closets so he can go, 'I'm in, I'm out, I'm in, I'm out!'").

- After this lightning-quick barrage of jokes, Robin acknowledged what it takes to appreciate his humor: "Right now people are going, 'What the hell's he doing now?' Ha, ha, ha! Catch up!"

- Robin then did an entire routine on California surfer lingo, which he called "Californese." According to Robin, the usual Californese answer to the simple question, "How are you?" was, "I'm just like totally here for a while."

- He also said there were only a handful of words and phrases in the entire "language": gnarly, fershurr, totally, I'm bummed, wow, I'm together for a while, okay, and go for it now.

- If Robin is good at anything, it's dealing with hecklers. During a bit about different color wines, some guy in the audience shouted out, "Yellow wine." Robin ran right to the edge of the stage, looked straight at the guy, and said (to riotous laughter), "A mind is a terrible thing to waste." He then spontaneously improvised a very funny TV commercial for the United Caucasian College Fund.

- From there, Robin went after another slew of cultural issues. His targets included McDonald's, fur coats, Liberace, the Elephant Man, Mean Joe Green, Thunderbird and Night Train wines ("Serve before Friday"), and the Napa Valley.

- Robin also did a variation on his all-time favorite joke (discussed previously) during this concert.

- After a few people in the audience got a little loud, Robin cracked that the people "from the hospital" were there and then did a flawless Jack Nicholson "I wanna see the damn World Series" impression from *One Flew Over the Cuckoo's Nest*.

- This led to a very funny bit about mental patients tasting wine: The Psychotics reacted with "I hate this fucking wine!" The Manic-

Depressives would say, "It's good," and then break into tears. And the Schizophrenics would get lost on their way to the tasting. He then did Sybil doing one of those American Express commercials: "Do you know us? We can't leave home without it!"

- Continuing his look at West Coast culture, Robin did bits on drunk driving in California, and on marijuana, which led to an extended bit about Jack Daniels, which he led off by stating, "If alcohol's a crutch, then Jack Daniels is the wheelchair."

- During this concert, Robin did a "Fosse Fosse" dance routine similar to the one he would do years later in *The Birdcage*, and he also used the "Oops, gravity works!" gag he has used elsewhere. (This gag usually revolves around somebody who is drunk or stoned falling down and then being surprised that "gravity works!")

- Robin then riffed on Chernobyl, truckers who use speed, hunters, the TV show *Wild Kingdom*, the New York City Zoo, weightlifters, Arnold Schwarzenegger, steroids, the San Francisco 49ers, marijuana (again), Oakland, the football strike, dyslexia, and the movie *ET: The Extraterrestrial*.

- Appropriately (considering that this *was* a "Mr. Happy" production), Robin then did an extended bit about his penis. He called it the Incredible Heat-Seeking Moisture Missile, the Throbbing Python of Love, Mr. Happy, and Mr. Tripod.

- There was a terrifically funny moment when Robin's performance was interrupted by the sound of a police siren outside and Robin instantly ad-libbed, "Oops, here comes my ride!"

- In honor of his mother, Robin recited her "I love you in blue" ("I love you in blue,/I love you in red,/But most of all,/I Love you in blue!") joke poem to the audience. (He would also recite this poem in his *Playboy* interview this same year; in his 1991 David Frost interview; and in his *Mrs. Doubtfire* appearance on Donahue in 1993. Hey, if something works. . . .)

- According to Robin, the word "condominium" comes from the Latin, meaning "to overcharge for no reason."

- As a setup for an extended routine on babies, Robin did a bit on masturbation, which referred back to one of the low points in his career, the 1977 movie *Can I Do It . . . 'Til I Need Glasses?*: Robin imitated a young boy locked in the bathroom; when his father pounds on the door and shouts, "What are you doing in the bathroom?" the boy cries out, "Going blind!"

- Robin's lengthy, funny, and very moving baby and childhood routine went from labor all the way through his son growing up and having to come get his father from a bar when he's old and decrepit. "Can you spare $40,000 a week?" was one line the "old" Robin came out with, perhaps revealing Robin's *Mork and Mindy* salary.

- At one point, Robin stopped the show and improvised a very funny routine on an audience member's trip to the bathroom, pretending that this woman, Alison, was being held hostage in the ladies' room.

- Robin talked about acting and again did the "John Houseman-Volvo" joke he had done elsewhere. (See the David Frost interview section on page 65).

- The first musical number Robin did was an imitation of John Davidson singing Devo's "Whip It."

- Robin's prop jokes included bits with a fan, a shield, an umbrella, a helmet, a fencing mask, and a red beret ("I am a Guardian Comedian.").

- Robin's final musical number—one which brought the house down—was Elmer Fudd singing Bruce Springsteen's "Fire"—("I'm dwivin' in my caw.").

This song concluded the performance, but then Robin returned for another skit as the newspaper vendor. Only this time, Robin Williams himself had a conversation with the vendor: The vendor asked Robin if he nailed Pam Dawber during his *Mork and Mindy* days, and Robin cracked that his cat wouldn't use the litter box if he lined it with the *National Enquirer*.

Robin has often told interviewers that one of his most prized possessions was Albert Einstein's autograph. He used this personal detail to conclude the concert by having the vendor give Robin an actual Einstein autograph, telling him to pass it on to his kid when he was through with it.

The two sides of Robin Williams then walked off into the night, chatting about life, God, and the right thing to do.

*An Evening with Robin Williams* is readily available on home video and is well worth renting. In fact, if you're a true Robin Williams fan, you should probably rent this concert *and* his *Evening at the Met* tape and watch them back-to-back.

Now that's what I call being a true Mr. Happy!

## What the Critics Had to Say

**Mick Martin and Marsha Porter:** "[A] remarkably good comedy video [that] provides ample proof why Williams was considered one of the finest live comedians of his era before scoring on television and in the movies." (From their *Video Movie Guide*)

**Videohound's Golden Movie Retriever** (1997 edition): "Robin Williams explodes all over the screen in this live nightclub performance."

**Director:** Don Mischer
**Cast:** Robin Williams
**Writer:** Robin Williams
**Music:** John Sebastian
Not rated; 60 minutes

# Robin Williams: An Evening at the Met (1986)

*"The people at the Met are going, 'You ain't comin' back, I'll tell you that right now. You ain't comin' back after what you did!' But we did it! Ha, ha, ha!"*

—Robin Williams, at the conclusion of his performance at the Met.

This August 1986 concert performance at the Metropolitan Opera House in New York City—the first ever by a solo comic—is probably the quintessential and defining Robin Williams "live" performance. (Robin, who was thirty-four at the time, performed two shows—one on Saturday, August 9th, and one on Sunday, August 10th, both at 8:30 P.M.).

Robin's performance is meticulously structured and extremely polished and it is obvious that at this point in his career, he was already a consummate stand-up performer with flawless timing and brilliant material. There were no props, other than a few set decorations belonging to the Met from which Robin ad-libbed a couple of gags. The only musical number was Robin's *a capella* "Opera Rap," which he probably wrote especially for this appearance, and performed during his encore.

This concert (which was originally broadcast as an HBO special presentation) begins with the viewer being ushered from home into a limousine, and driven to the Met, all to the accompanying strains of Mozart.

Inside the Met, just before the show begins, the voice of Robin Williams suddenly booms out over the audience:

> "Ladies and gentlemen, may I have your attention, please? There will be a minor change in the program tonight. The part of Robin Williams will be played by The Temptations."

Robin is then introduced and bounds onstage to a huge ovation, wearing black satin pants, a blue Hawaiian shirt, and red shoes. His first joke (after the improvised ballet steps he did as he came on stage) was, "Howdeeee! . . . Oops, wrong opera house!" The magnificent chandeliers were still rising up to the lofty ceiling as they do before all performances at the Met, and Robin then cracked a joke about them in which he thanked Imelda Marcos for the use of her earrings.

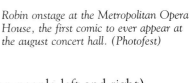

on people left and right).

Here are the highlights of Robin's rare appearance at the Met.

After admitting that he was "scared shitless," Robin's first topics for this concert included Prince Charles, Southerners, Abraham Lincoln, *Leave It to Beaver*, Robin Leach, and ballet.

Robin then did a lengthy routine on his drinking days. He told the audience he had to stop drinking alcohol because he used to wake up nude on the hood of his car with his keys in his ass. Topics for this bit also included wine with screw caps and hangovers.

After talking about booze, Robin then moved to the subjects of marijuana and cocaine, talking about paranoia, driving while stoned, freebasing ("It's not free! It costs you your house!"), and thoughtfully providing a three-part test to determine if you have a cocaine problem:

"1. If you come to your house, you have no furniture, and your cat's going, 'I'm outta here, prick!'—Warning!

"2. If you have this dream where you're doing cocaine in your sleep and you can't fall asleep, and you're doing cocaine in your sleep and you can't fall asleep, and you wake up and you're doing cocaine—Bingo!

"3. If on your tax form it says $50,000 for snacks—Mayday!"

Moving on, Robin then talked about football players on steroids, golf, marathon runners, yuppies, Japanese people, Hollywood cops ("Stop! Those shoes don't go with that bag!"), New York cops, Southern cops ("They wear sunglasses with the mir-

After rhetorically asking, "What the fuck am *I* doing here?", he then posed the traditional question, "How do you get to the Met?" But instead of the traditional answer ("Practice"), Robin supplied the eighties answer: "Money!"

A brief but hilarious bit follows in which he wondered aloud if Pavarotti was over at the Improv, saying, "Two Jews walk into a bar," (in a requisite Italian accent, of course). He then expanded this gag by imitating renowned tenor Placido Domingo doing *The Music Man*.

All of this hilarity took place within the first few seconds of Robin taking the Met's stage and from there, it only got better. Robin obviously prepared carefully for this performance and we get the sense that he did not leave too much room for freewheeling improvisation (as he clearly did for his 1982 San Francisco concert in which he wandered through the audience for several minutes, goofing

rors on the *inside*"), and Southern justice.

While speaking of the South, Robin came up with this observation (which got a *huge* laugh): "Isn't it strange to think that if you commit sodomy in Georgia, they're gonna put you in a cell with another man who's gonna sodomize you? That's Southern logic!"

From here, Robin tackled gun control, armor-piercing bullets, Pearl Harbor, and Ronald Reagan. While talking about Reagan, Robin did a routine in which he imagined politicians as actors in one giant, real-life movie. He did impeccable imitations of John Wayne as Tip O'Neill; Bela Lugosi as Casper Weinberger; Laurel and Hardy as George Bush and George Schulz; The Phantom of the Opera as Teddy Kennedy; and Obi Wan Kenobi and Princess Leia as Ronald and Nancy Reagan. He also mused that political summit meetings between world leaders should be held at Carmine's Clam Bar in the Bronx with a guy named Vinnie moderating. He said that the truth about Reagan is that he was really Richard Nixon wearing a Ronald Reagan mask.

Around the time of this concert, Richard Nixon had been on the cover of *Newsweek*. Robin's spin on that? "Richard Nixon on the cover of *Newsweek* is like John Hinckley on the cover of *Guns and Ammo*."

Robin then tackled the Middle East, South Africa, George Wallace, Lester Maddox, then South African Prime Minister Botha, alleged former Nazi Kurt Waldheim, and the United Nations.

Next were TV evangelists, pollution, Chernobyl, and spring fever, which led Robin to a lengthy (sorry!) discussion of his penis. From here he moved to the idea of a woman as President ("There would never be any wars. Just every twenty-eight days some intense negotiations"), menstruation, and the fantasy of Miss Right ("Or at least Miss Right Now.")

*A knight at the opera. Robin during his one-man show at the Met. (Photofest)*

Robin then let loose with a hilarious one-liner about sex therapist Dr. Ruth: "Here's a woman talking about oral sex and you know she doesn't even eat pork." He followed this with a lengthy and very funny routine about a black woman sex therapist named Dr. Roof, a no-nonsense sister who told men exactly where it was at and what they did wrong while making love. Taking on the persona of the good doctor, Robin discussed oral sex, foreplay, and condoms, which led him to his longest routine of the evening, a funny and touching segment on pregnancy, labor, childbirth, and parenthood.

In a truly clever and inventive routine, Robin talked about the Chromosome Square Dance, the Titty Fairy, the Hormone Fairy, and then explained what he called "Sharing the Birth Experience," the current fashionable attempt to involve the father in the birth process. (Three years earlier, Robin's first wife, Valerie, had given birth to their son, Zachary, so the "birth experience"—and all the hilarious chaos surrounding it—was a relatively recent memory for him.)

This is absolutely not possible, Robin declared. There is no way the father can actually share such a monumental and agonizing experience, he asserted, unless the man was: one, passing a bowling ball; two, circumcising himself with a chainsaw; or three, opening an umbrella up his ass. The women in the audience literally cheered when Robin finished this routine.

From labor he moved on to the actual birth, describing a newborn as looking like a little old man dipped in forty weight, or as if Gandhi and Churchill had a child together. He did another penis joke, saying he thought his son's umbilical cord was his penis, and then began a discussion of baby "ca-ca," a green substance ("What do you feed him? Algae!?") he described as being "part toxic waste and part Velcro."

After infancy comes childhood and Robin shared with the audience the experiences he had with his son Zachary during this period as well. He recounted a funny conversation:

**Zachary:** Why is the sky blue?

**Robin:** Well, because of the atmosphere.

**Zachary:** Why is there atmosphere?

**Robin:** Because we need to breathe.

**Zachary:** Why do we breathe?

> **Robin:** WHY THE FUCK DO YOU WANT TO KNOW? A YEAR AGO YOU WERE SITTING IN YOUR OWN SHIT, NOW YOU'RE CARL SAGAN??

Robin also talked about his son imitating his outbursts (he'd hear "Fuck it!" coming from the baby in the back seat of the car while driving); leaving his child with a babysitter ("Let's peel off these Pampers and party! You like Fisher-Price music?"); and knowing that in sixteen years or so, his son would come up to him and say, "God, dad. You're fucked." (And behind Zachary would be Robin's own dad, gleefully going, "YES!")

Winding up, Robin concluded his *Evening at the Met* with a moving dialogue between him and his infant son that brought him right back to one of his first jokes of the evening:

**Zachary:** Well, what's it gonna be?

**Robin:** I don't know, but maybe along the way, you'll take my hand, tell a few jokes, and have some fun. Hey, how do you get to the Met?

**Zachary:** Money.

**Robin:** Hey, you're not afraid, are you?

**Zachary:** No. Fuck it.

Robin then walked off the stage in character as his little son Zachary holding his daddy's hand.

Robin received a thunderous standing ovation and returned to perform the original *a capella* song, "Opera Rap," with the following lyrics:

> Say aria, aria, you're my man
> If he can't do, Wagner can!
> Say Wagner, Verdi, Puccini, too
> Come on everybody
> Do what you can do!
> Say opera rap, opera rap

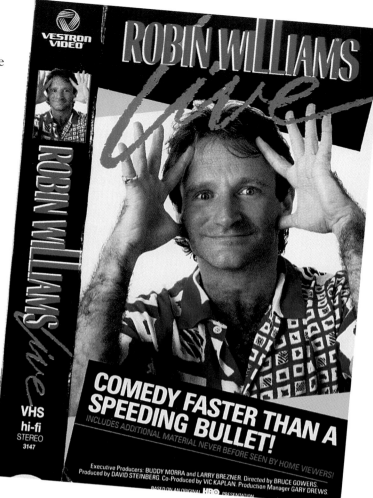

*(Photo: HBO/Vestron)*

Thus, Robin Williams concluded his triumphant *Evening at the Met*.

### What the Critics Had to Say

**Mick Martin and Marsha Porter**: "An always funny and sometimes hilarious live performance by one of comedy's premier talents. Irreverent and vulgar, Williams doesn't so much shock as he carefully picks sensitive factors of the human condition." (From their *Video Movie Guide*)

**Director:** Bruce Gowers
**Cast:** Robin Williams
**Writer:** Robin Williams
**Music:** "Opera Rap," written and performed by Robin Williams
Rated R; 65 minutes

# On the Road With Robin:
# A Talk With Barry Friedman of the
# Raspyni Brothers

*"I love to see Russian circus skills in American boys . . . you guys are great!"*
—Robin Williams, talking about the Raspyni Brothers

*The Raspyni Brothers opened for Robin during his concerts from 1986 to 1989. (Barry Friedman)*

The Raspyni Brothers are two terrific—but not actually related—guys named Daniel Holzman and Barry Friedman. Barry and Dan have been performing their comedy-juggling act together for almost fifteen years and have entertained audiences throughout the United States.

The Raspyni Brothers took their name from the legendary 1930s juggler Eduardo Raspini, and also from the juggling slang term *raspy*, which means (to mix sociocultural idioms), *gnarly*, as in, "Man, that was a raspy move!," or as Robin Williams's California surfer dude might say, "Dude! Gnarly move!"

The Raspyni Brothers have done it all: They have performed at corporate gigs (Apple Computer, MCI, and Toshiba, among many others), on talk shows, and in concert. Their TV work includes appearances on *The Tonight Show*, *Comic Strip Live*, *Entertainment Tonight*, *Evening at the Improv*, *The Jerry Lewis Muscular Dystrophy Telethon*, *Inside Edition*, and *George Burns' 95th Birthday Celebration*.

The Raspyni Brothers recently made a huge leap up the entertainment food chain by headlining in Atlantic City with their show, "A Laugh a Minute," the first time ever for a juggling act.

One of the more fascinating reviews of the Raspyni Brothers came from none other than Judge Lance Ito after the boys performed for the sequestered O. J. Simpson jurors to relieve the boredom. Judge Ito wrote a personal letter to the Raspynis, telling them "[Your] type of entertainment is much appreciated by both the Court and the jurors alike."

Some of the acts the faux brothers have opened for include Tony Bennett, Billy Crystal, Tom Jones, Jay Leno, Howie Mandel, Garry Shandling, Paul Anka, Roseanne, Dennis Miller, Dean Martin, David Brenner, Bob Hope, Steve Martin, and—the reason they are included in this book—Robin Williams.

I first "met" Barry Friedman on the Internet. Barry and I both subscribe to and participate in several TV and comedy-related Internet newsgroups, and he responded to one of my postings that mentioned I was looking for Robin Williams's memorabilia or anecdotes. Barry told me that he and his partner had toured with Robin in the mid-eighties and had gotten to be pretty good friends with the Whimsical One. Barry was immediately willing to be interviewed for this book and generously provided pictures and memorabilia from his personal collection.

After Barry told me a bit about their act and where he and Dan had performed, I remembered that I had actually seen some of the Raspyni Brothers' TV appearances. After he mentioned the "Ping pong balls in the mouth" element of his routine, I recalled a *Tonight Show* appearance of theirs. I remembered being amazed that these guys could do such stunning and amazing things with their mouths, not to mention tossing machetes back and forth as an audience member stands directly in the "line of juggling."

You can find out much more about the fabulous Raspyni Brothers by visiting their home page at http://www.raspyni.com.

Here is my talk with Barry, in which he treats us to some behind-the-scenes memories of working with Robin Williams.

**STEVE SPIGNESI:** You and your partner, Dan, toured with Robin during his comedy concert years as his opening act. Could you describe your act, The Raspyni Brothers, for our readers?

**BARRY FRIEDMAN:** We are an innovative two-man comedy/variety show. We specialize in the manipulation of very strange objects. Blowgun stunts, ping-

*Relaxing backstage with the "brothers." (Barry Friedman)*

pong-ball juggling in the mouth, bullwhips, cocktail-shaker cups, paddle balls, golf clubs—we use all of this and more in our shows!

**SS:** When did you first meet Robin and what were the circumstances?

**BF:** Let's see . . . the first time we met Robin was at St. Bonaventure College in upstate New York in October of 1986. We had been touring with Billy Crystal and Billy's manager, David Steinberg, told Robin that we would be a good opening act for him.

We walked into this huge theater and it was full of kids waiting to see Robin perform. David and Robin came up to us and David said, "Don't worry if they won't be quiet for you. If you get through ten minutes of your act and they won't stop, you can walk off." Great. Robin was very friendly and assured us that they would stop once we took the stage. He was right. We did our whole thirty-minute set and got a standing ovation. Robin was in the wings cracking up for the whole set and that made us feel really good.

**SS:** When did you tour with him and where did

*Robin tries to get in on the Raspyni's act, but instead comes across as a topless Dolly Parton! (Barry Friedman)*

you play? Could you put your time with him in some kind of perspective relative to his career: Pre-*Mork*? During *Mork*? What movies was he working on, if any, and did he ever discuss scripts with you?

**BF:** We did large arena shows with him during the period 1986 through 1989. We don't know what movies he was making during that time period. [See the film section for a listing of Robin's films in chronological order.] We never really discussed anything with Robin except live performing. Actually, one time we remember him talking about wanting to do a live concert movie and he thought it would be fun to have scenes of us doing the opening act while he was getting ready. We loved the idea! Never happened.

**SS:** How well did you know Robin when you were

touring with him? Were you close or was it a "strictly business" type of relationship?

**BF:** I would describe it as a friendly business relationship. Never unfriendly, very supportive. We would have some meals together on the road. Stop at restaurants between gigs. Stuff like that. We were invited to his fortieth surprise birthday party but were touring at the time and couldn't attend. Probably for the best anyway. Robin's wife, Marsha, invited us but I think we would have been out of place . . . too many big stars!

**SS:** What is your funniest memory of your time with Robin?

**BF:** He loved to overlap the end of our act into the start of his. That was neat.

I would do ping-pong-ball juggling in my

mouth, for example, and one night Robin loaded two into his mouth before going on stage. After a minute or two of crowd-roar, he would spit the balls into the crowd (they couldn't see them in his mouth so it was a surprise to them). More moments of roaring ensued!

Interestingly, Robin is not that funny offstage. He's very calm, reflective, and thoughtful. We would spend time in his suite after shows and would usually watch TV. We would talk between channel surfing.

My funniest memory of our time with Robin came after a show in Portland—but Robin wasn't the reason I laughed so hard.

It was the first time I met my future in-laws who lived about an hour away. I had been dating their daughter for about ten months at the time the show came up in Portland, so we had arranged to meet at the show. I was very nervous (about meeting them, not about the show!) as I walked to the arranged meeting place before the show.

My father-in-law is a marriage and family counselor and he made it very easy to get over the intimidated feelings I had. That was nice. After the show there was a meet and greet and it was there that we really got to talk. After about fifteen minutes I asked my future in-laws if they would like to say hello to Robin. They said they would and I went over and introduced them.

My father-in-law then asked Robin the most bizarre question I have ever heard. Remember, this is within the first half hour of knowing him! "It looks a little crazy in here," he began. "Would you like to sit down and talk for a few minutes?"

I was a bit freaked out—what have I done to my career? Doesn't he realize that there are about two hundred people in this room who want to shake Robin's hand and tell him a joke?

"Absolutely. That would be nice," is what Robin responded with, though. My mother-in-law and I chatted alone while Robin and my father-in-law sat alone talking for five minutes. People were hovering around wondering what important show-biz figure this man was who had Robin Williams in private conference!

**SS:** What was most *meaningful* about your time with Robin?

**BF:** It always amazed us how he would watch our show every night and laugh so hard at our routines. It pushed us to do something different every night so he could see something new. His laugh was coming right from the wings and it was a very reassuring feeling in a situation where we could have felt very intimidated.

**SS:** You and I are both in agreement that Robin is one of the most brilliant comedic geniuses to ever live. His invention and wit are legendary achievements in entertainment. Tell me, Barry, why do you *specifically* think Robin Williams is a genius?

**BF:** I think he is amazing at acting and performing. I would say he is a genius in his particular niche of performing. I think he is so versatile and that is a true gift.

I'll tell you one thing, we have opened for everybody you can imagine—from Patti LaBelle to Jay Leno to Dean Martin to Tom Jones to Billy Crystal—and there is *no other artist* whose show I stayed to hear EVERY SINGLE WORD of every night without exception. I just couldn't leave the theater when he was on stage. Nor, could I change or take off my makeup. I just hung in the wings every night. So, yeah, I would vote genius.

**SS:** When was the last time you saw or spoke to Robin?

**BF:** In 1990 we bumped into him at the Improv in Los Angeles. We sat at a table with a few other folks and had a really nice time. He was (as always) very interested in what we were doing, where we were working, and what we wanted to be doing. We talked about some of his recent movies and what we all thought. It was a very nice time.

The Raspyni Brothers continue to perform their very popular act throughout North America in both live venues and on TV. If the boys are ever in your neck of the woods, Big Steve suggests you "check 'em out!"

# Robin at Play:
## Robin Williams and Steve Martin
## in the Mike Nichols Production
## of Samuel Beckett's Waiting for Godot

*"In my first few days at [the Julliard] school, I learned that I didn't project out, that I talked too fast and that I swallowed my words. One of the first things I tried in class was a religious monologue Dudley Moore had done in [a play called]* Beyond the Fringe. *I thought I did fine, but my teacher, a man named Michael Conn, hated it so much that he said, "You have two choices: Come back and do it again or give up any thoughts you have about an acting career." He really was furious with me, and it was because I'd only imitated what I'd heard and hadn't tried to find new things that would make the piece mine."*

—Robin, about learning how to act(*Playboy*, October 1982)

Even though Robin Williams had been performing his comedy live on stage for years, his appearance as Estragon in *Waiting for Godot* in 1988 was his professional stage debut.

In the fall of that year, Robin starred in an 11-week run of Samuel Beckett's existential classic with Steve Martin, F. Murray Abraham, Bill Irwin, and Lukas Haas in a production at the Mitzi E. Newhouse Theater at Lincoln Center in New York City.

It is truly appropriate that a comic known for his free-form, stream-of-consciousness, often existential ramblings would choose as his first play the quintessential existential two-act masterpiece, *Waiting for Godot*. In *Godot*, Vladimir (Steve Martin) and Estragon wait patiently for the never-seen Godot, a figure who inexplicably gives meaning to their otherwise empty and incomprehensible lives.

As was expected with a high-profile cast of this caliber, the tiny Newhouse Theater sold out the entire run of *Waiting for Godot*. The production was helmed by noted director Mike Nichols who had previously done such acclaimed films as *Who's Afraid of Virginia Woolf* (1966); *The Graduate* (1967); *Catch-22* (1970); *Carnal Knowledge* (1971); *Silkwood* (1983); *Heartburn* (1986); and *Working Girl* (1988). Mike Nichols and Robin would again work together in the superb 1995 comedy, *The Birdcage*. [See the feature on *The Birdcage*.]

Steve Martin was, of course, as popular and as well-known as Robin and he contributed equally to the appeal and the box-office success of the play. The other cast members were also noteworthy: F.

Murray Abraham (Pozzo) was famous for his brilliant portrayal of Mozart's nemesis Antonio Salieri in 1984's *Amadeus*; Bill Irwin (Lucky) had been in *Popeye* in 1980 with Robin and in 1990 would work with Steve Martin in *My Blue Heaven*; and Lukas Haas (A Boy) had been superb in 1985's *Witness* and would go on to work with Steve Martin again in the 1992 film, *Leap of Faith*.

A few changes were made for this production. The 1954 Grove Press edition of the play opens with the stage directions, "A country road. A tree. Evening." Nichols and set designer Tony Walton changed the country road to the southwest American desert.

Whether at Mike Nichols's suggestion or not, Robin took some liberties with his portrayal of Estragon, often using accents, prop humor, and slapstick schtick. *New York Times* theater critic Frank Rich noted, "The most frenetic horseplay belongs to Mr. Williams, who at one point regurgitates the theme music of television's *Twilight Zone*, as if he were still playing his sitcom character of Mork. A brilliant mimic, the actor never runs out of wacky voices, but where is his own voice?"

That said, as critic Rich described it, Robin nevertheless gave an entertaining and inventive performance that at times made the audience feel "privileged" to be attending this rendering of Beckett's timeless classic.

For Robin, it was a chance to stretch and a chance to learn. In 1992, he spoke of what he gained from the *Godot* experience with *Playboy*,

*Robin admits to having learned something about timing from Martin during their hugely-successful, eleven-week Godot run. (Photofest)*

and when asked what he might have learned from costar Steve Martin, he said, "I learned about physical comedy and the nuts and bolts about timing from him, because, obviously, when I do my act, I have as much timing as an Uzi! [Steve's] is the comedy of pause, of waiting, of holding back." On what Steve Martin might have learned from Robin: "Perhaps about how not to be that anxious or obsessive."

Since *Waiting for Godot,* Robin has not done any theater work anywhere near as high-profile. From his "post-game" comments, one might get the impression that it could be a while before he tackles such a project again.

### What Robin Had to Say

**Before *Godot***: "You can do physical things, but you don't ad-lib Beckett. Just like you don't riff Beethoven. [Doing *Godot* is] interesting and terrifying at the same time. It's an ensemble piece, and you really have to put your faith in other people, and in yourself, too—you have to be there for them. It's the type of piece where you can't let up. If you slack off for a second, it goes. One word is gone and—scrunch!—the whole thing is like a quarter on the Japanese Osaka railroad track! It's hard to describe. . . . It's like having sex in a wind tunnel. Or it's like water skiing in quicksand. Or putting together a jigsaw puzzle in a hurricane. I heard that when Bert Lahr was doing Estragon, they asked him, 'What are you doing in this play?'

and he said, 'I don't know.' And then I heard that Beckett was real happy with that." (From the *New York Times,* September 13, 1988)

**After *Godot***: "[Doing *Waiting for Godot* was] painful. We put our ass out and got kicked for it. Some nights I would improvise a bit and the hardcore Beckett fans got pissed off. We played it as a comedy team . . . like these two guys from vaudeville who would go into routines that would fall apart into angst. Basically, it's Laurel and Hardy, which is how Beckett had staged it in Germany." (From *Playboy,* January, 1992)

### What the Critics Had to Say

**Frank Rich**: "As *Good Morning, Vietnam* seemed to evaporate whenever Mr. Williams had to forsake comedy routines for love scenes, so his Estragon vanishes whenever he has to convey genuine panic or despair." (From the *New York Times,* September 13, 1988)

**Director:** Mike Nichols
**Cast:** Robin Williams (Estragon), Steve Martin (Vladimir), F. Murray Abraham (Pozzo), Bill Irwin (Lucky), Lukas Haas (A Boy)
**Writer:** Samuel Beckett
**Sets:** Tony Walton
**Costumes:** Ann Roth
**Lighting:** Jennifer Tipton
**Sound:** Tom Sorce

**"Na-noo, na-noo."**

—Mork's all-
purpose greeting

*We shouldn't be surprised that an alien who drinks through his
fingers would ride a bicycle backward! (Photofest)*

# Chapter 2
## Mork and Mindy

his section looks at the TV series that brought Robin to almost-overnight stardom, *Mork and Mindy*.

It's all here: An in-depth look at the debut episode; complete summaries of all 91 *Mork and Mindy* episodes; details on the single most memorable episode of all time (in which Robin plays himself!); and a look at *MAD* magazine's irreverent take on the show.

We also look at the world of *Mork and Mindy* with a special feature on a rare *Mork and Mindy* book that was written for fans when the show was at its hottest. Na-noo, na-noo!

## "Mork Moves in"
## The One-Hour Debut Episode of
## Mork and Mindy

**Original Broadcast:**
Thursday, September 14, 1978, 8:00–9:00 P.M.
**Main Cast:** Robin Williams (Mork from Ork),
Pam Dawber (Mindy McConnell),
Conrad Janis (Frederick McConnell)
**Guest Stars:** Penny Marshall (Laverne DeFazio),
Henry Winkler (Arthur "The Fonz" Fonzarelli),
Dick Yarmy (Officer Tilwick)
**Written by:** Dale McRaven
**Directed by:** Howard Storm

ere is the first scene of the first episode of *Mork and Mindy*, the irreverent sitcom that catapulted Robin Williams to stardom and launched his movie career.

The opening scene of this hilarious one-hour, two-part episode takes place on Ork, where Mork is nervously awaiting a conference with his corpulent leader, Orson.

MORK

Boy, am I in for it now! Sent before the White Desk again! But what did I do? The Solar Lander, you fool! You painted a mustache on it! But Orson didn't know I did it! Then why am I here? If I knew that, I wouldn't be talking to myself!

ORSON

Mork!

MORK

Good morning, Orson!

ORSON

Orson. You call me Orson to my face but behind

my back you call me Fatso, Rocketship Thighs, and Star-Twit!

MORK

You forgot Laser-Breath! Aannhh! Aannhh! Sorry, Your Immenseness!

ORSON

See what I mean? These constant displays of humor are not acceptable behavior here on Ork.

MORK

You're right. We are rather a dull lot. The white bread of the universe.

ORSON

Emotions have been breeded out of us for the good of the race and you constantly make jokes! I'm afraid that won't do!

MORK

Uh, oh.

ORSON

There's an insignificant planet on the far side of the galaxy. From the fragmented reports we have on it, the people are, well . . .

MORK

Real nimnuls?

ORSON

Exactly. That's why I think you'll fit in there, Mork.

MORK

You're too kind, sir! What is the name of this hell-hole you're sending me to?

ORSON

Earth.

MORK

Earth. I was on Earth three bleems ago. I was sent there by a biology class to collect a specimen. I had to throw it back, though. Too small. I love that place!

ORSON

Well, don't enjoy it too much. It's not a vacation. We want you to learn all we can about primitive societies. Your mission is to report back to me men-

tally about the things you learn there. And remember, this is a serious mission!

MORK

You can count on me, Orson! D, D, and E! Dedicated, diligent, and efficient! Na-noo, na-noo!

ORSON

Na-noo, na-noo!

Mork lands on Earth and discovers that his luggage "egg" has lost one of his suitcases, one that was packed with Earth clothes. Mork does have one piece of luggage, though, and from it he puts on an Earth suit—backwards. He begins walking into town and soon runs into Mindy. She has just been dumped by her date when he got too "grabby" and she got mad at him. Because of Mork's backwards jacket, Mindy thinks he is a priest and is happy that she has met someone she can trust.

Mindy takes Mork back to her apartment where he asks for a drink of motor oil and talks to her plants. Mindy gets alarmed when she finally realizes that Mork has his suit on backwards and he then tells her that he's from Ork, a planet we later learn is 60,000,000 light-years away from Earth: "You follow the Big Dipper until it comes to a dead end and then you hang an up."

Mork then takes a picture with his Instamatic glove and drinks with his finger. Mindy is still frightened, and she is relieved when there's a knock on the door: But it's not someone to her rescue. Instead it's an Orkan travel egg with Mork's lost luggage.

Mindy eventually calms down when Mork formally introduces himself (with a two-fingered handshake and a "Na-noo, na-noo!") and she decides to study *him* as he proceeds to study Earth and Earthlings.

The following morning, young Eugene (a neighborhood boy who Mork calls "Munchkin-like person") brings Mork to the music store and introduces him to Mindy's suspicious father. Mr. McConnell is alarmed to learn that Mork is actually living with Mindy.

Later, back at her apartment, Mindy has a serious talk with Mork. He sits on his face and she tells him that he did a bad thing by telling her father they were living together. Mindy decides to help Mork by making him more Earth-like. Mork then tries on several voices, including Ralph Kram-

*Robin Williams as Mork from Ork, with Penny Marshall (as Laverne DeFazio) and Henry Winkler (as the Fonz). (Photofest)*

den and Ed Norton from *The Honeymooners*; a Munchkin from *The Wizard of Oz*; and Lucy and Ricky Ricardo from *I Love Lucy*.

Mork tells Mindy that he was on Earth twenty bleems earlier (he had told Orson it was only three bleems) and then gives her a mental flashback to the February 1978 *Happy Days* episode in which he came to Earth to visit his friend, The Fonz.

The remainder of this first episode is from the *Happy Days* segment in which Mork first appears. The Fonz is housesitting for the Cunninghams when Mork arrives, wearing a helmet (Fonz calls him "the nutso from outer space") and announces that he wants to be his friend.

Mork tells Fonzie that he doesn't understand the Earth ritual of men dating women. Parts are interchangeable on Ork, he tells Fonzie, so that's why he doesn't quite get Earth's courting rituals.

Fonzie tries to explain kissing to Mork. "Sliding lips sounds unappealing," Mork says, but he wants to be introduced to a "willing" Earth girl anyway.

Fonzie sends Mork upstairs to change into Richie's clothes so he will look more Earth-like. He then calls and invites over the "willing and able" Laverne DeFazio (Penny Marshall, who would later direct Robin in *Awakenings*) as a "willing" date for Mork.

This first half of this episode concludes with Laverne arriving at Richie's house, wanting to know why Fonzie invited her over.

The second half begins with Laverne introducing herself to Mork, who is so overwhelmed and probably nervous he gives her many more "Na-noo, na-noo's" than usual.

Fonzie then leaves Laverne and "Morkie" alone, counting on Laverne's romantic skills to indoctrinate Mork into Earth romance.

"Is it time to flatter you?" Mork asks Laverne. "Sure," she replies.

Mork the charmer then tells Laverne, "You have a lovely fungus growing out of your head."

Laverne decides that she wants to leave, but when Mork innocently tells her that he's new to the dating game, she stays.

Mork and Laverne sit on the sofa and she freaks when Mork sits on his face. He quickly straightens up and they sit on opposite ends of the couch and stare at each other. Mork mimics Laverne's actions and she gets mad because she thinks he's making fun of her.

Mork is crushed by her anger and anxiously tells her he wants to "return to hatchling state." She softens towards him but then has to kick him in the shin when he makes a move towards her earlobes. (He just wanted to tweak them, he later tells Mindy.) Mork, thinking Laverne's kick is a romantic overture, kicks her back and then chases her around the Cunningham living room, babbling Orkan. She flees ("I think he likes me," she tells Fonzie as she leaves), and we return to the present time, back in Mindy's apartment.

Mindy tells Mork that he needs to change his voice. He immediately speaks in a deep, Shakespearean cadence (he heard it on TV) and she tells him to use that voice because it sounds normal.

Mork tells Mindy that he has learned three things during his brief time on Earth: one, use a phony voice; two, don't drink with your finger; and three, don't sit on your face. Mindy adds a fourth: Don't tell her father that you're living with his daughter.

At this point Mindy's father bursts in, very upset about his unmarried daughter living with a man and he leaves her apartment in anger.

Back at his music store, Mr. McConnell drinks the bottle of champagne he had been saving for Mindy's wedding. His friend, Officer Tilwick, comes in and Mr. McConnell confides in him, recalling "when sharing a pad meant borrowing a notebook." Tilwick decides to help out by confronting Mork and trying to scare him into moving out.

Back at the apartment, Mork is talking to a bowl of eggs. He throws one up in the air, telling it, "Fly! Be free!" When the egg crashes to the countertop, Mork tells the other eggs, "Your brother bit the big one!"

Tilwick comes over and calls Mork a sponge and a low life, telling him he doesn't want to see Mindy hurt. Mork assures him he'd *never* allow Mindy to be hurt, but Tilwick tells him to take off, to which Mork replies, "I just landed." Tilwick then asks Mork, "Are your putting me on?" and Mork answers, "Putting you on? You're not even hollow!"

Shortly thereafter, Mindy and her father learn that Tilwick arrested Mork because he believed he was insane and there is a sanity hearing scheduled for tomorrow.

The scene then shifts to the courtroom where a judge is questioning a doctor who examined Mork. Mindy and her chastened father burst in and demand to speak on Mork's behalf as character witnesses.

The doctor tells the court that Mork is childlike, antisocial, unable to learn, and cannot function in society. Mork, who had watched *Perry Mason* and *Inherit the Wind* the night before, stands up, "na-noo, na-noo's" the judge, and then performs a scene from *Inherit the Wind*.

The court-appointed psychiatrist is outraged and tells the judge that during his psychological tests, Mork put a square peg into a round hole and now he can't get it out. Mork shows his ankle-watch and gives the doctor a word-association test which results in a woman named Pamela fleeing the room when the shrink blurts out that he has been having sex with her.

Mork tells the court that the defense rests and then sits on his face. The judge decides that there is no law against being eccentric and Mork's case is dismissed.

This one-hour debut episode concludes with Mork's first report to Orson in which he explains how everyone on Earth is an individual and that Mindy's coming to his defense had something to do with human emotions.

Orson gives Mork a new assignment: Investigate human emotions, but don't get involved too deeply with Earthlings. Mork agrees, but we all know there isn't a chance in Ork that Mork will follow his Immenseness's mandates.

This first *Mork and Mindy* episode hits the ground running. It is very funny and Robin Williams inhabits the character of Mork as if he were born into it. And in a sense, he was. [See the chapter at *The Mork and Mindy Story* for the story of Robin's audition for the role of Mork.]

The most effective moments in this episode

*Maybe Mork sent this photo to Orson with "Glad You're Not Here" written on it? Just wondering. (Photofest)*

are when Mork and Mindy interact. The scenes with Mindy's father and grandfather are kind of draggy and after a time, Mindy's grandmother was phased out and more future episode time was given to Mork and Mindy together.

The episode was a huge success and the start of Mork-mania. TV critic Tom Shales, in a review in the *Washington Post* that ran the day of the series debut, said that Robin's "gift for impromptu stand-up comedy is an awesome thing when seen live on a stage. His repertoire of voices, faces and verbal contortions is uncanny, and his energy level a wonder." As to how Robin's talents translated to the small screen, Shales described him as "like Henny Youngman hooked up to a nuclear reactor at full tilt, a Harpo Marx for the '70s."

Amen.

And na-noo, na-noo.

# Complete Plot Summaries of the Mork and Mindy Episodes

*"My father was an eyedropper and my mother was a sterile dish."*

—Mork, talking about his parents

**First Telecast:** Thursday, September 14, 1978
**Last Telecast:** Thursday, June 10, 1982
**Production Company:** Paramount TV

**Time Slots:**
September 1978–August 1979
Thursday, 8:00–8:30
August 1979–December 1979 Sunday, 8:00–8:30
January 1980–February 1982 Thursday, 8:00–8:30
April 1982–May 1982 Thursday, 8:30–9:00
May 1982–June 1982 Thursday, 8:00–8:30

(*Mork and Mindy* was broadcast solely on ABC during its prime time run. In 1995, the cable station Nick At Nite, a division of Nickelodeon, bought syndication rights to air the series during its very popular weekly prime time schedule. They started their run with a *Mork and Mindy* marathon.)

**Ratings High:**
**Season 1**: *Number 3 in the overall Nielsen with a final 28.6 rating.*

**Main Cast:**
Mork from Ork Robin Williams
Mindy Beth McConnell Pam Dawber
Frederick McConnell (1978–1979; 1980–1982)
Conrad Janis*
Cora Hudson (1978–1979; 1981–1982)
Elizabeth Kerr
Eugene (1978–1979) Jeffrey Jacquet
Orson (voice only) Ralph James
Franklin Delano Bickley Tom Poston
Remo DaVinci (1979–1981) Jay Thomas
Jeannie DaVinci (1979–1981) Gina Hecht
Nelson Flavor (1979–1981) Jim Staahl

---

*Janis's character was dropped from the show during the 1979 season and then brought back in the following season in an attempt to bolster ratings.

Exidor Robert Donner
Glenda Faye "Crissy" Comstock (1980–1981)
Crissy Wilzak
Mr. Miles Sternhagen (1981) Foster Brooks
Mearth (1981–1982) Jonathan Winters

Here is a rundown of all 91 episodes of *Mork and Mindy*, with brief summaries of the storyline, and guest stars who appeared in the show with Robin and Pam Dawber.

**Episode 1: "Mork Moves In" [Debut, Part 1]**
*Guest Stars: Penny Marshall, Cindy Williams, Henry Winkler, Dick Yarmy.* [See the feature on this episode.]

**Episode 2: "To Tell the Truth" [Debut, Part 2]**

**Episode 3: "Mork Runs Away"**
Mork believes that he is being a pain in the shazbot to Mindy and so he decides to run away.

**Episode 4: "Mork in Love"**
Mork is completely bewildered about this strange human emotion we call "love," and so decides to somehow find a way of experiencing it.

**Episode 5: "Mork Runs Down"**
One thing a good Orkan must never forget to do is to take his daily dose of gleek. Mork is not your typical Orkan, however, and he gets sick one day when he *does* forget.

**Episode 6: "Mork's Seduction"**
Mindy's gorgeous girlfriend makes a move on Mork—and Mindy doesn't like it one bit!

**Episode 7: "Mork Goes Public"**
A newspaper reporter gets suspicious about Mork and starts nosing around, suspecting Mindy of harboring an extraterrestrial.

**Episode 8: "A Mommy for Mork"**
Mork decides to experience life as an Earth baby.

*The competency hearing scene from the first episode of* Mork and Mindy. *(Photofest)*

### Episode 9: "Gullible Mork"
A prisoner convinces Mork to free him, assuring the good-hearted Orkan that he will return and turn himself in later.

### Episode 10: "Young Love"
Mindy is confused about whether or not she should marry her old boyfriend. Mork tries to help with typical "Morkish" advice.

### Episode 11: "Mork's Greatest Hits"
Orkans are unwaveringly nonviolent and, thus, when Mork is threatened by a neighborhood bully, he is torn about how to respond.

### Episode 12: "Mork and the Immigrant"
Mork befriends a Russian immigrant, convinced that he, too, is an extraterrestrial. (Robin Williams would, of course, go on to play a Russian "alien" in *Moscow on the Hudson*, later commenting that this character and Mork produced similar feelings in him, since both looked at American culture from the outside.)

### Episode 13: "Mork's First Christmas"
[See the feature later in this scrapbook that looks at the book, *The Mork and Mindy Story*.]

### Episode 14: "Mork the Tolerant"
Mork tries to teach the ever-nasty Mr. Bickley how to be tolerant and considerate of others.

### Episode 15: "Old Fears"
Mindy's grandmother Cora loses a friend when her card partner dies and she suddenly begins to feel old and depressed. Mork, of course, tries to help.

### Episode 16: "Snowflakes Falling"
Mork and Mindy travel to Exidor's secluded mountain hideaway.

### Episode 17: "Mork Goes Erk"
Oh, no! Mork gets word that his sojourn on Earth is over and that he is being transferred to another planet!

### Episode 18: "Mork's Mixed Emotions"
Orkans are not allowed to reveal their emotions. In

*Mindy with her best non-terrestrial friend. (Photofest)*

this episode, Mork defies his training and lets go of his feelings for the first time in his very long life.

### Episode 19: "Yes, Sir, That's My Baby"
Little Eugene has had it up to *here* with spinach and decides to run away from home to a place where no one's even heard of spinach.

### Episode 20: "In Mork We Trust"
Mork and Mindy are afraid that one of their friends is a crook.

### Episode 21: "Mork's Night Out"
Mindy's away, and so Mork (and Mr. Bickley) will play! Specifically, at a singles bar.

### Episode 22: "Mork's Best Friend"
Mork befriends a caterpillar named Bob and persuades Mindy to let him keep the furry millipede as a pet.

### Episode 23: "It's a Wonderful Mork"
There are such wonderful gadgets on Ork! In this episode, Mork uses an Essence Reverser to see what Mindy and company's life would have been like if his egg had never landed in their neighborhood. Shades of *It's a Wonderful Life!*

### Episode 24: "Invasion of the Mork Snatchers"
An early version of *The X-Files?* In this episode, Mork discovers that the United States military has been covering up a nuclear accident.

### Episode 25: "Clerical Error"
Yes, Mork *is* an alien, but not the kind the Immigration Department thinks he is! Mork receives a letter telling him to register with the government as a resident alien, or he will be forced to leave the country.

### Episode 26: "Hold That Mork"
Mork almost becomes a cheerleader.

### Episode 27: "Mork vs. Mindy"
Mork deliberately starts an argument with Mindy and she ends up throwing him out.

### Episode 28: "Mork Gets Mindy-itis"
How could it be? Mork becomes allergic to his beloved Earthling roommate Mindy!

### Episode 29: "Dr. Morkenstern"
Mork plays Dr. Frankenstein and transforms an otherwise quite content unfeeling robot into an emotional being.

### Episode 30: "Mork in Wonderland" [Part 1] (also

*Mork expressing . . . your guess is as good as ours! (Photofest)*

known as "The Incredible Shrinking Mork")
You never know how Orkans are going to react to Earth "stuff." Mork takes a cold medication and ends up shrunk and trapped in a parallel universe.

### Episode 31: "Mork in Wonderland" [Part 2]
The still tiny (but cold-symptom free!) Mork struggles to find a way out of the parallel universe and back to Mindy.

### Episode 32: "Mork Learns to See"
We learn what might be keeping Mr. Bickley so cranky: He has a blind son. Mork fights homesickness after meeting Bickley's boy and realizing that he should count his blessings.

### Episode 33: "Mork's Baby Blues"
Mork becomes a surrogate daddy when a gold digger leaves her child with him.

### Episode 34: "A Morkville Horror"
The house where Mindy used to live is rumored to be haunted. Now it's up for sale.

### Episode 35: "Mork's Health Hints"
Mork is nervous enough when he learns that Mindy has to go into the hospital for a tonsillec-

*Mork tries out for the Denver Broncos cheerleaders and creates an intergalactic uproar in Denver's Mile High stadium in the* Mork and Mindy *episode "Hold That Mork." (Photofest)*

tomy. He almost loses it when the hospital screws up and schedules Mindy for brain surgery!

### Episode 36: "Exidor Affair"
Mork's Orkan compatriot Exidor falls in love with an Earthling: a meter maid.

### Episode 37: "Exidor's Wedding"
Exidor is marrying his meter maid sweetheart and the news gets back to his sainted mother, a woman as strange as her son!

### Episode 38: "Mork Syndrome"
Nelson Flavor sends Mork on a mission: Obtain the political endorsement of the activist organization, the Committee to Clean Up Boulder. The only problem is that the members of the group aren't talking about trash: They want to rid Boulder of any and all ethnic minorities.

### Episode 39: "Raided Mind-Skis"
You know how Earthlings can trade condominium time-shares with fellow vacationers? Well, it's a little bit different with Orkans and other alien beings. Our alien friends trade *minds* with each other when they go on vacation. When Mork takes *his* little mind-swapping sojourn, Mindy is left dealing with extraterrestrials she doesn't know who are wearing Mork's clothes.

### Episode 40: "Dial N for Nelson"
Mystery and intrigue in Boulder. Mindy's cousin Nelson Flavor gives serious consideration to a political career—but then gets an anonymous threat.

### Episode 41: "Mork vs. the Necrotrons" [Part 1]
Ork and Necrotron go to war and the mayhem travels to Earth when our Mork becomes the target of an intergalactic undercover agent.

**Episode 42: "Mork vs. the Necrotrons" [Part 2]**
Mork has to defend himself against the Necrotron enemy agent sent to destroy him.

**Robin on the two-part "Necrotron" episode:** "We had a two-part show with Raquel Welch playing one of three dynamite-looking aliens who come down to Earth, take me prisoner and then try to get information out of me through sensuous tortures. Raquel was in a wild Bob Mackie outfit that had the guys on the set breathing very hard, and one of the other girls was a Playmate, Debra Jo Fondren, with long blond hair braided all the way down her back. The planned tortures included putting me in a hot tub and having the Playmate whip me with her hair. I was not unhappy when they decided against going with that." (*Playboy*, October 1982)

**Episode 43: "Stark Raving Mork"**
The good deeds of a priest genuinely impress and inspire Mork and so he decides to enter the seminary and become a priest himself.

**Episode 44: "Mork's Vacation"**
Mork and Mindy take another vacation retreat at Exidor's secluded hideaway.

**Episode 45: "A Mommy for Mindy"**
Nelson, Mindy's aspiring politician cousin, aggravates Mindy by his sexist and demeaning attitude toward women.

**Episode 46: "A Genie Loves Mork"**
Mindy edits a lonely hearts column and receives a letter from her friend Jeannie, who doesn't know that Mindy is the editor.

**Episode 47: "The Way Mork Were"**
A flashback episode in which Mork and Mindy reminisce about all their adventures since their first meeting.

**Episode 48: "Little Orphan Morkie"**
Mork and Mindy put together a kid's TV show in an attempt to help the political career of Mindy's cousin Nelson.

**Episode 49: "Loonie Tunes and Morkie Melodies"**
Mork becomes a walking encyclopedia of stupid commercials and ad jingles.

**Episode 50: "Putting the Ork Back in Mork"**
When Mork begins to forget his Orkan training and traditions, it becomes obvious that he's as close to an actual Earthling as he can possibly be.

**Episode 51: "Mork in Never Never Land"**
Mork brings home a nut who believes he's really Peter Pan.

**Episode 52: "Dueling Skates"**
Mork challenges the owner of a roller skating rink to a somewhat unconventional competition: a race across the Rocky Mountains!

**Episode 53: "Mork the Prankster"**

*Mork and Mindy enjoying a musical moment in a scene from the episode "It's a Wonderful Mork." (Photofest)*

Mork discovers practical jokes—but doesn't have the requisite humor or good judgment necessary for the jokes to be in good taste.

**Episode 54: "Mork's the Monkey's Uncle"**
Mork brings home an orphaned chimp.

**Episode 55: "Gunfight at the O.K. Corral"**
Mork is challenged to a shootout in a ghost town by a young boy at the day-care center who he tried to convert to nonviolence.

**Episode 56: "Mork's New Look"**
Mork considers plastic surgery.

**Episode 57: "Alas, Poor Mork, We Knew Him Well"**
A doom-and-gloom insurance salesman gives Mork some alarming statistics about accidents and Mork turns into a terrified Orkan who is afraid of almost everything.

**Episode 58: "Mork and the Bum Rap"**
Mork enlists the help of a bum to raise money for a children's hospital.

**Episode 59: "Mindy Gets Her Job"**
Mindy starts work at KTNS-TV.

**Episode 60: "Twelve Angry Appliances"**
Mork confronts an incompetent appliance repair man about his shoddy work.

**Episode 61: "Mork and the Family Reunion"**
Mork is delighted to welcome his hero from Ork—until he learns that the Orkan is there to replace him on Earth.

**Episode 62: "Mork Meets Robin Williams"**
[Read on for the full-length feature on this episode.]

**Episode 63: "Mindy, Mindy, Mindy"**
Mork builds a replacement Mindy when the real Mindy has to go out of town and Mork can't stand the loneliness.

**Episode 64: "Mork and the Swinging Single"**
Mork becomes a woman-crazy, man-about-town when Mindy suggests that he date women other than herself.

**Episode 65: "Mork and Mindy Meet Rick and Ruby"**
Remo DaVinci fires a musical act appearing at his restaurant because the woman in the group is seven

*Raquel Welch guest starred as a deadly agent sent to Earth by the Necrotrons in the* Mork and Mindy *episode "Mork vs. the Necrotrons." (Photofest)*

*Mork proposes to Mindy in this scene from the episode "Limited Engagement." (Photofest)*

months pregnant. Mindy and Mork won't stand for this and they picket the eatery until Remo comes to his senses.

### Episode 66: "There's a New Mork in Town"
Mork steps in when Mindy's blowhard uncle becomes unbearable to one and all.

### Episode 67: "Old Muggable Mork"
When Mindy's grandmother Cora is mugged during a visit to Boulder, Mork steps in and teaches the muggers a lesson: He uses his Orkan power to show them *exactly* what it's like to be old.

### Episode 68: "I Heard It Through the Morkvine"
Mindy becomes KTNS's gossip reporter and Mork goes overboard supplying her with "juicy" gossip.

### Episode 69: "Mindy and Mork"
Mork takes over care of the apartment when Mindy's job keeps her so busy that she can't do it anymore.

### Episode 70: "Bickley's Birthday"
At a fiftieth birthday party for Mr. Bickley, guests take turns revealing their biggest regrets and Mindy wants nothing to do with this little "game."

### Episode 71: "Limited Engagement"
Mork proposes to Mindy.

### Episode 72: "The Wedding"
Even though Orson told him *not* to marry Mindy, Mork goes ahead with the ceremony, prompting Orson to transform Mork into a sheepdog at the altar.

### Episode 73: "The Honeymoon"
Mork and Mindy go on a honeymoon to Ork. The only problem is that the bride is the biggest tourist attraction on the planet.

### Episode 74: "Three the Hard Way"
Upon their return from their honeymoon, Mork learns that he is pregnant. He ultimately gives birth to Mearth.

**Robin on Jonathan Winters joining the Mork and Mindy cast:** "[Having Jonathan] on the show was one of the main reasons I stayed with it. For me, it

*Mork and Mindy's wedding day. (Photofest)*

*The happy bi-planetary couple. (Photofest)*

was like the chance to play alongside Babe Ruth. I'd always wanted just to meet Winters. When I was a kid, my parents would say, 'All right, you can stay up a little longer to see this wonderful man fly around the room and do all his crazy stuff.' " (*Playboy*, October, 1982)

**Episode 75: "Mama Mork, Papa Mindy"**
The title says it all as little bi-galactic Mearth learns about life on Earth and grows up with a somewhat unusual parental arrangement.

**Episode 76: "My Dad Can't Beat Up Anyone"**
Mearth loves the Earth hero Superman and so, to win his son's admiration, Mork pretends that he, too, is a superhero.

**Episode 77: "Long Before We Met"**
Mork meets Mindy's high school sweetheart, gets jealous, and uses his Orkan powers to project himself back in time ten years to see how *he* would have fared in the battle for Mindy's affection.

**Episode 78: "Rich Mork, Poor Mork"**
Mork invests in an "all-Exidor" boutique.

**Episode 79: "Alienation"**
Mearth learns that he is only half human and runs away.

**Episode 80: "P.S. 2001"**
Mearth begins school on Ork but comes home crying when his classmates call him an "Earth-head."

**Episode 81: "Pajama Game II"**
Mork and Mindy allow Mearth to have a sleepover with a friend. The only catch is that Mearth's choice is the stunning Zelka.

**Episode 82. "Present Tense"**
Mork and Mindy have nothing to talk about when Mearth goes away for a few days.

**Episode 83: "Title Unknown"**
Mork and Mearth switch minds—on the evening Mindy's new boss wants to meet her family.

**Episode 84: "Drive, She Said"**
Mork becomes a danger to automobiles and pedestrians alike when Mindy decides he should learn how to drive a car.

**Episode 85: "I Don't Remember Mama"**
Orson cruelly deletes Mork's family from his memory because he doesn't think Mork can handle his past and his present lives.

**Episode 86: "Midas Mork"**
Mearth builds a super-computer named MLT which slowly takes over Mork and Mindy's home.

**Episode 87: "Cheerleaders in Chains"**
Mindy goes to jail rather than reveal a news source.

**Episode 88: "The Mork Report"**
Mork is up for an Orkan promotion—depending on what Orson thinks of the report about Mork's married life.

**Episode 89: "Gotta Run" [Part 1 of a 3-part series finale]**
Mork becomes friends with a guy from Neptune who has an Earthling wife.

**Episode 90: "Gotta Run" [Part 2]**
Mork decides to go public about being an Orkan in an attempt to stop Kalnik the Neptunian's attacks on Earth.

**Episode 91: "Gotta Run" [Part 3]**
After Mork admits he's from Ork, he suddenly has fans, marketers, TV producers, and Kalnik all after him at the same time.

### Robin on learning that Mork and Mindy was doomed:

"There was a period during which I thought, Oh, fuck, man, they're out to kill us all! After that, it was, All right, let us die gracefully. "My feeling now is that we did some good stuff—some strange stuff, too—and I know that we made an impact on our time." —*Robin, in the October 1982 issue of Playboy, talking about how the cast of Mork and Mindy all felt that the bigwigs at the network were no longer behind their show and were looking for any excuse to dump it.*

*Mork and Mindy with their child, Mearth (Jonathan Winters). (Photofest)*

# A Multitude of Morkisms

*"Q: How many martians does it take to screw in a lighbulb?*
*A: 8.2"*

—Typical Orkan Joke

**M**ork came to Earth from Ork much the way many European immigrants arrived in America: Possibly a *little* familiar with English, but much more comfortable with their own languages.

Since Mork had been on Earth earlier, and since Orkans can absorb information and languages quickly, Mork was able to immediately communicate with Mindy and other Earthlings.

But he still resorted to Orkan terms when English failed him.

Here is a look at a few of the more colorful Orkan "Morkisms" that our favorite alien sprinkled throughout his rapid-fire conversations. (Definitions are somewhat subjective. You'll have to check with an Orkan if you have further questions.)

**Ark, ark!**: Ha, ha!

**Bleem**: A span of time that doesn't really have an understandable counterpart on Earth. It is apparently an Orkan "year," although the actual time span of a bleem seems to be considerably longer than our terran twelve-month period. We know that Mork had been on Earth three bleems prior to his landing in Boulder but we *don't* know what that was in actual Earth time.

**Cholly-cho-cho**: Orkan term for a head.

**D, D, and E!**: "Dedicated, diligent, and efficient!" Mork's self-appraisal. Mork assures Orson during his first field report to Ork that he is, indeed, "D, D, and E."

**Geezbah!**: An exclamation of shock or surprise.

**Gleem**: The term for the space egg in which Mork arrived on Earth.

**Grebble**: An all-purpose noun-adjective.

**Gribbet**: Grip, as in a handshake.

**Har, har, har, har**: Ha, ha, ha, ha.

**Harf**: Hair.

**Little Hatchling Brothers**: Mork's term for Earth eggs.

**Munchkin-like persons**: Children.

**Na-noo, na-noo**: Think: Shalom or Aloha. This means hello, goodbye, how are you?, gosh!, really?, and serves as an all-purpose expletive-greeting for Orkans. Occasionally, Mork will throw out a single "Na-noo," which sort of

*Breakfast with an Orkan. (Photofest)*

serves as "Hi" in these instances.

**Nap-nap**: Please be quiet.

**-ness**: Mork's all-purpose suffix for addressing his superior, Orson, as in "Your Immenseness," "Your Cinerama-ness," etc. (He also once addressed Orson as "Your Fattitude.")

**Nimnuls**: Jerks, morons, idiots, fools, dolts, blockheads, etc.

**No sweat off my front!**: "I am not in the least bit distressed or dismayed by the recent turn of events."

**Ptooey! [To spit]**: This, believe it or not, means "Thank you!"

**Scrim**: Vamoose! Scram! Get outta here!

**Shazbot!**: Another all-purpose expletive, but a tad more profane, with Mork prone to using it in more charged situations.

**Thribets**: The Orkan form of currency.

**Tip my tripla**: Tip of the hat. (This must be accompanied by a squeeze of the nose and the words, "Doo-da, doo-da!")

**Toad-tush**: An Orkan insult.

Even though *Mork and Mindy* was very tightly scripted, the irrepressible Robin often ad-libbed hilarious contributions which were allowed to remain in the episode. Some of these Morkisms, then, more than likely sprang from the astonishingly fecund brain of the Jocular One.

# The Most Memorable *Mork and Mindy* Episode of All Time: "Mork Meets Robin Williams"

*"I'm a performing addict. I can't get enough of it."*

—Robin Williams

ohn Lennon is my favorite Beatle. Keep that in mind for now. The reason I'm telling you this will become clear at the conclusion of this feature.

The episode I consider the most memorable of the entire *Mork and Mindy* series took place in 1981, about two-thirds of the way through the series run. Robin had already done *Popeye* and his *The World According to Garp* was on the horizon. He was still doing comedy concerts and albums, and was very well known and popular. He could justifiably be called a big star.

Episode 62, "Mork Meets Robin Williams," was an attempt to capitalize on Robin's fame and give him a chance to make some personal statements about the nature of fame and what it means to be a celebrity in America. (The show's credits say that this episode was written by Dale McRaven and Bruce Johnson, but there are lines of dialogue and events mentioned that obviously came from Robin himself; he clearly had a great deal of input into what "Robin Williams" said.)

The episode begins with Mindy talking on the phone to some flunky in Robin Williams's organization:

> I know he's a big star. That's why I want to interview him for KTNS. Oh, I have to go through his manager, Mr. Morra [Robin's then real-life manager]? Well, could you have Mr. Morra's secretary return my call?

Mindy hangs up and muses to herself, "I wonder if Woodward and Bernstein had this much trouble trying to get to Nixon."

Mork enters from upstairs. He's wearing a tux and wants to know if Mindy likes his threads. "Do you think it's more Sears?," he wonders, striking a typical sedate Sears catalog pose; "Or GQ?," then hitting a smoldering *Gentleman's Quarterly* pose.

Mindy tells him he looks nice, but reminds him to hold in his stomach. Mork replies that she looks nice, too, but that *she* should remember to hold in her thighs.

Mindy then asks Mork to guess who she hopes to interview. "Rula Lenska?" Mork guesses. Mindy tells him Robin Williams and Mork blankly asks, "Who?"

Mork then tells Mindy that Robin Williams's parents must have had a sense of humor, because the word "Robin" on Ork means something utterly disgusting.

Mindy explains to Mork just who Robin Williams is: "He's a comedian. He's a star of TV, movies, and nightclubs."

She explains to Mork that "A lot of people on Earth are interested to hear what stars have to say."

Mindy tells Mork that he looks a little like Robin Williams.

"Scoff, scoff," Mork replies and, when Mindy shows him the cover of Robin Williams's latest comedy album, *Reality . . . What a Concept* (for which Robin won a Grammy in 1979), Mork proceeds to verbally tear apart the comedian's face:

> He looks like he does his hair with a Cuisinart! He's got a road map for eyes! You could pack a family in that nose, Minnd! And look at that mouth! They had to airbrush his entire face! I'm bright and cheery—this guy's got big problems!

The scene shifts to the TV station where Mindy works. Her boss, Mr. Sternhagen, gives her an ultimatum: Deliver the interview with Robin Williams or he himself will be out of a job. And if he goes, he tells her, she goes with him. Mindy protests that Robin is impossible to get in touch with. Sternhagen tells her that Robin performed for free at the Boulder Comedy Cabaret the previous night, and that the comic had lunch yesterday at DaVinci's Restaurant where he signed autographs and posed for pictures with all the patrons.

Mindy is stunned. Her dear friends Remo and Jeannie own DaVinci's and didn't call her, even though they knew she was desperate for an interview with Robin.

Mindy goes to DaVinci's for lunch to confront Jeannie, who apologizes and is forgiven. Mindy's dismay at missing Robin doesn't stop Remo from showing her his Robin Williams Polaroids, though, including pictures of Robin with Remo; Robin with Jeannie; Robin with Armando the Exterminator; and Robin autographing the chopped liver with his finger, complete with a happy face over the "i."

At this point, Mork comes in carrying a bumper from a car that rolled down a hill because the owner forgot to set his parking brake. Everyone in the restaurant thinks Mork is Robin and they chase him, tear off his clothes, and throw him up in the air as Remo and Nelson watch from the restaurant door.

Later, back at her apartment, Mindy pretends she is Barbara Walters in yet another futile attempt to get through to Robin on the phone. Her boss stops by after an alcohol-rich lunch and reminds her again that she really needs to get the interview with Robin. Because Mr. Sternhagen shouldn't drive, Mindy allows him to stay at her place and take a nap. Mork then arrives at the apartment with his clothes torn to shreds, convinced everyone in Boulder now knows that he's an alien. But he shouldn't be feared or attacked, he tells Mindy. He's just like everybody else:

> I say my prayers, I pet my vegetables, I put my pants on like everybody else—head first!

The mob pursued him with pens and called him filthy names, he tells Mindy. They

(*Photofest*)

called him "Robin!" Mork is terrified that if the horde of people catch him, they'll tar and feather him and put him on *That's Incredible!* (Remember that show?!)

Mindy tries to calm Mork, explaining that the people thought he was Robin Williams and wanted his clothes because they like Robin very much. Mork agrees to accompany Mindy to the concert hall that evening where he'll try to help her sneak backstage so she can meet Robin.

The next scene takes place outside the concert hall where Robin is performing that night. Mork and Mindy arrive. Mork is wearing a Groucho nose, mustache, and glasses as a disguise. Mindy persuades him that no one will think he's Robin, but when Mork removes his glasses, the crowd goes crazy and mobs him again.

A security guard (played by Rance Howard, Ron *Happy Days* Howard's father) hurries out and escorts "Mr. Williams" and Mindy into Robin Williams's dressing room. The guard asks Mork if there's anything more he can do for him and Mork replies, "A new pair of retinas would be very nice, please." The guard doesn't crack a smile and tells Mork, "Hard to believe you get paid for that."

Mindy is incredibly excited: She's finally going to meet a big star! Mork tries to talk some sense into her, telling her that a star "is just a big ball of glowing hot gas," and that Robin is just "a human being that's been hyped by an advertising campaign." Mork also revealed that if it were up to him, he'd prefer to be home flossing his ears.

At this point, the "real" Robin Williams (acting in a split-screen special effect) finally appears, wearing a black sportcoat, a garish Hawaiian print shirt, and a long white scarf. The first thing he does is tell Mork, "You know, you look a lot like . . . no, he's a woman now."

Mindy musters the courage to ask Robin for an interview and Mork chimes in telling Robin it's been a bad year for Mindy: She bet on Carter and Roberto Duran, and she bought Chrysler stock. (President Jimmy Carter lost his reelection bid, boxer Roberto Duran got beat, and automaker Chrysler's stock plummeted.)

Robin agrees to an interview, but before they start, he asks Mindy, "You're not from the *Enquirer*, are you? Little joke."

(In 1992, Robin talked to *Playboy* about what was behind this joke: "My mother's so naive about certain things. The *National Enquirer* called her and

said, 'We're doing a story and we'd like to have some photos.' She gave them photos of my father and me and some school photos. They used these pictures to imply that my father was this tyrant and I came from this horrible existence and that's why I was funny.")

To break the ice, Mindy tells Robin that he's got tighter security than the Pope. Mork tells Robin that Mindy couldn't get by his "manager's secretary's secretary's secretary's answering machine." Mindy signals him to be quiet and asks Robin her first question, "What's it like to be a celebrity?"

Robin replies that it's "not bad, really." He tells her that it's especially nice when he can get into really "chi-chi" restaurants whereas before they wouldn't even have let him wash the floor.

Mork once again chimes in with his own question: "Why do you wear baggy pants?" to which Robin immediately fires back, "I don't want a visible panty line!" Mork is excited: "There's your headline right there, Minnd! 'Robin Williams: Kinky!' " Robin also says to Mork, "You're a member of the Brotherhood of Bozo—why do *you* wear them?" Mork replies in a typical Orkan fashion, "Oh, that's where I keep my bees!"

Mindy brings up the subject of Williams's stamina. She reminds him that he flew all night on a plane from Hawaii, after which he lectured for three hours at the university. Then, he performed until three A.M. at the Comedy Cabaret, and now he was preparing to do two live shows.

Robin explains that he did the university lecture as a favor to the pilot that flew him to Colorado. The pilot had a daughter attending drama class at the school and he said that "if I'd lecture, he'd pull out of the dive!" ("Interesting concept," Mork mused. "Blackmail by gravity.") Robin also explained that the Comedy Cabaret was owned by "a friend of a cousin of a friend," and he couldn't say no.

Mindy considers this and tells him the angle for her story: "Robin Williams: The Comedian Who Can't Say No."

After giving Mork permission to eat some of his dressing room flowers ("A man's actually *grazing* in front of me!") Robin Williams gives a moving (and funny) speech in which he tries to explain his inability to say no to people.

I don't know why I can't say no. I guess

I want people to like me. I hate myself for that. I used to be able to say no.

Before all this craziness started, my friends used to call me up and go, "Robin, come on, we're all going outside. Really. There's some gnarly waves. We can all hang out." And I'd have to go, "No, my momma says I have to stay inside and read Nietzsche tonight."

Later on, I guess I felt really afraid to say no to them because then they'd all say, "Oh, Robin Williams! Mr. Smarty Pants! Mr. Big Shot! You forgot your old friends! You can't lend me ten thousand dollars for a new car! You won't do the Save the Shrimp benefit!"

Mindy tells Robin that if these guys were really his friends, they'd understand and reminds him that now, Robin Williams can't even say no to a total stranger. She also tells him that she thinks he's probably taken advantage of a lot and that if he learned to say no more often, then he'd have a lot more time to himself. Revealingly, Robin replies, "Maybe that's the last thing I want."

The guard steps in and says, "Five minutes, Mr. Williams," to which Mork replies, "Thank you," and the guard does a funny double take.

Robin tells Mindy that he'll come down to her TV station the next day and do an on-camera interview with her, but she refuses. She does not want to be one more person taking advantage of Robin's generous nature.

Mork then tells Robin that he was chased by Robin's fans—which Robin calls "Celebrity 1-A"—and found it a frightening experience. He asks Robin: "Why do you want to take a job where they tear your clothes off and throw you in the air?" Robin then humorously explains his genesis: "Actually, I became a performer by accident. You see, my dad used to have this job where he had to move around a lot. And sometimes he'd leave the forwarding address. Actually, he'd pack me in the crates with the dishes!"

Robin describes his somewhat lonely childhood, a childhood which created the person he was now as an adult:

I was always being the new kid in the neighborhood. And since I was suffering from a case of the Terminal Shy, I couldn't make friends that easily and I always spent a lot of time in my room and I created my own little world full of all these little characters that had strange and unusual qualities.

After a while, I realized that people found these characters funny and outrageous and then it got to the point where I realized that the character could say and do things that I was afraid to do myself. And after a little while . . . well, here I am!

We then hear Robin being introduced to the audience and he leaves to take the stage. Mindy notes the tremendous ovation for Robin and Mork muses that "all [that] applause might make torn clothes worthwhile."

And thus, "Mork Meets Robin Williams" concludes, except, of course, for Mork's report to Orson, one of the most poignant and powerful moments of the entire series:

**MORK**

Mork calling Orson! Come in, your Cinerama-ness! This week I learned what it's like to be famous on Earth.

**ORSON**

That's good.

**MORK**

Well, sir, sometimes it is and sometimes it isn't. You see, most Earthlings try very hard to be recognized for what they do, but when they become stars, sir, they realize they're recognized wherever they go.

**ORSON**

You mean they lose their privacy?

**MORK**

Well, sir, sometimes they can even lose their *clothes.* You see, being a star, sir, is a twenty-four-hour job—and you can't leave your face at the office!

**ORSON**

Isn't fame its own reward?

**MORK**

Well, yes, sir, it is. But when you're a celebrity, everybody wants a piece of you, sir. Unless you can say no, there will be no pieces left for yourself.

*Our favorite extraterrestrial and his dearest Earthling. (Photofest)*

ORSON

I thought all stars are rich, live in mansions, and drive big eggs.

MORK

I know, sir, that's the common misconception. But you see, to get to that you have to pay a very heavy price. You have responsibilities, anxieties, and, well, to be honest, sir, some of them can't take it.

ORSON

I'm not buying it, Mork.

MORK

Why, sir?

ORSON

It sounds to me like they have it made.

MORK

Well, most of them do, sir. But some are victims of their own fame. Very special and talented people. People like Elvis Presley, Marilyn Monroe, Janis Joplin, Jimi Hendrix, Lenny Bruce, Freddie Prinze. And John Lennon.

Fade to black.

I screened "Mork Meets Robin Williams" for this book on Sunday, December 8, 1996. As you might imagine, I was very moved by Mork's wistful and sad tribute to the show business icons no longer with us, especially his mention of my favorite Beatle, John Lennon.

It wasn't until the following morning that I realized that I had watched this episode on the sixteenth anniversary of John Lennon's December 8, 1980 assassination.

# *Shmork and Windy* The September 1979 Mad Magazine Parody of *Mork and Mindy*

In September 1979, *Mork and Mindy* was exactly one season old and was already the third highest–rated show in America, tied, ironically, with its boob tube progenitor, *Happy Days*, with each show garnering a stellar 28.6 Nielsen rating.

Such success brought overnight fame to Robin Williams—and made him an easy target for *MAD* magazine, that bastion of pop culture mockery and satire.

*Shmork and Windy* begins with the alien Shmork from Pork arriving on Earth after he is hatched from his egg by *Sesame Street*'s Big Bird. He convinces Windy from Boulder to let him move in with her.

We learn from Shmork that kneeling is a sex act on Pork ("Evidently, your father never told you about 'The Birds and the Knees'!!"); that he can drink through his fingers; and that he enjoys hanging upside down. Shmork then makes fun of *The Gong Show* and Tiny Tim, and when Windy's father

asks what he's doing, she tells him, "He's doing one of his time-killing shticks! That, and a few dozen na-noo's and Shazbots save our writers the trouble of having to come up with new gags or plots."

The parody then makes fun of Shmork's tendency to get confused with the way things are done on Earth (he thinks "holding up a bank" means lifting it up off the ground) and Windy asks him, "Isn't there ANYTHING on Earth that doesn't confuse you?", to which Shmork replies:

Of course there is! Paychecks, royalties, rerun rights, spin-offs, merchandising tie-ins, and the ever popular residuals! Two more seasons of "Na-noo, na-noo!" and I'll be able to buy me General Motors!

The music store that Windy's father owns is failing and Windy is quite concerned. When she expresses her worries to Shmork, he says "Look of concern . . . serious voice," which prompts Windy to ask him how he ever got into that "cute adorable habit" of verbalizing and describing his feelings. In a scorching critique of Robin's performance on the show, the *MAD* writers have Shmork respond, "Easy! At the audition for this show, I was so nervous, I read the stage directions out loud by mistake!"

The rest of this satirical piece focuses on an investigation by the Federal Bureau of Investigation of Windy's alleged sighting of an unidentified flying object (Shmork's flying saucer), which the government thinks is part of a Communist plot to plant a spy in the United States. Shmork contacts Awsom to tell him that Earthlings are hypocritical because they all complain that there's nothing worth watching on TV and yet they're all "running out and buying expensive gadgets to record any of these lousy shows they may have to miss."

Windy interrupts Shmork's communique with Awsom to tell him that a flying saucer has landed in their yard and the "things" in it are looking for him. These "things" turn out to be Darth Vader, Mr. Spock, and other famous aliens who are mad at Shmork for being the "first creature from outer space that's stupider than most Earthlings!!" The piece concludes with Darth Vader lambasting Shmork for ruining their "hard-earned alien image."

*Shmork and Windy* is a funny look at a popular show that was written when the show was at its hottest. Looking back at this *MAD* strip almost twenty years later, it is fascinating to realize that the ubiquitous VCR was still a new and expensive "gadget" and that not everyone was enamored of Robin's performance in the show.

Today, Robin's work in *Mork and Mindy* is universally considered to be a brilliant harbinger of his unquestioned comedic genius. *MAD* obviously felt that he wasn't anything special, which makes *Shmork and Windy* even funnier in hindsight.

# Fandom on Parade: A Look at The Mork and Mindy Story

*"We like to think of it as being 'intellectual slapstick.'"*

—*Mork and Mindy* writer-producer
Dale McCraven, talking about the show

*The Mork and Mindy Story* is a 75-page paperback by Peggy Herz published by Scholastic Book Services in 1979 to capitalize on the enormous popularity of Robin's hot new show.

This authorized book, now out of print and considered a collector's item, included a cover color photo of Robin and Pam Dawber, and eighteen black-and-white photos from the show. It also boasted new interviews with the entire cast, including Robin Williams, and provided some fascinating behind-the-scenes info on the making of the show as well as the private lives of the cast in the early days of the show.

*The Mork and Mindy Story* contained eight chapters and was aimed at a young teen-high school audience.

## The Flying Egg

The book's first chapter, "The Flying Egg," was a summary of the first episode of the series. This chapter was essentially a prose rewrite of the original script, with a final paragraph revealing that Robin Williams was not the original choice to play Mork when the character was first introduced on *Happy Days*:

Making a TV show into a big comedy hit isn't easy; it takes talent and time and hard work. It also takes luck—and luck was with the producers of *Mork and Mindy* when they were casting the show. They hired someone to play Mork in an episode of *Happy Days,* but the actor they had hired changed his mind. The producers had to replace him quickly. They held an open audition, and a young comic actor came walking in off the street. Nobody knew him. His name, he said, was Robin Williams.

The original actor who was supposed to play Mork was the versatile and malleable comedian John Byner. Byner had had a couple of failed sitcom attempts in the sixties and seventies, and was known in the late seventies primarily for his appearances on variety shows as an impressionist or skit player. Although Byner probably would have done a credible job playing Mork, he doesn't come close to manifesting the manic comic genius that Robin Williams brought to the role.

## Funniest, Sure, but Successful?

The book's second chapter, "Robin Williams: Voted 'Funniest' and 'Least Likely to Succeed,'" was a look at the beginnings of "Morkmania." It revealed that it was *Mork and Mindy* producer Garry Marshall's son Scotti, when he was only nine, who originally suggested that his dad add an alien to his *Happy Days* series.

The chapter looked at the *Happy Days* episode in which Mork made his first appearance and provided some background on Marshall's phenomenally successful career.

The author revealed that "Garry Marshall never intended to make Mork the star of his own series. Mork was to be in one episode of *Happy Days* and that was all. But TV viewers of all ages had something to say about that. They said it in cards and letters which poured into the network and the TV studio." No doubt about it, the producers realized Mork was hot and they saw a tremendous opportunity to capitalize on Robin Williams's new popularity.

The author then talked about her first meeting with Robin Williams, in 1978 when he was twenty-six. This meeting took place at a pivotal time in Robin's life and career. *Mork and Mindy* was just going into production and the following week,

(Author's collection)

Robin was getting married. He would be wedding a Connecticut dancer named Valerie Velardi in an outdoor ceremony in Tiburon, California. (My wife went to high school with Valerie and her family is very well known in southern Connecticut, having been in business in the area for years.)

Herz described Robin at their first meeting with a string of flattering adjectives: "warm, intelligent, friendly." So, in typical "Robin" form, one of the first things Robin did was lie to her: "I have a slight Scottish accent," he told her. "That's because I was born in Scotland and lived there for a year as a child." Herz later learned that Robin regularly changed his birthplace depending on his mood. Chicago, Detroit, Scotland, whatever. (He was actually born in Chicago in 1952.)

Herz then provided some interesting autobiographical background information on Robin. We learn that Robin had two grown half-brothers Todd and Loren (from his mother's earlier marriage) whom he didn't really see a lot when he was growing up. (In the nineties, Robin has often talked about how he had since grown closer to these half-siblings and expressed gladness that he now knew them better and is able to share in their lives and families.)

Robin told Herz that his father's job moved them around a lot when he was a kid and thus, he retreated into his imagination to keep

and humiliation with the beginning of his comedic sensibility: "I started wrestling and dieted off 30 pounds in a year. The comedy started then."

In a 1982 interview with *Playboy*, Robin spoke in more detail about getting beat up as a kid:

I started telling jokes in the seventh grade as a way to keep from getting the shit kicked out of me. Mom and Dad had put me in public school, and most of the kids there were bigger than me and wanted to prove they were bigger by throwing me into walls. There were a lot of burly farm kids and sons of auto plant workers there, and I'd come to school looking for new entrances and thinking, "If only I could come in through the roof." They'd nail me as soon as I got through the door.

After his father's retirement, the family moved to the San Francisco area and Robin got his first exposure to the world of stand-up comedy. He said that he wasn't into theater when he was in high school, instead preferring science and running, but then one day he discovered a place called The Committee, where young stand-up comedians often got their first shot at trying to make an audience laugh. "It fascinated me to watch them," Robin said. "I wasn't really thinking of doing comedy myself, but I loved watching the others do it."

After high school (as the chapter title indicates, Robin was voted "Funniest"—no surprise there—and "Least Likely to Succeed"—*big* surprise there, wouldn't you say?), Robin entered Claremont Men's College as a political science major. He lasted exactly one year. Robin's father was alarmed at his obvious penchant for acting and the theater, and wanted Robin to take up a trade like welding so he'd have something to fall back on. (Now *that's* a great idea: Put a blowtorch in the hands of a manic Robin Williams!) But Robin had a different dream and instead enrolled in the College of Marin

(*Author's collection*)

himself occupied. "During all that time," he explained, "my imagination was my best friend." Robin was heavy as a child and later told Herz that he "used to get beaten up a lot." He attributed this ostracization

to study Shakespeare, but not as an actor. Robin studied the bard's legendary work as *literature*, but this didn't last either, and shortly after he enrolled, he decided to leave school once again and move—where else?—to New York, New York, the town so nice they named it twice—and the place to go if you're just starting out a career in show business.

## American Cheese, Steve Martin, and a Lizard

The next chapter, "A Hit TV Show—and a Lizard Under the Refrigerator," tells of Robin's adventures in the Big Apple.

Once in New York, Robin managed to win a scholarship to the prestigious Julliard School (ironically, the audition for the scholarship was held in San Francisco), where he learned acting, singing, how to move, how to speak, juggling, mime work, physical comedy, and everything else that was necessary to become a successful entertainer.

He began doing improvisational workshops and, finally, stand-up comedy. He lived with a group of fellow students and he remembered that their diet consisted mainly of cottage cheese, yogurt, and American cheese sandwiches. (Mmmmm, tasty!)

As he also discussed in his 1979 *Playgirl* interview [see the feature on that interview], to earn money, Robin often performed street mime in front of the Metropolitan Museum, sometimes making over $100 a day.

After his scholarship ran out, Robin left Julliard in 1976, and quickly learned that it really didn't matter to casting directors where you studied; they were mainly interested in what you could do. Robin subsequently returned to San Francisco and began looking for a career path:

> I wanted to get into an acting company, but there was only one, and they weren't holding auditions right then. So I had to wait, and one night, I went to a comedy workshop. I started to work there regularly.

Robin didn't get paid at the workshop, however, so he took odd jobs to support himself, including painting houses, waiting tables, and other types of mundane work.

During this "dues-paying" period, Robin worked in some horrible places. "I've performed in

discos," he recalled, "while they were still dancing!" All this time, though, he was learning, and diligently fine-tuning his comedic persona. "You have to start finding your own style," he told Herz. "When I was a kid, I loved Jonathan Winters. He is my inspiration, but I've never met him." (This situation was remedied, of course, when Winters took a recurring role on *Mork and Mindy* as the son, Mearth.)

Robin and the author then talked about some of his early stand-up routines, and Robin described a few of the various characters he created and performed during this period, including an old hippy poet named "Grandpa Funk" and a Russian stand-up comedian named "Joey Stalin" (who was later renamed "Nicky Lenin"). Giving us a glimpse into the creative process, Robin then talked about how he created his own unique brand of comedy: "I don't write out my routines, but I write down concepts—or very general ideas."

Robin also reminisced about his first big concert appearance. It was in 1978 and Robin performed before seven thousand people in San Francisco. Steve Martin and Joan Baez were also on the bill and Robin recalled that "It was like performing in the Roman arena." Robin got a standing ovation for his performance at this concert. (Robin and Steve Martin would again work together in 1988 in the Samuel Beckett play, *Waiting for Godot*. [See the feature on that production.])

## Did You Know . . .

. . . that Robin's portrayal of the "Mork" character was inspired by Steven Spielberg's film, *Close Encounters of the Third Kind?*

It turns out that Robin had seen the classic sci-fi movie the week before he tried out for the Mork role on *Happy Days* and shortly thereafter, an amazing juxtaposition of creative elements occurred: Robin, after seeing the film, added "The Alien Comedian" to his cast of characters, and gave him a whole repertoire of weird noises and behaviors—which was *exactly* what the *Happy Days* (and subsequently, the *Mork and Mindy*) people wanted from the Mork character!

Here is Robin describing his audition in an October 1982 *Playboy* interview:

> When I auditioned for Mork, I made every bizarre noise and gesture I could

think of, and the director, Jerry Paris, hired me and pretty much let me play it the way I wanted to. The show got some positive feedback, and for whatever reason, ABC decided to use the Mork character in a spinoff series.

Robin was at first unsure about Mork's narrative longevity. "I didn't see how they could develop the character," he said. But Garry Marshall said they would give the character two distinct personality traits, craziness and humanity, and that was enough for Robin to take it from there.

Robin found the fairly rigid structure of weekly television a bit daunting. "My favorite thing is to improvise—to make up things as I go along," he explained. "But the time limits of TV make that difficult to do. I managed to do *some* improvising, though."

Even though *Mork and Mindy* was a huge success, with Robin already a star and on his way to even greater accomplishments, he still felt the need to perform comedy in clubs. He used his stand-up performances as a tool to find new material and new ideas. This makes sense. Robin often used his comedy as a means of self-discovery. Now, because his opportunity for improvisation was limited on his weekly television show, he still felt the need to get out there and try and make people laugh spontaneously. "Comedy gives you a chance to really connect creatively," he explained. "I'm still learning." But sometimes improvisation can backfire. Robin told Herz the story of a night when he stayed on stage too long and could not find the courage or means to gracefully exit—long after he knew he had exhausted his time. "I wanted to leave, and the audience wanted me to leave," he candidly admitted. "I don't write my act—and, that night, I just couldn't get myself off stage."

As is often the case with comics and actors who have a manic stage presence, when Robin is not "on," he is quiet and subdued. He likes to read science fiction, run, and go to the beach when not performing. And, of course, he loves going to the movies. In a fascinating foreshadowing of one of his most memorable roles—the Genie in *Aladdin*—Robin talked about animation, revealing that he loved going to animation festivals because "great things are being done in animation!"

This chapter closed with Herz telling her readers that Robin was currently living in Los Angeles in an apartment with Valerie (They have since divorced). They had a parrot, an iguana, and two lizards, and, thus, we learn where the title of this chapter came from: "One lizard lives in a cage," Robin told his interviewer. "The other lives under the refrigerator."

## "I Don't Do Martians"

The next chapter, "Finding A Comedian Who Could Act," told the story of the birth of the *Mork and Mindy* series.

When Garry Marshall originally approached TV writer-producer Dale McCraven with the idea for the series, McCraven was less than thrilled with the concept. "[Garry] said to me, 'Do you want to do a show about a Martian?'" he recalled to Herz. "And I said, 'I'm sorry. I don't do Martians.'"

Marshall also called writer-producer Bruce Johnson and asked him the same question. Like McCraven, though, Johnson had never seen the "Mork" episode of *Happy Days* and was also underwhelmed by the concept.

McCraven and Johnson's reluctance vanished, however, after Garry Marshall showed them the episode of *Happy Days* in which Robin made his first appearance as Mork from Ork.

They were unanimous: "Robin Williams impressed us."

And they immediately recognized the comedic potential of little Scotti Marshall's idea and agreed to give the "Mork" series a try.

Production began in July of 1978, with a script cowritten by McCraven and Johnson. Their conceptual approach to the series was a tried-and-true sitcom theme: the fish out of water. "Mork is like a newborn babe in a grown-up body," McCraven said. They would write about Mork reacting to his new environment and bringing to it his Orkan traditions and customs. This type of show could fail miserably (as it has many times in the history of TV) but these guys had one element hugely in their favor: Robin Williams. They were all delighted to learn that not only was Robin very funny, but he could act as well.

During her discussion with McCraven and Johnson about how the show was written and produced, Herz brought up the persistent rumor that Robin ad-libbed the majority of his dialogue. The two TV veterans were both adamant that that simply was not the case. "Not true," they both insisted. "A half-hour TV show couldn't possibly be done that way." McCraven explained how the scripts were infused with that special Robin Williams touch:

> Robin contributes a great deal. But we don't leave holes in the scripts! Robin can take lines that have been written and make them sound like ad-libs, which is great. He comes off as being spontaneous, but he is a very studied man. He may try some ad-libs during rehearsals. But when we film the show on Thursday, he knows exactly what he's doing.

To further confuse matters, here is Robin himself, in a 1982 interview with *Playboy,* weighing in on the scripted versus improvised question:

**Robin Williams** The show was a crapshoot that worked out, and the freedom I had on it was incredible. If *Mork and Mindy* had been totally scripted, I don't think we would have lasted more than seven weeks, but the producers saw an energy happening between Pam and me, and they didn't want to mess with it. So they let me improvise, and in the script, there'd be notes for me to say something on the theme of such and such, and I'd just go off and expand on it.

**Playboy:** Isn't that unusual in a TV series?

**Robin Williams:** As far as I know, it is. But you have to remember that Mork supposedly was an open book, a sieve who'd picked up his knowledge of the planet from years of watching Earth television. He was a little like a comic book character called Zippy the Pinhead, somebody who absorbs everything that comes in but who puts it back out a little out of context, like a word processor with dyslexia. It helped that Mork was an alien, because in some ways there were no real boundaries as to what he could say or do.

And finally, here is Robin's costar Pam Dawber offering *her* spin on this question:

> Robin is the main energy of our show. Obviously, he is the star of the show. And there are times when he doesn't follow the script. He improvises. When he does that, all I can do is stay loose. I remind myself: "I'm here because I'm

having a good time." And I tell myself before I go out in front of the studio audience that if I blow a line, we'll all laugh, and so will the studio audience.

(In another late seventies interview, cited in Rick Mitz's *The Great TV Sitcom Book,* Robin said, "I improvise about one-third of my dialogue. The director gives me a time slot and I fill it. I walk all over the script. I pick up a verbal shotgun and go berserk. Otherwise you end up giving in to TV. The pressures on TV writers are so great they'll do the silliest things over and over. My job is to fight that voodoo repetition.")

The two producers also talked about how they "toned down" the Mork character once he had his own show. They took away some of his supernatural powers, including his ability to walk through walls, making the point that the more "human" Mork was, the more vulnerable he would be to the audience, thereby making him more popular and more endearing. After all, if Mork could simply levitate his way out of an awkward situation or vanish through a wall on a whim, it would take away a lot of the humor potential intrinsic to an alien trying to deal with life on Earth. (This is a valid point, but characters with incredible supernatural powers, most notably Samantha on *Bewitched* and Jeannie on *I Dream of Jeannie,* were successes even though they wielded their powers at will. Then again, these mystical ladies weren't sprinkling their magic in front of a live audience.)

Another interesting piece of *Mork and Mindy* trivia revealed in this chapter was the fact that the show was originally scheduled to air in the deadly time slot of 8:00 P.M. on Mondays—directly opposite the enormously popular *Monday Night Football.* (Back in the late seventies, *Monday Night Football* was shown live in every time zone *except* the Eastern, which meant that only on the East Coast would *Mork* be shown at 8:00 on Mondays. Because football was time-delayed on the East Coast, all the other time zones would have shown *Mork* whenever they could squeeze it into their schedules— like Sundays at 6:00 A.M.!)

A studio executive who saw the taping of a couple of shows quickly intervened, however, and gave *Mork and Mindy* the time slot they deserved, Thursdays at 8:00 P.M. (This is probably one of the hottest time slots on network prime time TV: Today, almost twenty years later, that slot is occupied by a show that has consistently been in the top five of the Nielsens since its debut, *Friends*.)

## The Christmas Episode

The next chapter of the *Mork and Mindy Story*, "Mork Learns About Christmas," looks at the very first *Mork and Mindy* Christmas-themed episode, "Mork's First Christmas," which featured guest stars Morgan Fairchild and Dave Ketchum.

This episode is quite touching and Robin does an amazing job at conveying to the audience his excitement about Mork's very first Christmas season on Earth, while also showing us just how confusing all the holiday traditions and rituals can be to someone unfamiliar with them.

Author Herz attended the rehearsal for the episode and was able to observe how Robin could switch from manic mayhem to poignant drama in an eye blink.

The story centers around Mork learning that he is supposed to give gifts to his friends at Christmas. But being Mork, he doesn't quite *get* it. His Christmas gift to Mindy? A bracelet made of dead flies. "There are lots more upstairs!" he excitedly tells a stunned and repulsed Mindy. Mindy and her dad and their guests try to pretend that they are thrilled with Mork's bizarre gifts, but he overhears them talking about how strange and inappropriate they are and realizes he has made a huge blunder.

He decides to make it up to them by giving them each something he knows they would appreciate: A thought. Mork has the ability to put images into people's minds, and so, he gives them each a memory.

To Mindy, he gives the memory of the day a beloved childhood dog she thought was lost forever returned home.

To Mindy's grandmother, he gives the memory of her first Christmas with her late husband, Mindy's grandfather. They had no money, but they were passionately in love with each other and that was enough.

And to Mindy's dad, Mork gives the memory of the happiest moment in his life, the day Mindy was born.

In this episode, Mork is supposedly the one who learned what Christmas was all about and how to give gifts. But the truth is that it was the *others* (including the viewers) who learned the *real* meaning of Christmas, and from an alien who had gone many, many bleems without ever even seeing a Christmas tree!

## Pam Dawber

The next chapter of the book, "A Girl From Detroit Meets Mork From Ork," is a look at how Pam Dawber got started in show business and how she got her big break, playing Mindy to Robin Williams's Mork in their hot series.

Pam did all the usual things young aspiring actors do to break into the business. She modeled, did car shows, sang in small productions of Broadway musicals, and continually auditioned for TV shows and movies.

One of those interesting entertainment business coincidences occurred when Pam auditioned for and got her very first movie role in the 1978 film *A Wedding* (pre-*Mork and Mindy*), which was directed by Robert Altman. Altman would go on to direct Robin Williams in *his* first film role, *Popeye* (1980).

Herz's interview with Dawber, which took place in a restaurant during a lunch break from *Mork and Mindy*, revealed some intriguing bits of info, one of which was that Dawber once had a weight problem as well as an apparent eating disorder, both of which came about when her sister died and her own career seemed to be going nowhere. But then came *Mork and Mindy* and her career took off like a comet.

(Note: After *Mork and Mindy* was canceled, Pam went on to do TV movies: *Holocaust Survivors*, 1983; *The Little Mermaid*, 1984; *Wild Horses*, 1985; *Through Naked Eyes*, 1987; and feature films (*Stay Tuned*, 1992). She also starred in her own sitcom, *My Sister Sam*, from 1986 to 1988. Her costar and TV "sister," Rebecca Schaeffer, was later murdered by a deranged fan compounding the untimely loss of her own real-life sister at an early age.)

In Herz's interview, Pam Dawber commented level-headedly on success:

> I don't ever want to have everything. The quickest way to unhappiness is to buy everything. Then nothing is special.

## Conrad Janis

The next-to-last chapter of Herz's book is called "From Football in the Living Room to an Alien in the Attic," and consists of an interview with show-biz veteran Conrad Janis, the actor who plays Mindy's often-bewildered dad, Frederick McConnell.

Herz talked with Janis about how he got started in show business and the many roles he played over the years (he'd been acting since he was thirteen). But the musician-actor obviously had a warm spot in his heart for Robin Williams and *Mork and Mindy*. "Being on the show is a fantastically lucky break for me," he told Herz. (He got the part after he appeared as a dad on *Happy Days*.) "Robin Williams is a new kind of comedian. He is very funny and very fresh, and I think they've come up with a format that gives him freedom to express what he is as a person and as an actor," Janis explained. "When he plays Mork, we see ourselves through new eyes. We can't lie to Mork, and that makes us examine ourselves and what we are really like."

Janis also talked about what it was like on the set with Robin, and he, too, said that Robin often improvised and that they, as his fellow actors, had to be ready to respond.

## In Conclusion

The last chapter of Herz's book, "A Kind of Magic Takes Over," sums up her time spent with the cast and crew of *Mork and Mindy*, calling it "a special time with a very special group of people."

Peggy Herz's book offers us a glimpse into the making of a hit TV show. But it also provides us with a look at Robin Williams when he was just starting out, long before we met Mrs. Doubtfire and the Genie, and it shows us that, even in his early years, the spark of creative genius was already burning in this odd, brilliant, hairy young man.

*Robin Williams and Pam Dawber. (Photofest)*

**"You the guy on TV? You suck!"**

—A typical New Yorker; and one of the reasons Robin loves New York

*A rare photo of Robin and Bette Davis from a 1977 episode of Laugh-In. (Photofest)*

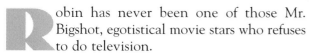

# Chapter 3
# *Robin on TV*

*"Doing television sucks material out of you like a vacuum cleaner on speed."*

—Robin (*Playboy*, January 1992)

Robin has never been one of those Mr. Bigshot, egotistical movie stars who refuses to do television.

Being the comedic Renaissance man that he is, Robin has done countless TV talk shows, as well as appeared in cable movies, TV series, many specials, and other productions for the small screen.

This section looks at some of his more notable TV appearances and also provides a chart listing much of his TV work over the past couple of decades.

## The Robin Williams TV Chart

*"Laugh-In sure sobered my ass up. The show lasted fourteen weeks, and most of the time, I played a redneck or a Russian. My best line: Frank Sinatra was on Laugh-In one week, and I went up to him and said, "Mr. Sinatra, I'm so happy to meet you I could drop a log." I was afraid they'd want to fire me and that I'd have to explain that I'd never meant to upset Uncle Frank. Thank God, he laughed."*

—Robin talking about his early days on television (*Playboy*, October 1982)

This chart provides, at a glance, an overview of many of Robin Williams's more notable TV appearances and performances over the past two-plus decades.

As this career review makes abundantly clear, Robin's work on television has been eclectic and unpredictable, veering from standard talk show appearances to roles in childrens' shows. He has hosted *Comic Relief* and appeared with Carol Burnett in variety specials. He has guest-hosted *Saturday Night Live*—as well as an animated series of Shakespeare's plays.

Robin's TV "choices"—like his feature film choices—paint a picture of a vibrant creative artist who refuses to be pigeonholed and who is willing to try almost anything.

Lately, Robin's TV appearances have been limited to talk shows to plug a new movie, and cable presentations such as *Comic Relief* (as well as an occasional rare guest spot on a prime time series such as *Homicide* and *Friends*).

The odds are greatly against Robin ever getting back into series television (although that's what they said about Michael J. Fox when he was a hugely successful film star and now he has a new series called *Spin City*, which is a hit).

*Robin and legendary actor Jimmy Stewart in a scene from a late seventies episode of the* Laugh-In *revival Robin starred in before* Mork and Mindy. *(Photofest)*

Robin's film career keeps him busy and allows him enormous creative freedom and control. Robin will probably keep popping up on TV now and then, though. Don't you get the feeling that the zany Mr. Williams just *loves* to work and isn't so caught up in an ego trip that he'd turn down a terrific TV spot?

Yeah, me too.

### 1977

- *The Richard Pryor Show* (NBC, as a regular)

### 1977–1978

- *Happy Days* (ABC): "My Favorite Orkan" (guest star, 1978)

- *Laugh-In* (NBC, as a regular)

## 1978

- *Fernwood 2-Night* (Syndicated, as a guest)

## 1978–1982

- *Mork & Mindy* (ABC, series co-star)

- *Happy Days* (ABC): "Mork Returns" (guest star, 1979)

## 1979

- *Out of the Blue:* "Random's Arrival" (ABC, guest star)

## 1982

- *Faerie Tale Theater* "The Tale of the Frog Prince" (Showtime)

- *E.T. and Friends* (special; host)

## 1983

- *An Evening with Robin Williams* (HBO)

## 1984

- *Saturday Night Live* (NBC, guest host)

## 1985–1986

- *Comedy Tonight* (syndicated, as a guest)

## 1986

- *Robin Williams: An Evening at the Met* (HBO)

- *The 58th Annual Academy Awards Presentation* (ABC, co-host)

- *Saturday Night Live* (NBC, guest host)

- *A Carol Burnett Special:* "Carol, Carl, Whoopi, and Robin" (ABC)

- *Comic Relief I* (HBO, host)

## 1986–1988

- *Robert Klein Time* (USA, as a guest)

## 1987

- *Comic Relief II* (HBO, host)

- *A Carol Burnett Special* (ABC, Emmy)

- *Will Rogers: Look Back in Laughter* (HBO, host)

- *Dear America* (HBO, documentary; narrator)

## 1988

- *All-Star Toast to the Improv* (HBO)

- *ABC Presents a Royal Gala* (ABC, Emmy)

- *Saturday Night Live* (NBC, guest host)

- *Late Night with David Letterman* (NBC, as a guest)

## 1989

- *Comic Relief III* (HBO, host)

## 1990

- *Comic Relief IV* (HBO, host)

- *An Evening With Bette, Cher, Goldie, Meryl, Lily, and Robin*

## 1991

- *Robin Williams Talking With David Frost* (PBS, guest)

## 1992

- *The Whoopi Goldberg Show* (Syndicated, as a guest)

- *Comic Relief V* (HBO, host)

## 1992–Present

- *The Tonight Show With Jay Leno* (NBC, guest)

## 1992–1993

- *Shakespeare: The Animated Tales* (Showtime, series host)

## 1993

- *Late Show with David Letterman* (CBS, guest)

## 1994

- *Homicide* (NBC, guest appearance)

- *Comic Relief VI* (HBO, host)

- *In Search of Dr. Seuss* (TNT)

## 1995

- *Dolphins* (PBS documentary; star and host)

- *Comic Relief VII* (HBO, host)

## 1996

- *E! Entertainment Television* (various interviews and appearances)

## 1997

- *Father's Day,* Robin's cine-collaboration with Billy Crystal, was released in May 1997 and, as is common for Robin, he made the rounds of the talk shows and did other TV appearances to promote the movie's opening.

His most memorable appearance was with Crystal on the May 8, 1997 episode of the hit NBC sitcom *Friends*. During their very brief (about a minute and a half) cameo appearance, these two geniuses proved why they are two of the biggest stars on the plantet. (I still say that Billy Crystal's *Mr. Saturday Night*—anemic box office notwithstanding—is absolutely brilliant and one of the best things he's done.)

At the beginning of the show, Robin and Billy enter the Friends' coffeehouse Central Perk and ask the Friends to "scooch" over on the couch so they can sit down.

Robin's character is an immigrant (could be Italian, could be Russian—it's sort of Robin's "generic foreign guy" accent) and Billy is his friend. They begin to have a conversation which mesmerizes the six friends. It seems that Robin suspects his wife of having an affair:

###### ROBIN

I have a feeling my wife is sleeping with her gynecologist.

###### BILLY

Really? How do you know?

###### ROBIN

Well, you know, he's got access! It's a feeling you get, you know?

###### BILLY

Like when you go bowling and you know you're in somebody else's shoes?

###### ROBIN

That's the one! Why is this happening to me? I don't know! (contemplatively) Maybe it's my wound?

###### BILLY

It's not healed yet?

###### ROBIN

It's ooooozing! Could you pass the cream?

###### BILLY

This is gonna be hard but I wanted it to come from me and nobody else.

###### ROBIN

What is it?

###### BILLY

It's me. I've been sleeping with your wife.

###### JOEY

So you're the gynecologist?

###### BILLY

Hey, I'm trying to have a private conversation here, okay?

###### ROBIN

(Sobbing) Can I have a napkin . . .could you please pass me a . . . GIVE ME THE THING! (grabs napkin dispenser from Rachel) (To Billy) Enough! You are no longer my friend! We're finished! Nada! No more! You are a bastard for doing that! Get away from me!

(They exit)

Robin and Billy owned this segment. The larger-than-life presence and sheer star power of these two guys elevated an already wonderful sitcom to something even better. Robin and Billy have had so much experience playing in all kinds of venues and to all kinds of audiences that they were easily able to hit a home run during this short segment (much of which, I'll bet, was improvised). Not all movie stars can pull off this kind of guest spot and still retain their movie star luster.

An example of someone who failed is Sharon Stone when she did a guest spot as a trailer park bimbo on *Roseanne*. She was not convincing, and was not able to translate her undeniable talents to the small screen. Because Billy and Robin both got their starts in sitcoms, they were more easily able to make the necessary adjustments required to be effective on the small screen. Whatever the actual process, it worked like a charm and their appearance was one of the highlights of the series. (Their guest appearance did not do much to help *Father's Day* at the box office, though. It was not the success everyone had hoped it would be.)

In addition to *Friends*, Robin, along with Billy, also made the rounds of the late night talk shows (Leno and company) in the spring of 1997, as well as the morning programs, including one of Robin's favorites, *The Today Show*.

Some of Robin's more notable TV appearances will be discussed in depth. Read on!

# The Tale of the Frog Prince
## (1982)

*"You're very beautiful in your own bitchy way."*
—The Frog Prince to the spoiled Princess

This one-hour *Faerie Tale Theatre* production from Showtime may not hold a very warm spot in Robin Williams's heart, even though he is quite good in it.

As he revealed in an interview with David Frost [see the feature in this volume], Robin found out that his TV show *Mork and Mindy* was being canceled while he was off working on *The Tale of Frog Prince* with Eric Idle. Thus, there may always be a negative association with this production in Robin's mind and heart because of the accompanying series cancellation.

But then again, maybe not.

The upside for Robin was that he got to work with some truly talented people in this film, including *Seinfeld*'s "Kramer," Michael Richards, as his father the King; and the always superb Teri Garr, as the spoiled Princess and the love of his frog's life.

And speaking of frogs, Robin spends the majority of this movie wearing a green frog suit. The rest of the time, he's naked, and sporting a Prince Valiant-esque wig. As they say, there's no business like show business.

This short feature tells the story of the Frog Prince, who is the son of a King and Queen named Geoffrey and Gwynneth. Geoffrey and Gwynneth forget to invite a sorceress named Griselda to the christening of their child. Griselda is livid because she had magically helped them conceive the child and had made them promise that she would be invited to the baby's christening. Because of this egregious slight, Griselda the Crone turns the infant Prince into a frog and the only way he can be freed is by a kiss from a real Princess.

The Frog Prince, now grown, meets the spoiled daughter of King Auric and Queen Beatrice and connives his way into a dinner party in her honor, where he wins over her parents and the crowd with his charming personality. He spends the rest of the evening convincing her that he loves her. She kisses him, he transforms into Prince Robin, they wed, and everyone lives happily ever

*Robin (right) and Teri Garr in a scene from "The Tale of the Frog Prince," produced by Shelly Duvall for* Fairie Tale Theatre. *(Photofest)*

after. (This is, after all, a fairy tale.)

Robin gives a very mannered and specific performance as the Frog Prince, which is even more impressive when we factor in the costume: For most of the film, he does not have the opportunity to utilize his always-expressive face, and instead, must

*Robin and Teri in "The Tale of the Frog Prince" after Teri's kiss transforms him back into the Prince. (Photofest)*

depend on body language and vocal intonations. He does a terrific job.

Overall, kids will love *The Tale of the Frog Prince* and Robin Williams's fans might want to rent it just for the curious experience of watching Robin emote in green latex.

## What the Critics Had to Say

**Mick Martin and Marsha Porter:** "Perhaps the best of the *Faerie Tale Theatre* presentations. . . . It's witty and well acted." (From their *Video Movie Guide*)

**Videohound's Golden Movie Retriever:** "Superb

edition of Shelley Duvall's *Faerie Tale Theatre*." (From the 1997 edition)

**Director:** Eric Idle (of Monty Python fame)
**Cast:** Robin Williams (The Frog Prince, Prince Robin), Teri Garr (The Princess), Candy Clark (Queen Gwynneth and Candy), Roberta Maxwell (Queen Beatrice and Griselda), Michael Richards (King Geoffrey), Donovan Scott (Hendrix and The French Chef), Charlie Dell (The Page), Van Dyke Parks (The Musician)
**Writer:** Eric Idle
**Music:** Lenny Niehaus
Rated G; 55 minutes

# The David Frost PBS Interview

*"It's like jazz . . . when it works."*
—Robin Williams, talking to David Frost
about improvisational stand-up comedy

In May of 1991, Robin Williams sat for an hour-long interview with acclaimed British broadcast journalist David Frost. This interview, which was broadcast in the United States on the Public Broadcasting System, was one of the most important interviews Robin has ever granted.

This was an important time in Robin's life. After finishing filming *Hook* (in which he was a tad overweight), he lost twenty-five pounds by giving up drinking and drugs. (Frost mentions that Robin lost the weight for his next movie but doesn't name the flick. Actors often work on films that are released in a different chronological order than the order in which they were filmed.) The movie could have been *Shakes the Clown*. Robin plays a mime in that film and wears skintight stretch clothes during all his scenes. (It would make sense that he did not want to look chunky in such an outfit.) Also, he was less than a couple of years away from two of his most important career achievements, the films *Aladdin* and *Mrs. Doubtfire*.

All of these changes in Robin's life had acted to create a gentle and reflective man who was less manic, less frenzied, but not less funny. This interview was superbly conducted by Frost, who carefully listened to Robin's answers and asked astute

follow-up questions that didn't just go for a laugh.

It is a sure sign of Robin's brilliance that he was able to thoughtfully (and honestly) answer Frost's questions while still doing bits, cracking jokes, and throwing out a panoply of hilarious voices, including Jesse Helms, George Bush, and Robin's beloved California surfer dude ("Fershurr!").

Interviews on PBS are much classier and are presented with a far more restrained and dignified tone than broadcast network TV interviews. Plus there's an added bonus when you watch a PBS program: No commercials!

Frost's one-hour show began with a clip of Robin onstage performing in concert. The clip showed him doing the following gag:

> And they also say, in case of a water landing, you can use your seat cushion for a flotation device. If you make it out the door, there you are, floating on your seat cushion. Two sharks go by and go, "Oh, isn't that nice, Tom. Canapes!"

They then showed clips from *Good Morning, Vietnam*; *Dead Poets Society*; and *Awakenings*; followed by rare footage of Robin in a cap and gown (goofing around with his cap and pretending it was a Frisbee) receiving an honorary Doctor of Fine Arts degree from the Julliard School, from which he never graduated.

## Culture Shock

The interview began with Frost and Robin playfully joking about Robin now being a doctor. Robin used the mention of the Julliard School (which he described as "theatrical Darwinism") to make the point that today, the graduates were all hopeful and optimistic but that in a year, they'd all be crying, "You lied!"

As he has done in many other talks, Robin told the story of coming to New York from San Francisco and experiencing the kind of startling culture shock that only the Big Apple offers.

Robin also admitted to Frost that the pressures in New York were so overwhelming that he almost had a nervous breakdown his first year in the city. But he loved show business enough to stick it out and would often look to something his former teacher, the great John Houseman once told him. "Don't be in this business if you don't love it," he told Robin. "Because it's too brutal otherwise."

## The Army of the Theater

The mention of Houseman prompted a question from Frost about whether or not the legendary thespian had taught Robin a lot when he was at Julliard. Robin replied that Houseman didn't really do a lot of teaching at the school but would, instead, speak to classes now and then, often enlightening them with some wonderful piece of wisdom about acting, or the theater, or show business in general.

Houseman was wonderful, Robin recalled. He then did a very funny bit in which he imitated Houseman's voice and diction cadence flawlessly. "The theater needs you," Robin said as Houseman. "You must become soldiers in the Army of the Theater." But this was clearly a setup, as Robin quickly followed with the punch line: "And then the next week we saw him selling Volvos."

Robin went on to tell Frost that he got to know Houseman much better years later and that he considered him a revolutionary, especially the early work he did with the great director Orson Welles. Robin credited John Houseman with inspir-

ing him to study both comedy and theater and not just the movie business.

Frost picked up on this and remarked that Robin was originally an actor who became a comedian, instead of the other way around.

This spurred Robin to remember his early years doing stand-up in clubs in San Francisco. Some of these clubs were shady places, he recalled, and then told the story of a comedian friend of his who once got shot at while on stage. "The guy even had a comeback," Robin laughed. "This is a two-shot minimum!'" (Robin obviously loved this line: A year later, talking in *Playboy*, he said "[Los Angeles] is strange for me. It's a fantasy life, just very surreal. It's a city where they have drive-by shootings, two-shot minimum.")

Frost then asked a perceptive question. He asked Robin if there was ever any evidence in the first few years of his career that he would end up doing what he does now? Robin answered that now he realizes he was a "closet comedian" and doing improvisation freed him.

## Mom and Dad

The talk turned to Robin's parents. His father was a strict man but knew deep down that Robin had found something he loved. Robin's dad encouraged him but did suggest that he take up a trade like welding (an anecdote Robin has used elsewhere) as something to fall back on. Robin told Frost that he actually did sign up for and take a welding class. During the first class, the instructor made a point of telling them that it was possible to be blinded by the acetylene torch. Upon hearing that, the ever-cautious Williams got up and left.

Robin then talked about his mother; she was the one with the sense of humor in the family. She would black out her teeth or put a rubber band up her nose and then pull it out to make him laugh. He told Frost she was like a character out of Tennessee Williams (a line he used on the *Donahue "Mrs. Doubtfire"* show—see the feature on that show), only this time he added a funny coda to his remark. He said his mother smoked cigars and was "a Christian Dior Scientist, which means she only wore certain types of makeup."

Robin acknowledged that his mother's wit and comic sensibility influenced the development of his own comedic style and that mother and son were able to interact through their humor. Robin

*Robin's talk with David Frost was one of the most important interviews he has ever granted. (Photofest)*

then recited his mother's "I love you in blue" poem covered elsewhere in this volume. Then the conversation moved to a discussion of Robin's father, Robert.

Robert Williams was a "wonderful, ethical" man, Robin began, and he credited his father's deep-seated sense of morality as the reason why he became so interested in social issues, such as the homeless crisis and AIDS causes. He told Frost that his father actually quit the automobile business when his conscience told him to, because of the shoddy workmanship and deceptive business practices prevalent at the time.

Robin really got to know his father before his death, and was later comforted to know that his dad finally realized that his son was doing what he loved—and succeeding at it.

This was an emotional moment in the interview, and Robin decided to lighten up the mood by suddenly becoming a psychiatric patient involved in "one-way therapy," telling "Dr. Frost" (while lying back on the couch, of course), "And then I stopped touching myself. I don't *want* to have the operation anymore—even though I've got the breasts!"

## Making It Up as He Went Along

The talk then turned to improvisation as a tool for developing comedy. Robin again talked about how improv freed him:

> It was total freedom. There was no dictating where or what you would have to do. And it was a chance to use everything you knew in one place—to do a Shakespearean play on George Bush: [In George Bush's voice] "Neither a borrower nor a savings and loan default. . . ."

Robin then commented that when improv didn't work, "It's like really bad piano practice," and offhandedly compared it to long-distance running. This prompted an exchange that is evidence of just how quick Robin Williams's mind works. Frost casually commented to Robin that he had heard that running eight miles stimulated an endorphin release in the brain similar to what was released during sex. Robin immediately fired back with, "So a marathon . . . wow!" This cracked up David Frost

and Robin added, "It's not the size of the shoe!"

Frost mentioned that Mitzi Shore (one of the owners of the Improv nightclubs) once told him that one of Robin's funniest stand-up bits was two California surfer dudes reciting Shakespeare. Robin then did—from pure memory—a lengthy speech from *Hamlet*, but in the voice of a "fershurr" surfer guy. After this truly impressive performance, he veered off into Richard Nixon as Richard III, lamenting, "My kingdom for a splicer!"

Robin then did a funny bit about performing in clubs late at night, when the only patrons were either really into comedy or "had had three or four pina colonics," recycling yet again one of his funniest lines.

## On TV

Next, Frost asked Robin about his early TV work, specifically his stint on *Laugh-In*, and whether or not it had led to bigger things. It most assuredly did not, Robin responded, and admitted that he had been surprised when his appearances on the show did not lead to more offers and instant stardom.

Instant stardom *would* soon be Robin's, though, and the interview then turned to *Mork and Mindy*. Robin has said previously that, in the beginning, no one was sure the show would survive. Here, he told how studio executives were impressed with the audience reaction to the first episode and agreed to give it a trial run. Robin told Frost how they aimed the show at a dual audience—kids and adults. They knew that kids would respond well to Mork and his antics, but they also would sneak in jokes that no kid would get, but that would definitely register with the grownups. He cited one reference he made in the show to "Catherine the Great and *My Friend Flicka*," a genuinely raunchy allusion. (He was referring to the historical legend that Catherine the Great was killed when the horse she was having sex with fell on her and crushed her to death.)

## On Fame

Frost then asked Robin if instant fame had been unsettling and Robin responded with an analogy that truly encapsulated what instantaneous celebrity felt like. Robin said that such overwhelming success coming so quickly felt like "being taken from the bottom of Death Valley to the top

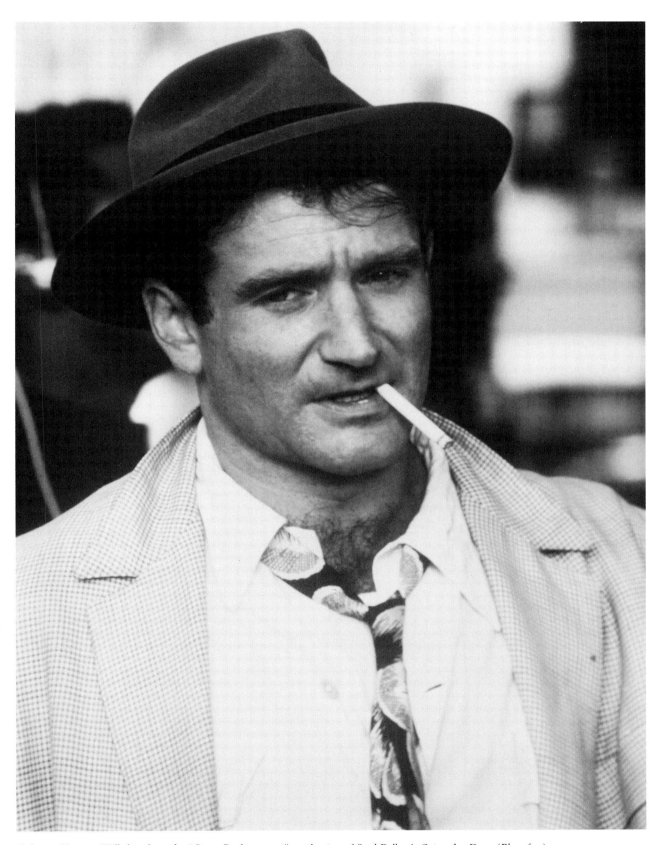

*Robin as Tommy Wilhelm, from the "Great Performances" production of Saul Bellow's* Seize the Day. *(Photofest)*

hooks up with an eccentric doctor (who might not actually *be* a doctor) named Tamkin (Jerry Stiller), who convinces Tommy to put his last seven hundred dollars into lard and rye commodities which, of course, he promptly loses.

Then Tommy's weekly hotel rent comes due and he can't pay it, and Tommy's wife calls and demands immediate payment of his (late) child support or she'll prevent him from seeing his kids. On the verge of a complete mental breakdown, Tommy swallows what's left of his pride and literally begs his father for help.

Tommy's father, however, is a heartless despot who tells Tommy that he does not want to carry anyone on his back—including his own son—and that he will not bail him out under any circumstances.

Tommy leaves his father and runs through the streets of New York, screaming for Dr. Tamkin, hoping to get some of his money back. (It turns out Tamkin didn't even put in his own half of the commodities investment.)

Thinking he sees Tamkin walking into a building, Tommy chases the man (who turns out not to be Tamkin) and ends up crashing into a funeral and falling in the aisle as the shocked mourners stare in disbelief at this wild man who has disrupted their ceremony.

Tommy composes himself, puts on the proffered yarmulke, and sits in a seat at the front of the synagogue. While two women gossip about which side of the family he might be from, Tommy sits there and alternately sobs, laughs, moans, and cries out loud, now completely beaten and broken, in the midst of a total mental collapse. It is obvious to us that Tommy interprets his crashing into a funeral of all things at this lowest point of his life as the ultimate metaphor for his future prospects. To Tommy, the universe seems to be telling him that he's already dead.

Robin Williams gives a bravura performance in *Seize the Day*. He plays Tommy Wilhelm with such an edge, we can't help but relate to the pressure the character is experiencing and vicariously see the thin, fragile thread by which his sanity hangs.

At one point in the movie, Tommy's father (Joseph Wiseman) tells Tommy that he is turning into "a mountain of tics," and that is an apt and evocative description of how Robin Williams plays Tommy.

Robin gives one of the most powerful dramatic performances of his life, and it is yet another example of what a magnificent dramatic actor he has become in the decade or so since he first burst onto the scene.

## What the Critics Had to Say

**Mick Martin and Marsha Porter:** "Robin Williams is watchable in this drama, but like so many comedians who attempt serious acting, he is haunted by his madcap persona." (From their *Video Movie Guide*)

**Tom Wiener:** "Williams is first-rate in this sleeper." (From his *The Book of Video Lists*)

**Richard Zoglin:** "In odd but inspired casting, Robin Williams plays Tommy and delivers the best dramatic performance of his career. In past roles, Williams has sometimes seemed mechanical and pinched. Here his hyperactive face and vocal tics are orchestrated into a wrenching portrait of panic and desperation." (From a review in *Time* magazine, May 4, 1987)

**Director:** Fielder Cook
**Cast:** Robin Williams (Tommy Wilhelm), Richard Shull (Rojax), Glenne Headly (Olive), Joseph Wiseman (Dr. Adler), Jerry Stiller (Dr. Tamkin), Tony Roberts (Bernie Pell), Jayne Heller (Mrs. Adler), Katherine Borowitz (Margaret), John Fiedler (Carl), William Duell (Joey), Saul Bellow (Man in Hallway), Fyvush Finkel (Shomier)
**Writer:** Ronald Ribman, based on the novel by Saul Bellow
**Music:** Elizabeth Swados
Not Rated; 93 minutes

# Robín Says Goodbye
# to Johnny Carson

Some of Robin Williams's most inspired performances have been on talk shows.

There is a unique sensibility on late night American talk shows: Appearances on the *Tonight Show With Johnny Carson* or the *Late Show With David Letterman* (or Conan, or Tom Snyder, etc.) are not really interviews, as an appearance with David Frost or Barbara Walters would be. They are really nothing more than performances done as a tradeoff for a chance to plug an artist's latest project.

Actors appear as themselves (something actors are usually loathe to do) in the hope that people will be so intrigued by them *personally* that they will flock to their latest movie. Sometimes an appropriate clip is shown, which taken out of context, makes little sense.

In Robin Williams's case, his comedic abilities are so overwhelming that many of his talk show appearances end up being not so much about his latest movie, but a chance for Robin to do ten or fifteen minutes of brilliant stand-up comedy—sitting down.

This feature looks at one of Robin's more memorable talk show appearances, the night he bid farewell to Johnny Carson.

## Robin's Appearance on the Second-to-Last *Tonight Show* With *Johnny Carson* (May 21, 1992)

This penultimate *Tonight Show* (which took place shortly after the Los Angeles riots that followed the first Rodney King verdict) could easily have been a sappy and maudlin lovefest but, to Robin's credit, he never lost sight of what show business is all about—*entertainment*—and he ultimately gave one of his most hilarious performances ever, including coming up with a couple of lines that had Johnny Carson laughing so hard he was almost in tears.

Here's how Johnny introduced Robin:

In this business, there are comedians, there are comics, and once in a while—rarely—somebody rises above and supersedes that and becomes a comic persona unto themselves. I never cease to be amazed at the versatility and the wonderful work that Robin Williams does. Would you welcome him please . . . Robin Williams!

Robin then came out pushing a rocking chair that had guitar runners. "I brought you a little something from the Elvis estate!", he told Johnny, who then asked Robin if he could sit in the chair. Robin told him, "Sit down and we'll give you a piña colonic!" (a line that cracked up Ed McMahon big time).

Johnny sat down and began to rock and then ad-libbed a line about wanting to sit in the sun. Robin responded by yelling in his ear, "We're going to Spago!" Robin then told Johnny that he had brought him the new L.A. medical alert. It says, "I've fallen and get the hell away from me!" Continuing with his "riot" theme, Robin went on:

This is a wild night . . . I was going to bring you a VCR, but the stores had none! Somebody I guess had done a little political shopping! You see people going, "Yeah, man! This is for Rodney King! And the five TVs are for me!"

They always catch the one wino, "Yeah, man! I'm really pissed off about Don King! The whole Don King thing has got me down man!"

And they brought in the National Guard. They didn't bring bullets. They couldn't find them! So they're out in the streets "All right everybody . . . [singing] We are the world!"

They saw BMWs pulling up to the Radio Shack . . . "Oh, fabulous! This is great! I wonder if we can get store credit if you already have it?"

At this point, Johnny chimed in with,

"Thank God for Quayle. He's kept us alive for two more nights!" This set Robin off on a whole new riff:

> They sent him down to the 'hood! That was great! He thinks he's now a homey! Yeah, Dan's hangin'! Look! It's *Goys in the Hood!* [Quayle voice] "Hi, there. You have got to chill, yeah, yeah! This is real def [screwing up intricate handshake] What it is, what it was." "Oh, man, you dumb!"

> This guy is like one taco short of a combination plate!

The "taco" line got a huge laugh and Robin continued goofing on Quayle, informing Johnny that then-President George Bush had told Quayle to go out and talk about Jerry Brown. Robin then imitated Vice President Quayle trying to remember who he was to talk about: "Jerry Brown, Jerry Brown; Buster Brown, Buster Brown; Audie Murphy, Audie Murphy; Murphy Brown, Murphy Brown!" This also got a big laugh and Robin exclaimed, "He's Rain Man!" Robin then imitated Dan Quayle as Rain Man: "Five minutes to *Murphy Brown* . . . Air Force One—safest plane—never crashed."

Robin then told Johnny that Quayle was Bush's greatest insurance in the world. He then transformed into a guy with a shotgun taking aim at Bush. The guy suddenly stops and has a dialogue with himself—"I pop *him,* and *he* becomes . . . oh, man!"—and then puts down his gun. Robin immediately followed this with a George Bush impression, with Bush proclaiming, "Thousand points of light . . . they're not burning anymore . . . come on down!", riffing once again on the Rodney King riots.

Next Robin did a bit that got the biggest laugh of the night from Johnny. He called it "How To Do George Bush." Robin stood up, swaggered a few steps, and told Johnny, "You take John Wayne . . . and you tighten up his ass!", and then immediately transformed into a riotous clone of the President. Carson—who has played straight men to the greatest comedians in the world—involuntarily exploded into genuine laughter, completely losing his legendary control. Johnny then did his own impression of Bush which Robin added to by noting that, with Bush, "instead of cowboy boots, there's Topsiders!"

Robin offered a little political commentary by remarking that Bush first blamed all of the country's woes on the welfare programs of the Sixties, then on *Murphy Brown,* and said pretty soon the Republican administration would be blaming Lincoln. Robin illustrated this by saying in his best "George Bush" voice, "Lincoln, did it all wrong. Freed people before he had the plan in place. All wrong."

Johnny then asked Robin what he thought of Ross Perot, noting that, "The guy's ahead in the polls and he hasn't said anything!" Robin immediately fired back with, "Well, you know he's not gonna write a bad check!" Robin then mused that he had the feeling if Perot were elected, at his inauguration, he'd rip off his mask and reveal that he was actually Richard Nixon underneath.

Robin then imitated Paul Tsongas (a former Democratic Presidential candidate who died in early 1997) as Elmer Fudd, and Johnny scored with a couple of lines that even Robin didn't see coming:

### JOHNNY

I think Clinton made his big mistake when he said, "I didn't inhale."

### ROBIN

That's a tough one to pull off!

### JOHNNY

And Jerry Brown's problem was that he never exhaled!

This struck Robin so funny he almost fell off his chair. He then went off on the Jerry Brown reference by saying that "People look at Jerry Brown and go, 'Oh, my God, the man's gonna have a bake sale for the Army!' He's like the gestalt President!" He then described Pat Buchanan as "The Anti-Bush," and finished this segment with a blast at pro-lifers: "Right-to-life people, the moment they [the babies are] born, it's 'I'm outta here! See ya!'"

This got a huge laugh and Johnny went to a commercial.

The second half of Robin's appearance started with Johnny asking him about his ranch. Robin replied in a Mexican accent and then went off on a riff about Ronald Reagan and *his* ranch. He imitated Nancy Reagan barking at her husband, "Move it, old man!"

The conversation then moved to a discussion of Robin's youngest child, Cody, who was six months old at the time.

"When they're born, they're so exquisite; they're perfectly formed," Robin began, "with these incredibly huge *cojones*. As we say, big balls!" Interestingly, the *Tonight Show* replaced Robin's use of the word "balls" with his previous use of "cojones." Apparently NBC has an aversion to English-language testicular humor, but Spanish slang is acceptable. (Two years later, during an interview on *Late Night with David Letterman*, Robin said, "Very few people have the balls to wear an ottoman!", and again, "balls" was bleeped out by NBC censors.) During this bit, Robin acknowledged his questionable language by telling Johnny, "And if that's bleeped, good luck!" Johnny then asked Robin if his son's big "cojones" were a family trait, and Robin responded by pretending he was talking to his infant son: "Your grandfather had a great set, too!"

Robin also admitted, "I hope he grows into these!" and then imitated an adult whose testicles grew at the same rate as the rest of his body until they were big enough to sit on.

Johnny laughed hysterically and said, "We're outta here tomorrow night! What do I care? What are they gonna do? Can me?"

Robin played off these remarks by imitating an offended woman writing a letter: "Dear Mr. Carson . . . Oh, damn!"

Johnny then switched gears and asked about Robin's new blond hair color. Robin at first answered that it was for a movie, but then immediately went off on a riff in which he was the effeminate host of a public access cable talk show. He started off by saying, "Hi, welcome to *In Your Ear*. My guests tonight are Mother Teresa. . . ." and then something interesting happened. Johnny Carson apparently did not register that Robin had mentioned the name of his fictitious "show" and he interrupted the bit to say, "*Rappin' with Robin*." Robin was thrown for a split second and came out with, "*Rappin' with Robin*. We'll be right back!", a non sequitur that really didn't make much sense, either logically or comedically, but Robin was improvising on the spot and had to come up with *something* after Johnny distracted him and broke his concentration. Robin quickly recovered and said, "It feels like one of those things that has guests like . . . 'My guests are Mother Teresa and Ruta

Lee,' " which is proof positive of Robin's razor-sharp mind. Johnny again tried to contribute and came up with the line, "And later, Mason Reese will be along," which fell flat.

Robin forged ahead with the bit, however, coming up with a joke that got huge laughs:

Mother Teresa is here pushing her new cologne. It's called Compassion—the scent of sentiment!

The performing Robin then reverted back to the real Robin and told Johnny that he had dyed his hair for his latest movie, *Toys*. Johnny then asked Robin, "Is this a comic picture with serious overtones, or a serious picture with comic overtones?" to which Robin replied, "Yes," which got a big laugh. He then told Johnny that he had to have his hair redone every three weeks and said it was very difficult to be sitting under a hairdryer going, "Hey how about those Bulls?"

The talk then shifted to a discussion of Robin's work with Comic Relief. Robin revealed that their latest effort had raised six million dollars for the homeless, which, he remarked, is the "tire for one airplane." Johnny then remarked that to help people you would think the government could do without one $900 million bomber, and Robin corrected him by noting that $900 million would just cover the spare parts for the plane.

Robin then switched to George Bush saying, "Gotta make it happen," which led him to ask Dan Quayle (as Bush), "Dan, what do you think about Roe vs. Wade?" Quayle's reply? "Uh, I prefer to float." This line also scored enormously with the audience.

Johnny then asked Robin what he did in his spare time and Robin said he ran cross-country because it was "so much cheaper than the old ways," a veiled reference to his cocaine days. He said people don't come up to you when you're running and ask you if you're strung out for a new pair of shoes. He said he runs for the endorphin rush which he explained was "your body's way of saying, 'This really hurts, I'm going to medicate you!' " He also said he plays with his kids, and then asked Johnny what he was going to do when he retired. Robin jokingly suggested that Johnny run for political office, a suggestion that Johnny immediately (and quite adamantly) rejected because he said that if he did, it wouldn't take long for the media to find out what he did in the backseat with his old girlfriend when he was in high school.

Robin then joked that Johnny could run for office with Gorbachev, although Gorbachev "doesn't have a green card. He's truly an independent!"

Robin's segment ended here, although he did stay on stage during Bette Midler's musical performance and follow-up chat with Johnny. Robin expertly came up with a few perfectly-timed one-liners that played off Bette's schtick (which was brilliant), including a bit about crotch-grabbing that concluded with Robin imitating Jack Nicholson reading Henry Miller to his kids.

All in all, Robin's *Tonight Show With Johnny Carson* swan song was a truly memorable event in the history of late night television and, of course, in Robin Williams's career.

---

# Robin on *Homicide: Life on the Street*

On Thursday, January 6, 1994, Robin Williams returned to series television, albeit briefly, for a heart-wrenching guest appearance on the acclaimed NBC police drama, *Homicide: Life on the Street.*

Robin played a tourist visiting Baltimore with his wife and their two children. The tourist is thrust unexpectedly into a surreal nightmare when his wife is gunned down by a punk holding them up, because she wouldn't give up a beloved locket. "I lost my wife, but I joined a club," his character tells the police.

Robin's performance in this episode is brilliant: He shows us sadness, pain, anger, frustration, shock, and complete confusion with nothing but a glance, a turn of the head, a look in his eyes.

*Robin's brief return to series television was considered by many to be brilliant . . . and unexpected. (Photofest)*

*Robin and* Homicide *regular Richard Belzer. To ease the drama, you would expect these two veteran stand-up comics provided moments of off-camera zaniness. (Photofest)*

When this episode originally aired in early 1994 it was *not* a surprise to see how good Robin was or how easily he inhabited this tragic role. *This* Robin Williams had almost nothing to do with the brilliant and beloved lunatic from *Good Morning, Vietnam.* After the first few seconds of temporary disorientation at seeing the "funny man" we know so well walk into a Baltimore police station with a stunned and horrified look on his face, we instantly forget his comedic past and instead embrace him as an unwitting "casualty of violence," as TV critic John Leonard so aptly described Robin's character.

There is an especially edgy scene when Robin's character asks the cops if he could just hold one of their guns. He doesn't want any bullets in the gun and he doesn't want to shoot it—he just wants to hold it to see how it feels and, possibly, we can guess, to imagine what *might* have been if he had had one of these just a few short hours ago.

Robin Williams is always making movies and, thus, the timing had to have been just perfect to get him for such a high-profile guest appearance on a network program. We have not seen him visit a TV series since.

Pity. This kind of work deserves the audience numbers weekly TV series can generate, if only to show us how *good* network TV can actually be.

## What the Critics Had to Say

John Leonard: "Williams hasn't had so straight a role since he played Tommy in a PBS production of Saul Bellow's *Seize the Day.*" (From *New York* magazine, January 10, 1994)

**Director:** Stephen Gyllenhaal
**Cast:** Robin Williams, Andre Braugher, Daniel Baldwin, Ned Beatty, Clark Johnson, Yaphet Kotto, Melissa Leo, Jon Polito, Kyle Secor
**Story:** Tom Fontana
**Teleplay:** David Simon and David Mills

**"Show business is in my blood. Or maybe it's in my feet."**

—Robin Williams's biology of humor

*Our favorite sailor man caught at a time when his pipe wasn't spinning. (Photofest)*

*Robin looking especially youthful, don't you think? (Photofest)*

*The illustrious novelist himself, T. S. Garp. (Photofest)*

each day to go teach at "gradual school" and Garp stays home and does the laundry, cooks, takes care of the kids, and writes.

Tragedy becomes a constant in Garp's life, however, and true happiness seems to deliberately evade him. Terrible events dog him, including an airplane crashing into his house (flown by *Garp* director George Roy Hill in a cameo appearance), an assassination attempt on his mother, an adulterous affair between his wife and one of her "gradual" students, and a destructive affair between him and an 18-year-old babysitter. But the worst thing to happen to him is an auto accident that breaks his jaw; puts his wife in a neck brace; blinds one eye of his son, Duncan; and, most tragically, takes the life of his youngest son, Walt.

The pivotal event that causes this terrible series of tragedies was Garp's car crashing into the car of his wife's lover, Michael Milton, as Helen was performing "farewell" fellatio on him in the front seat. The force of the crash caused Helen to bite down and amputate Michael's penis. The reason Garp hit the car with such force was because he had turned off the engine and the lights and was coasting into the driveway at a high rate of speed. He liked to do this because he said it felt like flying.

Flying is an important theme running throughout *The World According to Garp* and it is significant that the movie begins and ends with Garp "flying": first, in and out of his mother's arms, and lastly in a helicopter after a crazed "Ellen Jamesian" shoots him three times in the chest.

*The World According to Garp* ends sadly with two dreadful events: The first is the assassination of Garp's mother; the second, the assassination attempt on Garp himself.

Jenny is shot by an anti-feminist zealot; Garp

*Garp is tended to by his mother, the feminist nurse, Jenny Fields (Glenn Close) in* The World According to Garp. *(Photofest)*

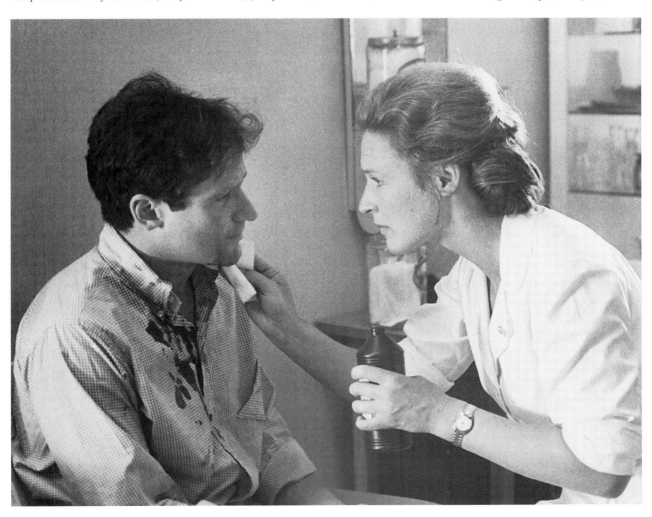

is shot by an anti-male radical.

Interestingly, *The World According to Garp* provided Robin with his first opportunity to dress in drag in a movie. (He dressed as a cheerleader in a *Mork and Mindy* episode, and the classic *Mrs. Doubtfire* wouldn't come for another decade.) In order for Garp to attend the women-only, feminist memorial service for his mother, Roberta the transsexual (John Lithgow) dresses Garp as a woman. Garp's former next-door neighbor, the sexually-repressed Ellen Jamesian Poo, spots him and screams "Arp!" (That's all she could get out without a tongue.) Poo later sneaks into Garp's wrestling class and shoots him point-blank.

*The World According to Garp* is a layered, metaphorically complex morality tale that works on many levels and provides Robin Williams with a role that is as rich and textured as some of his important later roles in such films as *Awakenings* and *Dead Poets Society*. It is both a serious drama and at the same time a sardonic black comedy.

Wouldn't it have been interesting if *Garp* had been Robin's first feature film role, followed by *Popeye* and then the others? Would *Popeye* have been savaged by the critics the way it was if it followed Robin's superb performance in *The World According to Garp*?

Just wondering.

## Bizarre Epilogue

It is truly a strange world when a Robin Williams movie can figure into, of all things, the O. J. Simpson civil trial. In November of 1996, Kato Kaelin

boyfriends in April of 1992. O. J. surreptitiously watched the two have sex through a window of Nicole's condo. This incident prompted a huge fight between Nicole and O. J. in October of 1993 that resulted in the infamous 911 call that brought several police officers to Nicole's home.

## What Robin Had to Say

"[*The World According to Garp*] was like an oil drilling. I had to dig down and find things deep inside myself and then bring them up. Heavy griefs and joys, births and deaths— *Garp* is an all-encompassing look at a man's life." (*Playboy*, October 1982)

## What the Critics Had to Say

**Roger Ebert:** "While I watched *Garp*, I enjoyed it. I thought the acting was unconventional and absorbing (especially by Williams, by Glenn Close as his mother, and by John Lithgow as a transsex-

was called to testify in the civil trial against O. J. brought by the families of murder victims Nicole Brown Simpson and Ronald Goldman. During Kaelin's testimony, he revealed that the day before the slayings, he and O. J. had watched the Robin Williams movie, *The World According to Garp*. When the movie got to the scene in which Garp's wife Helen performs oral sex on one of her students in the front seat of his car (and subsequently bites off his erection), Kaelin said that O. J. talked about how the scene reminded him of the time he had spied on Nicole performing oral sex on one of her

*The ever-serious Garp at his typewriter.*
*(Photofest)*

acted by all." (From his *Movie and Video Guide*)

**Videohound's Golden Movie Retriever:** "Ultimately pointless, perhaps, but effectively and intelligently so." (From the 1997 edition)

**Director:** George Roy Hill
**Cast:** Robin Williams (T. S. Garp), Mary Beth Hurt (Helen Holm), Glenn Close (Jenny Fields), John Lithgow (Roberta), Hume Cronyn (Mr. Fields), Jessica Tandy (Mrs. Fields), Swoosie Kurtz (Hooker), Amanda Plummer (Ellen James); with James McCall, Warren Berlinger, Brandon Maggart, Jenny Wright, John Irving (Wrestling Coach). **Writer:** Steve Tesich, based on the novel, *The World According to Garp,* by John Irving **Music:** David Shire
Rated R; 136 minutes

ual). I thought the visualization of the events, by director George Roy Hill, was fresh and consistently interesting. But when the movie was over, my immediate response was not at all what it should have been. All I could find to ask myself was: What the hell was that all about?" (From his review on CompuServe)

**Leonard Maltin:** "An absorbing, sure-footed odyssey through vignettes of social observation, absurdist humor, satire, and melodrama; beautifully

# The Survivors
## (1983)

*"You know, I never had a friend like you."*

—Donald Quinelle to Jack Paluso

Robin Williams's 1983 film, *The Survivors*, came with a fairly impressive "pedigree." In its favor were the following:

1. *The Survivors* was an original script and the feature film debut for Emmy-winning writer Michael Leeson, who would later script 1989's biting and hilarious divorce comedy-drama, *The War of the Roses* (starring Kathleen Turner, Michael Douglas, and Danny DeVito).

2. It was directed by Michael Ritchie, who had previously helmed such memorable flicks as *The Candidate* (1972), *Smile* (1975), *The Bad News Bears* (1976), and *Semi-Tough* (1977).

3. And perhaps most significantly, *The Survivors* starred three major talents in the film industry: veteran actor Walter Matthau, a genius at creating meticulously crafted characters, often through nothing more than the raise of an eyebrow or a flawlessly timed glance; the 1980s country music superstar Jerry Reed, (Burt Reynold's costar in the *Smokey and the Bandit* canon), who proved that he was even a better actor than a singer-songwriter; and, of course, Robin Williams, who had just come off a phenomenally successful run on *Mork and Mindy*, as well as two *truly* unique films, *Popeye* and *The World According to Garp*.

So, with all this high-priced talent and Hollywood history in its favor, does *The Survivors* work?

Well, yes, it does . . . sort of.

*The Survivors* was extremely topical when it was released in 1983. As recently as November of 1982, the United States had been in the midst of a raging recession, unemployment was the highest it had been (10.8 percent) since 1940, and paranoia gripped our land like an iron hand. *The Survivors* mined this fertile socioeconomic territory by telling the story of three disparate characters, all in dire financial difficulty, whose paths crossed in an unlikely turn of events that, frankly, could probably only happen in a movie script.

Donald Quinelle (Robin Williams) is a midlevel manager who is confident that he is on the fast track to corporate success. He's a "three-piece suit" kind of guy who drives the same model station wagon to work as all his colleagues. One morning he is summoned to company president Mr. Stoddard's office and he rushes there eagerly: He thinks he's in line for some big promotion or some other well-deserved accolade from the big man himself. He is greeted, instead, by an empty office . . . and a parrot. The parrot, who Mr. Stoddard spent months personally training, looks at Donald and tells him, "You have been a valuable asset to this company, so this is not easy for me to say. You're fired."

At first Donald thinks it's a joke, but when Mr. Stoddard's secretary pulls a gun on him and calls him an "ungrateful turd," he knows it's for real.

Donald leaves the building shell-shocked and isn't really paying attention when he stops at Sonny's Service Station to fill up his car's gas tank. Donald distractedly misses his car's gas spout with the nozzle and instead, pumps at least ten gallons of gasoline all over the ground. He gets in the car and drives off, and then, through his rear window, we see the entire gas station explode into a raging inferno, thanks to a carelessly thrown cigarette dropped by none other than the gas station's owner, Sonny Paluso (Walter Matthau).

This catastrophe puts Sonny out of business and ends up being the pivotal event that throws him and Donald together.

Donald and Sonny both end up at the Unemployment Office where Sonny gets Maced by an Indian civil servant when he refuses to accept that he cannot collect unemployment because he was a business owner. Donald spends hours in line trying to make sense of the ramblings of a well-dressed man who speaks nothing but Spanish.

After their experiences with the unemployment system, the two of them both end up at the Pit Stop Diner, where Donald sits at the counter weeping, while Sonny continuously wipes his inflamed, Maced eye.

The third member of the motley triumvirate that makes up *The Survivors*, professional hitman Jack Locke (Jerry Reed), chooses this very moment to hold up the diner wearing a ski mask and speaking in an ethnic dialect.

Donald and Sonny have been pushed just a tad too far, however, and being held up is apparently the final insult. Sonny grabs Jack's gun, and it goes off. Donald gets shot in the arm, and Jack's mask comes off in Sonny's hand. Jack flees the diner and Donald ends up in the hospital where he is forced to endure a TV editorial blasting him for his foolish heroics and calling him and Sonny "hotshots with dumb luck."

The robbery was a defining moment for Donald, however, and he decides to go on TV and issue a rebuttal to the editorial during which he mentions Sonny Paluso by name. Jack Locke (a killer who claims to have killed Jimmy Hoffa), happens to be watching Donald as he blathers on and on about the Constitution while also offering a few ludicrous observations ("the root cause of crime is criminals"). Jack, hunting for both Donald and Sonny (eliminate the witnesses is, after all, the first rule of good crimesmanship), is able to track down Sonny after learning his last name.

Jack shows up at Sonny's house to kill him; Donald arrives to apologize to Sonny; they hit Jack in the head with a trophy, and take him to the police station where he is arrested.

On the way home, Donald makes Sonny stop at a gun store where he buys enough artillery to arm his own private army. Donald also signs up for a Survivalist retreat where he will learn how to defend himself against the marauding "vermin" that will be everywhere when society ultimately collapses.

This is where *The Survivors* falters. The remainder of the movie is a convoluted (and unlikely) chain of events in which Jack gets out on bail and forces Sonny to take him to the Survivalist camp. He wants to kill Donald, who knows that he was the one who killed Jimmy Hoffa (even though Jack admits that he made that story up because no one else was taking credit, so he figured, what the hell).

The scenes at the camp are slow-paced and forced. Robin's character devolves from a poor sap dumped on by a cruel economy into a cartoon soldier who seems to have lost all grounding in reality and transformed himself into a militaristic buffoon.

Walter Matthau is, as always, superb. And to be fair, Robin does have some funny moments and he does what he can with the character. But the scenario is so farfetched and poorly paced that we cannot suspend our disbelief and simply enjoy the "wacky" antics of *The Survivors*, as we *were* able to with the comedy, *Stripes* (1981), a movie made up of an equally bizarre and unlikely series of events, but one which nonetheless allowed us to enjoy its characters and storylines.

There are some interesting elements in *The Survivors*, including a few obvious Robin Williams–contributed one–liners, such as: "He has a face like somebody in the road company of *Deliverance*"; "Does this make you realize that men have nipples too?"; "A professional killer with colitis? They must hear you coming!"; and "Oh, God, I love the smell of malamute in the morning!" (No disrespect to screenwriter Leeson, but I'd be willing to wager that those lines were not part of the original script but were, instead, improvised during shooting by the inimitable Mr. Williams.) *Roseanne*'s TV-husband John Goodman, in one of his earliest screen roles, plays one of the fanatical survivalists.

*The Survivors* has what I guess you could call a happy ending, although it is an anemic conclusion to what can only be described as an average script. The ending? Donald takes off his clothes in the snow because he's freaked out by his depressing "lot in life," Walter Matthau reassures him and calms him down, and the three of them, now friends, drive off down a snowy road after they successfully escape the bloodthirsty survivalists.

## An Interesting Bit of Cinematic Synchronicity

There is a scene in *The Survivors* (quoted in the epigraph to this chapter) which will resonate with Robin Williams's fans who also saw *Aladdin*. In *The Survivors*, Robin's character tells Walter Matthau's character, "You know, I never had a friend like you," which is very similar to what Genie tells Robin's character Aladdin ("You ain't never had a friend like me!") in the movie *Aladdin*, which came out almost ten years later. Coincidence? Perhaps.

*Robin and costar Walter Matthau seen in the closing moments of* The Survivors. *(Photofest)*

## What the Critics Had to Say

**Mick Martin and Marsha Porter:** "Generally a black comedy, this movie features a variety of comedic styles, and they all work." (From their *Video Movie Guide*)

**Leonard Maltin:** "Combination black comedy and social satire. Likable stars do their best with [a] scattershot script." (From his *Movie and Video Guide*)

**Roger Ebert:** "The story gets so confused that the movie can't even account for why its characters happen to be in the same place at the same time; in desperation, it gives us a scene where Williams actually calls Reed and tells him where he can be found. Uh-huh." (From his *Movie Home Companion*)

**Director:** Michael Ritchie
**Cast:** Robin Williams (Donald Quinelle), Walter Matthau (Sonny Paluso), Jerry Reed (Jack), James Wainwright (Wes), Kristen Vigard (Candice), Anne Pitoniak (Betty), Annie McEnroe (Doreen), Bernard Barrow (TV manager), Marian Hailey (Jack's wife), Joseph Carberry (Detective Burke), Marilyn Cooper (waitress), Skip Lynch (Wiley), Meg Mundy (Mace lover); with John Goodman, Sanford Seeger, Yudie Bank, Michael Moran, Norma Pratt
**Writer:** Michael Leeson
**Music:** Paul Chihara
Rated R; 102 minutes

# *Moscow on the Hudson*
## (1984)

*"America is magnificent."*

—Vladimir Ivanoff, Robin William's character
in *Moscow on the Hudson*

*"I have a defector. We're between Estee Lauder and Pierre Cardin."*

—Bloomingdales security guard Lionel Witherspoon
informing his superiors of Ivanoff's defection

*Moscow on the Hudson* tells the story of a Russian saxophonist named Vladimir Ivanoff who plays in the Russian circus and who defects to the United States during a visit to New York City.

Robin Williams plays Vladimir Ivanoff flawlessly. He easily communicates the meek and timid demeanor so common to immigrants and makes us feel what it must be like for someone from a foreign country to suddenly have to make sense of our often chaotic culture and labyrinthine bureaucratic agencies.

The movie begins in Russia where we see how people lived before the collapse of the Soviet Union's Communist government. There is a macabre fascination in these early scenes and some telling moments stand out.

For instance, citizens walking through the streets of Moscow would automatically get into a line they saw forming, no matter what the line was for. These lines often snaked around entire city blocks and they usually meant that some merchant had gotten a shipment of some kind of commodity. It could be toilet paper or shoes. It didn't matter. The Russians would get into the line.

In one of these scenes, Robin's character finds that the line he is on is for shoes. When he gets to the front of the line, he learns that they do not have either of the pairs he wants in his size. No matter. He buys two pairs that are several sizes smaller because he knows he can trade them for something else he can actually use.

In another scene, as Robin and his circus clown friend Boris are driving through Moscow, they see a truck parked under a bridge and immediately know that the driver has black-market gaso-

line for sale. They make a u-turn and stop. The most revealing moment in this scene occurs when they open their trunk and take out two large containers for the gasoline: In Russia, one has to always be prepared to take advantage of any opportunity that might come one's way. This element of Soviet life is hammered home again when another car pulls up to the truck and *its* driver likewise removes two gasoline containers from *his* trunk.

Vladimir is resigned to this type of life in Russia, though, and is not interested in hearing Boris's talk of defection.

Boris plans on defecting to the United States when the Russian circus visits New York. The KGB knows of his plans and is prepared to do everything to stop him. Vladimir advises his friend to abandon his plans but Boris is committed to the idea.

During their stay in New York, however, Boris chickens out and, uncharacteristically, *Vladimir* makes a spur-of-the-moment decision and defects to a security guard at Bloomingdales. He hides under the skirt of an Italian immigrant sales clerk named Lucia (Maria Conchita Alonso) and eventually goes home with Lionel, the guard to whom he defected.

Vladimir, with the help of a Cuban lawyer (in *Moscow on the Hudson*, ironically everyone in America is from somewhere else), secures political asylum and embarks on a career path that includes selling hot dogs, bussing tables, driving a cab, and ultimately, driving a limo. He develops a relationship with Lucia and eventually gets his own apartment. He writes to his family back in Russia but doesn't know if they receive his letters.

After a time, Vladimir becomes a little disillusioned by the freedoms in America. Instead of seeing opportunity, he now sees the crime and the poverty. He becomes jaded after getting mugged. Robin plays this shift in his character's perceptions with passion and makes it completely believable. Vladimir ultimately recognizes his overreaction as too extreme, however, and the movie ends with him regaining his love for his new homeland and coming to a new understanding of the social dynamic of America.

Robin effectively shows us that Vladimir was only seeing the glories of America and that, with time, he came to a more balanced understanding of what it's like to live in the United States.

In *Moscow on the Hudson,* Robin Williams plays Vladimir with skill and confidence. Even his Russian and Russian American accent are completely believable.

Coming so quickly after *The World According to Garp,* this film was a very strong addition to Robin's dramatic filmography, and showed that here was one of our better young dramatic actors.

Other than the little-seen *Seize the Day* in 1986, though, it would be a good five years before Robin tackled another dramatic role that was worthy of his talents, that of the English teacher John Keating in 1989's *Dead Poets Society.*

## What the Critics Had to Say

**Roger Ebert:** "Robin Williams . . . disappears so completely into his quirky, lovable, complicated character that he's quite plausible as a Russian. . . . [This is] a rarity, a patriotic film that has a liberal, rather than a con-

*Robin as Russian defector Vladimir Ivanoff in* Moscow on the Hudson. *(Photofest)*

servative, heart. It made me feel good to be an American, and good that Vladimir Ivanoff was going to be one, too." (From his *Movie Home Companion*)

*Robin and* Moscow on the Hudson *costar Maria Conchita Alonso. (Photofest)*

**Leonard Maltin:** "Fine original comedy-drama. . . . Full of endearing performances, perceptive and bittersweet moments—but a few too many false endings. Williams is superb in the lead." (From his *Movie and Video Guide*)

***Videohound's Golden Movie Retriever:*** "Williams is particularly winning as naive jazzman. . . . Be warned though, it's not just played for laughs." (From the 1997 edition)

**Director:** Paul Mazursky
**Cast:** Robin Williams (Vladimir Ivanoff), Maria Conchita Alonso (Lucia Lombardo), Cleavant

Derricks (Lionel Witherspoon), Alejandro Rey (Orlando Ramirez), Savely Kramarov (Boris), Elya Baskin (Anatoly), Olag Rudnik (Yury), Alexander Beniaminov (Vladimir's grandfather), Paul Mazursky (Dave), Yakov Smirnoff (Lev)
**Writers:** Leon Capetanos and Paul Mazursky
**Music:** David McHugh
Rated R; 115 minutes

# *The Best of Times*
## (1986)

*"Let's play some football!"*

—Jack Dundee

The biggest problem I have with *The Best of Times* is that the story is utterly unbelievable.

The fundamental premise of the film is that Robin Williams's character, Jack Dundee, has been so emotionally traumatized by blowing a critical catch in a pivotal high school football game that it has affected his entire life and left him crippled in the self-esteem department. (As evidence of his neurosis, we learn that Jack's doorbell plays his high school anthem.)

The writer of *The Best of Times*, Ron Shelton, would go on to better things, including *Bull Durham* (1988), *White Men Can't Jump* (1992), and *Tin Cup* (1996); but here, because he starts with a premise that the audience really can't buy into, the remainder of the movie collapses like a house with a cardboard foundation.

Jack Dundee is a bank manager in a bank owned by his obnoxious blowhard father-in-law, "The Colonel," (Donald Moffat) a staunch supporter of the Bakersfield football team that beat Jack's team in that all-important final high school game. Jack visits a massage parlor once a week on the outskirts of town, but not to have sex. Instead, he pays sixty dollars just to talk about the big game, a game that has been over for a dozen years, and yet still haunts the obsessive and tormented Jack. (*The Best of Times*, by the way, is an alleged comedy.)

Reno Hightower (Kurt Russell) was the all-star quarterback who threw Jack that critically important pass and he, too, has apparently been scarred by the debacle of Jack dropping the ball. He has also never left the gritty, rundown town of Taft and now owns and operates a van-painting shop. His marriage to Gigi (Pamela Reed) is a disaster and his knees are a mess.

During one of Jack's therapeutic massage parlor sessions, his masseuse (Margaret Whitton), also a Taft High alumni, gets so sick of hearing Jack whine about the dropped pass, she impulsively blurts out that he should just play the game over again and get on with his life.

Rather then dismissing this suggestion as ludicrous and unrealistic (the way people in *real* life would), Jack warms to the idea and decides to propose to The Colonel and Reno Hightower replaying the game.

The Colonel, seeing yet another opportunity to humiliate his loathed son-in-law, readily accepts. Reno, on the other hand, takes a bit more persuading. Jack reminds Reno that he's behind on his mortgage payments and that he has been covering for him at the bank. Jack calls in this debt and Reno reluctantly agrees to the game, telling Jack, "You're a low life, blackmailing, chickenshit squid."

Once the game is scheduled, the Taft team, all of whom are now overweight, out-of-shape, and in their late thirties, must train and prepare for this seemingly futile attempt at redemption. The Bakersfield team, on the other hand, has coaches, uniforms, and equipment, and they are fit and more than ready to play. Although Taft has none of the above, the town rallies around the team anyway and spruces up for the big game.

In the midst of all this football stuff, there are several romantic subplots involving Jack and Reno and their wives, with all of these scenes *really* slowing the film.

The last third or so of the movie consists of the game and, of course, as you would predict Jack is called in at the last minute and does catch the winning touchdown pass. Hurray, do the wave, sis-boom-bah.

Robin Williams's work in *The Best of Times* comes off as confused and erratic. He has a few moments when the kick-ass Robin surfaces (he does a little riff about "Mr. Weasel" and throws a mini-tantrum in the massage parlor that has possibilities) but overall he is not given a sharply defined character to play and, his performance suffers.

*The Best of Times* is one of the films that Robin considers to be part of his Trilogy of Failure.

*Robin as Jack Dundee in* The Best of Times. *(Photofest)*

(The other two he has mentioned as regrettable career choices are *The Survivors* and *Club Paradise*.) He's got a point: *The Best of Times* is slow-paced, rambling, and boring.

Even a serious Robin Williams fan could skip *The Best of Times* and not miss a thing. Too bad. Good and talented people were involved with the project. Director Roger Spottiswoode would go on to direct the TV movies *The Last Innocent Man* (1987) and the powerful AIDS drama, *And the Band Played On* (1993); we've already talked about writer Ron Shelton; and the caliber of the cast is obvious.

But in the end, regrettably, the whole was less than the sum of its parts.

## What the Critics Had to Say

**Leonard Maltin:** "Some quirky, offbeat touches highlight Ron Shelton's script and the wives (Reed, Palance) are a treat but seemingly surefire film becomes too strident (and too exaggerated) to really score. (From his *Movie and Video Guide*)

***Videohound's Golden Movie Retriever:*** "With this cast, it should have been better." (From the 1997 edition)

**Director:** Roger Spottiswoode
**Cast:** Robin Williams (Jack Dundee), Kurt Russell (Reno Hightower), Pamela Reed (Gigi Hightower), Holly Palance (Elly Dundee), Donald Moffat (The Colonel), Margaret Whitton (Darla), M. Emmett Walsh (Charlie), Donovan Scott (Eddie), R. G. Armstrong (Schutte), Dub Taylor (Mac), Carl Ballantine (Arturo)
**Writer:** Ron Shelton
**Music:** Arthur G. Rubinstein
Rated PG; 105 minutes

*The cast of* The Best of Times *(from left): Holly Palance, Robin, Kurt Russell, Pamela Reed. (Photofest)*

# *Club Paradise*
## (1986)

*"Jump off with your passion, not as a whore."*

—Robin Williams, talking about how to
make career choices

Club Paradise holds an ignoble place in Robin Williams's body of film work: It is the only movie he has admitted to making *only* for the money.

It is easy to understand Robin's initial enthusiasm for the commercial potential of *Club Paradise*. The cast was made up of some of the hottest comic actors and stars of the eighties: Eugene Levy, Rick Moranis, Andrea Martin, Brian Doyle-Murray, and Mary Gross; as well as the legendary Peter O'Toole,

the sexy model-turned-actress Twiggy, and hot reggae star, Jimmy Cliff. The script was cowritten by Harold Ramis and Brian Doyle-Murray. Ramis had just come off the enormously successful 1984 hit *Ghostbusters* (which he cowrote and starred in); and Doyle-Murray (Bill Murray's brother) had previously cowritten the 1981 Bill Murray military comedy, *Stripes*. *Club Paradise* was also to be directed by Ramis, who had previously been behind the camera for the two giant hits, *Caddyshack*

*Robin and Twiggy with their* Club Paradise *costar, world-famous reggae musician Jimmy Cliff. (Photofest)*

*Robin as retired fireman Jack Moniker in* Club Paradise. *(Photofest)*

(1980) and *National Lampoon's Vacation* (1983).

Yes, all the elements were in place and everyone believed *Club Paradise* would not only be a terrific movie, but that it would also mimic the box-office success of the previous comedies that all these creative dynamos had been involved in.

So what happened?

*Club Paradise* is about a Chicago fireman Jack Moniker (Robin Williams) who is completely fed up with his job. He uses an on-the-job injury as an opportunity to take a disability retirement package,

move to a Caribbean island owned by Great Britain, and live the good life in a tropical resort (Club Paradise) for the rest of his life.

As he settles in and gets to know more about the island and its people, he learns that the resort, owned by his reggae musician friend, Ernest Reed (Jimmy Cliff), is behind on its taxes. The slimy bureaucrat who owns the majority of the rest of the island is intent on closing Club Paradise for back taxes, and selling the whole island to foreign developers who will build condos and high-rise hotels.

Jack and Philipa (a tourist, played by Twiggy, who falls in love with him and stays on the island) put together a gorgeous (but intentionally misleading) brochure to lure vacationers to the resort and hopefully raise enough money to save the place.

Robin's character in *Club Paradise* is essentially a wisecracking straight man. There is none of the manic craziness common to some of his more memorable performances and much of the humor in the movie comes from the secondary characters played by Levy, Moranis, Martin, and O'Toole (playing the figurehead governor of the island).

*Club Paradise* could have been funnier if Robin Williams had been given better material and especially if he had been allowed to improvise some of his scenes. The supporting cast are all consummate pros and do the best with what they are given, but overall, the script seems too slow, too convoluted, and it doesn't have enough truly funny lines or scenes.

There is an unnecessary subplot about a revolution that seems to come out of nowhere, and there is not enough interaction between Robin and the other comedic stars. It would seem to be the logical move that if you have Robin Williams in your movie, unless it's a drama like *Awakenings* or *Seize the Day*, you should really make as much use of him as you can and let him *be* Robin Williams. He is collared in *Club Paradise*; his performance is subdued and restrained and he has almost no memorable funny lines, except for a few scripted wisecracks.

Andrea Martin is very funny as a housefrau set loose (the first thing she tries upon her arrival on the island is hang gliding), and Rick Moranis is terrific as the pot-smoking "wild and crazy" ladies' man who ends up wind-surfing twenty miles out to sea in the middle of a monster storm. Eugene Levy is good, as always, and Peter O'Toole is perfect as the lazy, flat-broke governor who is quite aware of his station in life, thank you very much, and is perfectly content to wile away his days drinking umbrella drinks and cavorting with the attractive female guests on the island. Twiggy is a surprisingly natural actress, and cinematic veterans Joanna Cassidy (as Terry Hamlin) and Adolph Caesar (Prime Minister Solomon Gundy) round out the cast.

The music in *Club Paradise* is mostly reggae, mostly by Jimmy Cliff, and it is one of the few truly superb elements in the film.

*Club Paradise* could have been better considering the caliber of talent involved. Is it worth a rental? Sure, if you don't bring it home expecting *Ghostbusters* or *Stripes*. It's not that it's a bad film—it's just average (or slightly below average). But when you're talking about this cast, "average" for them is almost unacceptable. For the guys who made *Stewardess School II* or *Smokey and the Bandit III*, *Club Paradise* would be a three- or four-star movie. For Williams, Ramis, and company, however, it's a major disappointment, but still worth seeing if you're a fan of any of the talented people involved.

## What Robin Had to Say

PLAYBOY: Are there any films you've made for reasons other than artistic ones?
ROBIN WILLIAMS: *Club Paradise.* They said it would be a box-office smash, a great combination of people, we'll kick ass, etc. And then [explosion sound] my ass got kicked. That's when you get screwed. (From *Playboy*, January 1992)

## What the Critics Had to Say

Leonard Maltin: "Pleasant cast in pleasant surroundings, lacking only a script and a few more laughs." (From his *Movie and Video Guide*)

*Videohound's Golden Movie Retriever:* "Somewhat disappointing with [Robin] Williams largely playing the straight man. Most laughs provided by [Andrea] Martin, particularly when she is assaulted by a shower, and [Rick] Moranis who gets lost while windsurfing." (From the 1997 edition)

**Director:** Harold Ramis
**Cast:** Robin Williams (Jack Moniker), Peter O'Toole (Governor Anthony Croyden-Noyes), Rick Moranis (Barry Nye), Andrea Martin (Linda White), Jimmy Cliff (Ernest Reed), Brian Doyle-Murray (Vot Zerbe), Twiggy (Philipa Lloyd), Eugene Levy (Barry Sternberg), Adolph Caesar (Prime Minister Solomon Gundy), Joanna Cassidy (Terry Hamlin), Steven Kampmann (Randy White), Mary Gross (Jackie), Joe Flaherty (pilot), Carey Lowell (model), Robin Duke (Mary Lou), Simon Jones (Toby Prooth)
**Writers:** Harold Ramis and Brian Doyle-Murray
**Music:** David Mansfield, Van Dyke Parks, Jimmy Cliff
Rated PG-13; 96 minutes

*The always-hairy Robin, seen here with his costar Twiggy in a scene from* Club Paradise. *(Photofest)*

*Robin in action during the only scenes from* Good Morning, Vietnam *that he was allowed to improvise. (Photofest)*

# *Good Morning, Vietnam*
## (1987)

*"Goooooooooood morning, Vietnam!"*
—Adrian Cronauer

**G**ood Morning, Vietnam was Robin Williams's break-out film and the movie that transformed him from a working actor into a huge star.

His earlier film work (most notably *The World According to Garp, Moscow on the Hudson,* and the little-seen but unquestionably brilliant *Seize the Day*) had shown that he had cinematic potential and was undoubtedly a talented actor (and, of course, a comedic genius), but *Good Morning, Vietnam* was ultimately the perfect vehicle to wholeheartedly utilize his unique blend of manic comedy and dramatic acting capabilities. Prior to *Good Morning, Vietnam,* Robin had not made a film in which he could act *and* perform. That duality of character is exactly what he needed to fulfill his potential, and that is what he found in Adrian Cronauer's story and Mitch Markowitz's *Good Morning, Vietnam* script.

*Good Morning, Vietnam* was directed by the talented Barry Levinson (*Diner* (1982), *The Natural* (1984), *Tin Men* (1987), *Rain Man* (1988), *Avalon* (1990), *Bugsy* (1991)) who would later direct Robin in 1992's *Toys.* In his book, *Levinson on Levinson,* the director talked about how the film ended up being a combination of scripted action and dialogue blended with Robin Williams's amazing improvisations:

> I thought the idea of the DJ was interesting. The real man [Cronauer] was not as funny as Robin. Not too funny at all. Very serious, in fact. . . . So we ended up changing about 40 percent of the script. Working with Robin on his routines was a little like playing football when we

were kids. . . . Robin would do a take and I'd say, "I like the thing about so-and-so. I don't think that bit works, but this is good. What about that thing you talked about the other day, about the nudist monk? Let's give that a try." Then he'd go and do another take, we'd go over it again and say, "This is good, save this. Drop that. Add this. I think we're in fine shape. Let's see if you've got any other ideas." Then another idea would emerge that wasn't really developed; we'd talk about it and explore it a little more, and then start shooting again. We shot very fast, a lot of footage, and basically hammered out that whole section of the movie. We shot it in an incredibly short period of time considering the impact it has in the movie.

Robin's performance won him a Golden Globe Award for Best Actor in a Musical or Comedy, and earned him a Best Actor Oscar nomination. His transformation from the exhausted, sullen airman newly arrived in Saigon, into the raucous, multi-voiced DJ when he sits in front of the microphone for the first time is an amazing thing to see and hear. Here is how Robin began this first radio scene:

Goooooooooood morning, Vietnam! Hey, this is not a test, this is rock and roll! Time to rock it from the Delta to the DMZ! Is that me or does that sound like an Elvis Presley movie? [Sings in Elvis Presley voice] Viva Danang. Oh, Viva Danang. Danang me, Danang me, why don't they get a rope and hang me! Hey, is it a little to early for being that loud? Hey, too late! It's o six hundred. What does the "o" stand for? Oh, my God, it's early.

*Robin and Good Morning, Vietnam costar Forest Whitaker. (Photofest)*

*Robin as maverick DJ Adrian Cronauer in* Good Morning,
Vietnam. *(Photofest)*

In this first bit, Williams does his interpretation of: scenes from *The Wizard Of Oz* (with himself doing all the characters); Rod Serling doing the *Twilight Zone* opening narration in which he finds himself in "The Demilitarized Zone"; visits from Gomer Pyle, President Johnson, Hanoi Hannah, a GI named Roosevelt E. Roosevelt who told Adrian he was stationed in Poon Tang; Lawrence Welk; Mr. Leo, a fashion consultant for the army whose motto was "If you're going to fight, clash!"; and Bob Fribber from artillery who wanted Adrian to "play anything . . . just play it loud!" All rapid fire, with the sequence, from start to finish, lasting exactly 3 minutes and 20 seconds.

*Good Morning, Vietnam* tells the story of the aforementioned Cronauer, an armed forces DJ who gets reassigned from Crete to Saigon in an attempt to bolster the morale of the ever-increasing numbers of GIs being shipped to Vietnam.

In the tradition of M*A*S*H's irrepressible Hawkeye Pierce, Williams's Cronauer is an irreverent, somewhat disrespectful, defiantly anti-mainstream rebel who eschews the accepted army playlist of Percy Faith, Ray Conniff, and "certain ballads by Mr. Frank Sinatra" and instead plays The Beach Boys, Martha and the Vandellas, and James Brown. Not surprisingly, the GIs love him, (especially his friend and aide Edward Garlick, played by Forest Whitaker in one of his earlier film roles), but, aside from General Taylor (played by Noble Willingham), the brass can't stand him. J. T. Walsh's character Sergeant Dickerson (who is inexplicably in Saigon because of prostate problems) in particular works diligently (and ultimately succeeds) at getting rid of Cronauer.

*Good Morning, Vietnam* is very entertaining and most effective when (not surprisingly) Robin's character is on the radio or interacting with his fellow military types. The film could have done with less of him teaching the Vietnamese English and playing softball with them, as well as the subplot involving his romantic pursuit of a young woman from his class. These moments are less successful but do not seriously detract from the overall excellence of the film or Robin's performance in it.

DJ Adrian Cronauer entertains the troops. (Photofest)

## What Robin Had to Say

"Barry Levinson, [Paul] Mazursky, they were comics. So they understand the beast. And that's why they can work with someone like me. And know when to say no, and to put up like those kind of rubber road cones when you're learning to drive and you hear that—bang!—but you didn't break the car. And that's why [Barry Levinson] was great." (From a PBS interview with David Frost)

*Robin and the cast of* Good Morning, Vietnam. *(Standing left to right) Bruno Kirby, Floyd Vivino, Richard Portnow, Robert Wuhl, Forest Whitaker. (Photofest)*

## What the Critics Had to Say

**Leonard Maltin:** "Williams is the whole show here. . . . His manic monologues are so uproarious that they carry the rest of the film, which has a weakly developed story and often irrelevant musical interludes." (From his *Movie and Video Guide*)

**Roger Ebert:** "*Good Morning, Vietnam* works as straight comedy, and it works as a Vietnam-era M*A*S*H, and even the movie's love story has its own bittersweet integrity. But they used to tell us in writing class that if we wanted to know what a story was really about, we should look for what

changed between the beginning and the end. In this movie, Cronauer changes. War wipes the grin off of his face. His humor becomes a humanitarian tool, not simply a way to keep him talking and us listening. (From his *Movie Home Companion*)

**Mick Martin and Marsha Porter:** "Williams's improvisational monologues are the high points in a film that meanders too much, but Forest Whitaker also shines." (From their *Video Movie Guide*)

**Videohound's Golden Movie Retriever:** "[Robin] Williams spins great comic moments that may have been scripted but likely were not, as a man with no history and for whom everything is manic radio material. The character ad-libs, swoops, and swerves, finally accepting adult responsibility. Engaging all the way with an outstanding period sound track." (From the 1997 edition)

**Director:** Barry Levinson
**Cast:** Robin Williams (Adrian Cronauer), Forest Whitaker (Edward Garlick), Tung Thanh Tran (Tuan), Chintara Sukapatana (Trinh), Bruno Kirby (Lieutenant Hauk), Robert Wuhl (Marty Lee Dreiwitz), J.T. Walsh (Sergeant Dickerson), Noble Willingham (General Taylor); with Richard Edson, Floyd Vivino
**Writer:** Mitch Markowitz
**Music:** Alex North
Rated R; 121 minutes

# The Adventures of Baron Munchausen (1989)

*"I don't have time for flatulence and orgasms! I hate that face you make me make! Please, please, no! I don't want any more bodily functions!"*
—The King of the Moon's detached head, (Robin) speaking to his piggish body

This $46 million special effects extravaganza was Robin's first collaboration with Terry Gilliam (*Fisher King* director). It tells the story of the legendary Baron Munchausen, a mythic figure about whom stage plays were written and who everyone believed perished in some amazing adventure.

The movie is, without a doubt, an enchanting viewing experience, but it speaks volumes about the extraordinary and inestimable talents of Robin Williams that his brief ten minutes of screen time (in a two-hour plus movie) provided (for this somewhat biased viewer) the most enjoyable moments of the film. Robin's performance, short enough to be considered a cameo, is funny, engaging, and the liveliest sequence in the film. He isn't even credited under his real name, but rather as "Ray D. Tutto,") which is a play on the name of Robin's character, the King of the Moon, also known as "Re di tutto,"the "King of Everything."

Robin's scene takes place on the Moon. The Baron (John Neville) and his young companion Sally (Sarah Polley) have flown to the Moon in a hot-air sailing ship (the balloon is made from ladies' undergarments—don't ask) to seek help from the Baron's dear friend, the King of the Moon, in saving Sally's beseiged hometown.

Robin's character *literally* illustrates the idea of the mind and body being two distinct and separate entities. The King of the Moon (and his wife, the Queen, played by Valentina Cortese) have detachable heads. The heads are actually screwed on and the two parts of their person—head and body—are in constant conflict. The head wants to disconnect from the vile and repulsive body and concern itself only with the "higher things" of existence, while the body is only interested in the baser pursuits, primarily, sex and food.

When the Baron and Sally first arrive on the Moon (a surrealistic place where the buildings travel around like pedestrians on a sidewalk), the King has freed himself from his body and his stark white head is floating around in space. After greeting the Baron ("*Bene venuti a luna, Baroni!*"), the King informs Munchausen that he is now King of Everything, not just the Moon, and he proves his point by making some chirping noises and telling them that he just invented Spring. His new title is Re di tutti—"but you can call me Ray."

The King tells the Baron that the Moon is now just a small part of his domain and that without him, there would be nothing: "*Cogito, ergo, es,*" the King tells the Baron. Translation: "I think, therefore, you is."

This prompts young Sally to inform the Baron, "Your old friend's a lunatic." The King then tells them that Munchausen's many adventures are a distraction to him and that he considers the

111

Baron to be "like a mosquito in the Taj Mahal." The Baron reminds the King that without his adventures, there would *be* no King of the Moon and this irritates old Ray. He imprisons the Baron and Sally in a room atop a giant pedestal and then the King laments the existence of his "revolting body," which is busy chasing the body of his Queen. "It's hard to believe my body and I were ever connected," he whines to the Baron and Sally. "We are so totally incompatible. He is just dangling from the food chain and I am in the stars!"

The King's body recaptures its head, screws it on tight, and immediately changes into a flesh-colored glutton. "I'm baaaaack!" he exclaims to one and all. "I got lips again and I'm gonna use 'em, baby!" he tells his Queen.

The King then proclaims, "I'm your elephant of joy!" and raises his "trunk," with the appropriate accompanying screeching sound. (This would seem to be an improvised Robin Williams bit.) He then begins disgustingly stuffing fruit into his mouth and belching and when he sees the Baron, there is food and juice all over his face. Apparently, the King's body doesn't know what its head does when it's separated because the King then says to the Baron, "Hey, I know you! You're the little guy tried to make off with my Queen last time you were here! We'll have no more of that, piccolo Casanova!"

Sally and the Baron are then put into a cage, but the King's head again escapes from the body and rhapsodizes that it is now free again "to concentrate on higher things!"

The body quickly recaptures the head with a butterfly net, though, and leads it off. The head cries out, "Let me go! I've got tides to regulate! Comets to direct!"

Later, the Queen's detached head frees the Baron and Sally and informs them that the King is home in bed with her body. The Queen's head repeatedly makes little orgasmic noises while speaking to them and when the adolescent Sally asks the Baron why she's doing that, the Baron embarrassedly tells her that the King is off "tickling her feet." We then see the King in bed with the Queen's body . . . tickling her feet! The King eventually discovers that her head is gone ("Where is your head? No wonder you're so quiet.") and then figures out that she's with the Baron: "You are with that little man! You told me size don't make a difference!"

The King vows to kill the Baron and sends a

three-headed vulture after him. The bird dives for the Baron and Sally, but they split up and the bird rips itself apart trying to chase both of them at the same time. The King's body dies when the center bird crashes into the ground, and the head cries out, "The body is dead! Long live the head!" He decides that he doesn't need a body after all, but then he sneezes and flies off into space.

And thus ends Robin Williams's ten minutes of screen time in *The Adventures of Baron Munchausen*. The rest of the film is no less bizarre and fantastic.

Robin's performance in this movie is terrific fun and, again, one of the most engaging and exciting sequences in the film. The movie as a whole does have some sluggish spots, but it also boasts appearances by the supremely gorgeous Uma Thurman (as Venus) and cameo appearances by Sting, and Elton John's percussionist, Ray Cooper.

Is *The Adventures of Baron Munchausen* worth renting? Yes, if you're a Robin Williams fan and want to see one of the odder entries in his filmography. Just be aware, though, that after Robin's scenes, (which occur about a third of the way through the movie) you can watch the rest of the movie a little less attentively and still enjoy it for its spectacular and amazing effects.

## What the Critics Had to Say

Leonard Maltin: "Breathtaking special effects go hand in hand with Gilliam's outlandishly funny and far-out ideas; a visual feast that's worth staying with through its occasional lulls." (From his *Movie and Video Guide*)

**Director:** Terry Gilliam
**Cast:** Robin Williams (King of the Moon—Robin was credited as "Ray D. Tutto"), John Neville (Baron Munchausen), Eric Idle (Desmond/Berthold), Sarah Polley (Sally Salt), Oliver Reed (Vulcan), Charles McKeown (Rupert and Adolphus), Winston Dennis (Bill and Albrecht), Valentina Cortese (Queen and Violet), Sting (Heroic Officer); also, Uma Thurman, Ray Cooper, Jonathan Pryce, Bill Patterson, Peter Jeffrey, Alison Steadman, Jack Purvis
**Writer:** Terry Gilliam
**Music:** Michael Kamen
Rated PG; 126 minutes

# Dead Poets Society
## (1989)

*"We are food for worms, lads. Because believe it or not, each and every one of us in this room is one day going to stop breathing, turn cold, and die."*

—John Keating

*Robin as English teacher John Keating in* Dead Poets Society. *(Photofest)*

There are some viewers who will interpret the subtext of *Dead Poets Society* as validation of a rigid and harsh disciplinarian style of upbringing and education. These advocates do have a point, but one's ultimate assessment of this absorbing period piece will depend largely on how one views life and our time on this globe: Is life a harsh and merciless battle to be won through denial, steadfast focus, and, of course, structure and discipline? Or is it a wondrous journey that should be savored and enjoyed through the embrace of spontaneity, love, and an honest acknowledgment of the fleeting nature of the brief time we all have above ground?

In *Dead Poets Society*, Robin Williams plays John Keating, an unorthodox English teacher at the New England all boys' prep school, The Welton Academy. Keating's first instructions to his students are to tear out an essay in their poetry text because he believes that the guy who wrote it doesn't know what he's talking about (he calls it "excrement"); and then for them to stand on his desk, one at a time, in order to get a different view of the world. Keating's code of conduct is based on the axiom *carpe diem*: "Seize the day." He believes his young charges should challenge authority and conventional wisdom and make bold and daring moves, for such actions, he assures them, will undoubtedly

(Photofest)

be considered rebellious reading poetry aloud to each other. And yet, the story and the excellent performances take over and we are caught up in the life-and-death struggle between one student and his father, a struggle that ultimately ends in tragedy.

Robert Sean Leonard, in only his third theatrical film (his first two were forgettable: 1987's *Bluffing It* and 1988's *My Best Friend Is a Vampire*), plays Keating's student Neil Perry, the son of a man who is a cold and controlling authoritarian.

Neil wants to act; his father (Kurtwood Smith) wants him to be a doctor. Keating encourages Neil to stand up for what his heart wants and Neil subsequently defies his father by acting in the school play, against the old man's orders. Mr. Perry shows up at the play, drags his son home, and tells him he is pulling him out of Welton and sending him to a military academy because of his disobedience. Later that evening, Neil puts a bullet through his brain (with his father's gun) and his father is the first one to find him.

Back at Welton, the powers-that-be need a scapegoat . . . and John Keating ends up the unlucky winner. The Headmaster makes the surviving members of the Dead Poets Society sign a declaration that Neil killed himself because Mr. Keating encouraged all of them to act in a self-indulgent and reckless manner. Keating gets fired and the Headmaster takes over his English class.

The first day with the Headmaster as teacher is the day Keating is departing for good. He stops in to his old classroom to retrieve his personal belongings and while he is in the back room, the Headmaster asks one of the students to read aloud the very essay Keating had made them tear out of their books. The students cannot bear this painful irony for very long and as Keating is leaving, the mem-

yield growth and enlightenment.

When Keating was a student at Welton, he and a few like-minded classmates formed a club they called the Dead Poets Society. They would gather in a cave and read poetry aloud in an attempt to acquire some of the transcendental wisdom of such writers as Tennyson, Blake, Emerson, Thoreau, and other "free thinkers." As an instructor, Keating rouses the adolescent frustrations of his students (*all* students, actually) to break free from the rules and demands of school, their parents, society, etc. A group of his students accept his challenge, reincarnate the Society and begin holding secret meetings—gatherings that are completely against the rules of the school.

As with any period piece (this one takes place in the 1950s), the sensibility of the times takes some getting used to. Today it is unfathomable to believe that a group of 16- and 17-year-olds would

bers of the Society all stand on top of their desks in tribute to him and his philosophies.

Robin Williams's performance in *Dead Poets Society* is a very good dramatic achievement (he received Golden Globe and Oscar nominations), though he cannot help veering off into the Land of Robin now and then. John Wayne doing Shakespeare? Sure, why not. A surfer dude on *American Bandstand*? Okay. Robin also adds a touch of sadness to Keating's character that is quite effective. And Australian director and Academy Award nominee Peter Weir, responsible for such thoughtful and textured films as *Picnic at Hanging Rock* (1975), *Gallipoli* (1981), *The Year of Living Dangerously* (1982), *Witness* (1985), and *The Mosquito Coast* (1986), brings a unique sensibility to the film, often eliciting from Robin a more nuanced performance that American directors have not often demanded from him.

All in all, a worthwhile achievement for all concerned.

## What Robin Had to Say

"[*Dead Poets Society*] is not a performance as much as it is a statement of philosophy." (From a PBS interview with David Frost)

"Originally, my character was supposed to have leukemia, which would have been *Dead Poets Love Story*. Then Peter Weir said, 'Let's lose that. Focus on the boys.'" (From *Playboy*, January 1992)

"I like the point of the movie, of trying to find the passionate thing in your life, finding some sort of passion." (From the *New York Times*, May 28, 1989)

## What the Critics Had to Say

**Roger Ebert:** "[Williams's] performance is a delicate balancing act between restraint and schtick. For much of the time, Williams does a good job of

*An example of* Dead Poets Society's *John Keating's unorthodox teaching style. (Photofest)*

playing an intelligent, quick-witted, well-read young man. But then there are scenes in which his stage persona punctures the character—as when he does impressions of Marlon Brando and John Wayne doing Shakespeare. There is also a curious lack of depth to his character . . . Keating is more of a plot device than a human being." (From his *Movie Home Companion*)

**Leonard Maltin:** "Well made, extremely well acted, but also dramatically obvious and melodramatically one-sided." (From his *Movie and Video Guide*)

***Videohound's Golden Movie Retriever:*** "Williams shows he can master the serious roles as well as the comic with his portrayal of the unorthodox educa-tor. Big box office hit occasionally scripted with a heavy hand to elevate the message." (From the 1997 edition)

**Director:** Peter Weir
**Cast:** Robin Williams (John Keating), Robert Sean Leonard (Neil Perry), Ethan Hawke (Todd Anderson), Josh Charles (Knox Overstreet), Gale Hansen (Charlie Dalton), Dylan Kussman (Richard Cameron), Allelon Ruggiero (Steven Meeks), James Waterston (Gerard Pitts), Kurt-wood Smith (Mr. Perry); with Norman Lloyd, Lara Flynn Boyle, Alexandra Powers
**Writer:** Tom Schulman
**Music:** Maurice Jarre
Rated PG; 124 minutes

# *Cadillac Man*
## (1990)

*"I do for you; maybe one day you do for me?"*
—Robin as Joey O'Brien

*Cadillac Man* is another unique entry in the Robin Williams film catalog: It is one of the nearly three dozen movies he's done in which he does almost none of his manic, patented Robin Williams schtick. (*Awakenings, Seize the Day,* and *Being Human* are some of the others.) In fact, in *Cadillac Man,* the car dealership's customers and Lauren Tom's Chinese restaurant waitress character are funnier than Robin.

Robin's performance is an edgy, dramatic one with some comedic overtones that do not really provide him with the opportunity to mimic or improvise even for a moment. Sure, he has several funny lines and scenes, including a scene that cracks up costar Lori Petty (who plays his girlfriend Lila) in which he dons a wig and imitates a foreigner asking to see a Cadillac Allante, and then tells her eagerly, "We're gonna play Mandingo again!" But throughout the film there is none of the complex, stream-of-consciousness type of material he is so famous for. Even in the heavy drama

*Joey and Joy are held hostage by the lovesick maniac Larry, played by Tim Robbins, in* Cadillac Man. *(Photofest)*

116

*Robin with costar Tim Robbins from* Cadillac Man. *(Photofest)*

*Dead Poets Society*, he did John Wayne doing Hamlet and a few other bits that were classic Robin.

Robin's *Cadillac* character, Joey O'Brien, is overwhelmed by his life: He has an antagonistic ex-wife Tina (Pamela Reed), who threw him out because of his womanizing and ended up with the house he paid for; an unmanageable daughter to whom he is a stranger; a high-maintenance, demanding married mistress Joy (Fran Drescher), who wants to leave her husband for him but insists on a full emotional commitment from Joey (something he is incapable of); a naive, ditzy girlfriend, who designs bizarre clothing that she wants Joey to help her sell; and a mob loan shark (Paul Herman) Joey owes twenty grand to who begs him, "Joey, don't make me wait too long. Please, Joey."

But Joey *loves* to sell. *Cadillac Man* opens with Joey shamelessly trying to sell a widow a new car—at her husband's funeral. When he arrives at work, Joey learns that he needs to sell twelve cars in two days or be one of the salesmen who loses his job in a staff reduction when the dealership he works for, Turgeon Auto, moves to a new location.

As if all this personal turmoil was not enough, on Sunday during the big sale, the husband of Donna the receptionist (played by Annabella Sciorra), Larry (Tim Robbins), drives his motorcycle into the dealership and takes everyone—the salespeople, the customers, and even Joy's pain-in-the-ass dog (played by Drescher's real-life dog Chester)—hostage. Larry suspects Donna of having an affair with someone at the dealership (she is—her boss Jackie Turgeon Jr.) and finally, he just can't take it anymore.

The remainder of the movie consists of the hostage standoff, which Joey orchestrates so that he, instead of the others, is the focus of Larry's obsessive attention. He does this by telling Larry that he was the one having the affair with Donna and that there was no one else at the dealership involved with her. Joey "takes the hit" for Jackie and it isn't long before he bonds with Larry and convinces him to give himself up.

*Robin as salesman Joey O'Brien in* Cadillac Man. *(Photofest)*

The film concludes with Joey's life regaining some semblance of order: The loan shark forgives Joey's loan in gratitude for Joey saving the life of his son (who worked at the dealership washing cars); the grateful Turgeons give him a guaranteed spot at the new place; his ex-wife Tina actually considers taking him back; and he becomes a minor celebrity. The only losers are his mistress Joy and girlfriend Lila, but throughout the ordeal it becomes rather obvious that those were both dead-end relationships anyway.

In *Cadillac Man*, Robin Williams stretches himself yet again. After the success of *Good Morning, Vietnam*, he could have easily gone for another broad comedy. Instead he did what could be called his dramatic trilogy, *Dead Poets Society, Awakenings*, and *Cadillac Man*.

## What the Critics Had to Say

**Mick Martin and Marsha Porter:** "Well acted and often hilarious." (From their *Video Movie Guide*)
**Leonard Maltin:** "Williams is terrific as usual [but] wildly uneven film tests the mettle of even the staunchest Williams fan, swinging helter-skelter from comedy to melodrama, dragging and then picking up again. Infuriating at times, then occasionally redeemed by a great moment." (From his *Movie and Video Guide*)

*Videohound's Golden Movie Retriever:* "A lesser comedic talent might have stalled and been abandoned, but [Robin] Williams manages to drive away despite the flat script and direction. . . . Williams and [Tim] Robbins are often close to being funny in a hyperkinetic way, but the situations are dumb enough to rob most of the scenes of their comedy." (From the 1997 edition)

**Director:** Roger Donaldson
**Cast:** Robin Williams (Joey O'Brien), Tim Robbins (Larry), Pamela Reed (Tina), Fran Drescher (Joy Munchack), Zack Norman (Harry Munchack), Annabella Sciorra (Donna), Lauren Tom (waitress), Lori Petty (Lila), Paul Guilfoyle (Little Jack Turgeon), Bill Nelson (Big Jack Turgeon); Elaine Stritch (The Widow)
**Writer:** Ken Friedman
**Music:** J. Peter Robinson
Rated R; 95 minutes

*Cadillac man Joey O'Brien and his girlfriend Joy Munchak, played by the irrepressible Fran Drescher. (Photofest)*

# Awakenings
## (1990)

*"There is deity within you."*

—Robin Williams, from a
PBS interview with David Frost

One might make a case that Robin Williams's performance in *Awakenings*, for all its gravity and sincerity, does not succeed and should not be counted as one of his better roles.

Why?

Because on first viewing, Robin's Dr. Malcolm Sayer seems to be passionless—which is all the more ironic when one considers that the theme of the film is the reigniting of passion in the hearts and souls of the newly-awakened catatonics.

But Robin's restrained, understated delivery is exactly why his performance *does* work. He is playing a man whose life is devoted to science. Dr. Sayer (modeled on Oliver Sacks, the author of the film's source book) is, after all, a man who spent five years trying to extract one decagram (ten grams) of myelin from four tons of earthworms only to prove that it's impossible—something his new boss, Dr. Kaufman (played by John Heard), knew as soon as he heard the experiment described.

We need to also remember that Robin Williams was in his thirties when he made *Awakenings* and yet his Dr. Sayer bears the weight of many more decades than three or four. Robin carries himself as a much older man and it is a tribute to his genius that we can believe wholeheartedly that we are watching a man in his fifties, possibly nearing sixty. Dr. Sachs is bearded and burly; Robin is bearded but *plays* burly. He uses his physical presence to communicate illustrative information about this quiet, dedicated doctor.

The movie begins with Dr. Sayer taking a job at a chronic hospital in the Bronx, a place where they have wards nicknamed "The Garden" because all they do there is feed and water its residents. Sayer is astounded by the resignation on the part of the staff to the hopelessness of the patients, many of whom have not moved or spoken on their own for thirty years.

Sayer begins researching their histories and learns that a great many of them had encephalitis as children. He theorizes that they may all be in a stage of Parkinson's disease that has them hopelessly trapped in bodies that will not respond to their brain's commands. He tries treating one patient, Leonard Lowe (played with penetrating honesty by Robert De Niro), with the drug L-dopa and to his wonderment, he finds the previously catatonic man up one night writing his name. He then convinces the hospital and its supporters to fund L-dopa therapy for all of the vegetative patients. The hospital does, and one by one they all come back to our world.

Robin Williams plays Dr. Sayer's amazement at this development with subtlety and grace, and yet he also allows us to see how overwhelmed he is by suddenly having to deal with all the myriad personalities he is now responsible for. Again, we remember that Dr. Sayer is a man who rarely interacts with people. He is a research scientist and now—look at what his research hath wrought! In the scenes in which the newly awakened patients reacquaint themselves with the wonder of life, Robin allows some of the manic energy he is so well known for to surface, albeit in a restrained and tentative way.

It isn't long, however, before Leonard begins developing tics and manifesting strange physical behavior and Dr. Sayer realizes that the drug is failing. The final third of the film, focusing on Leonard's rapid degeneration and eventual return to a vegetative state, belongs almost completely to Robert De Niro. But it is through Robin Williams's eyes that we see Leonard's downfall and it is with Robin Williams's emotions that we experience the heartbreak and feelings of helplessness Dr. Sayer must live with as his patient—and his friend—ends up catatonic once again.

The interaction between these two great

*Robin and Robert De Niro from* Awakenings. *(Photofest)*

actors is spellbinding to watch. In the January 1992 issue of *Playboy*, Robin Williams talked about working with De Niro on *Awakenings*:

**PLAYBOY:** That touching scene when Leonard awakens—were you off camera doing things to make him laugh?

**ROBIN WILLIAMS:** Bob would say, "Surprise me." So I did Harvey Fierstein talking to him. "Leonard, sweetheart, lose the puppy on the pajamas. Come over here, darling, did Mom bring you that terrycloth robe? Do you want some slippers?" I could drop him doing that.

*Awakenings* touches on many themes, including appreciating life and not taking it for granted; the ecstasy of new love; the painful quandary of not being able to provide experimental, possibly helpful medical care because of the cost; and the problem of what to do with patients who are quite simply not going to get better, no matter how committed and optimistic their doctors may be.

*Awakenings* is a powerful and moving film that, coming so soon after *Dead Poets Society*, proves that Robin Williams is not only one of our best comedians, he is also one of our finest dramatic actors as well.

The film also boasts terrific performances by Julie Kavner as sympathetic nurse Costello; Penelope Ann Miller as Leonard's love interest, Paula; Ruth Nelson as Leonard's mother, Mrs. Lowe; and especially Anne Meara, as the awakened patient Miriam.

## What Robin Had to Say

"[*Awakenings* is] deeply sad, but also so exhilarating, the way that all of Oliver's work is. He makes you examine these supposedly negative and horrifying things from another perspective and say, yes, there is great pain . . . but he also says, look at the power of the human spirit and more than just the spirit, the power of the mind. There is deity within you. That is that spark, that divine thing. And it stems from creation, that thing that is soul. *Anima* is what the Greeks call it. And that's what I was fascinated by with Oliver's writing and with *Awakenings*: That which can shine through." (From a PBS interview with David Frost.)

## What the Critics Had to Say

**Roger Ebert:** "Dr. Sayer, played by Williams, is at the center of almost every scene, and his personality becomes one of the touchstones of the movie. He is shut off, too, by shyness and inexperience, and even the way he holds his arms, close to his sides, shows a man wary of contact. He really was happier working with those earthworms. This is one of Robin Williams's best performances, pure and uncluttered, without the ebullient distractions he sometimes adds—the schtick where none is called for." (From his *Movie Home Companion*)

**Leonard Maltin:** "Powerfully affecting true-life story . . . Williams is superb as the doctor." (From his *Movie and Video Guide*)

***Videohound's Golden Movie Retriever:*** "Occasionally over-sentimental, but still providing a poignant look at both the patients—who find themselves confronted with lost opportunities and faded youth—and at [Oliver] Sacks, who must watch their exquisite suffering as they slip away. De Niro's performance as the youngest of the group is heartrending, while Williams offers a subdued, moving performance as the doctor." (From the 1997 edition)

*Robin as Dr. Sayer with his costar Julie Kavner (Nurse Costello) from Awakenings. (Photofest)*

*Robin (as Peter Banning) and his* Hook *costar Dustin Hoffman (as Captain Hook). (Photofest)*

*Robin with Dustin Hoffman. (Photofest)*

capable of much more playful performances, as in *Tootsie* (1982), *Dick Tracy* (1990), and, now, *Hook*. Dustin's Hook wears a long, curly black wig and boldly flaunts his shiny, steel hook, which probably for his own personal safety, he tops with a cork and covers in red velvet when he sleeps. The hook, appropriately, almost becomes a character in the film.

This brings us to a discussion of the sets in *Hook*. They are spectacular, yet oddly sterile. Neverland—with all its bridges, and trees, and strange structures—is reminiscent of Sweethaven, from Robin's film, *Popeye*, but, in this case, the patently artificial "comic book" feel of Sweethaven doesn't work as effectively for the realm of Neverland. There are a few gorgeous special effects matte shots in *Hook* that are breathtaking, but the main sets where most of the action in the (at times, interminable) Neverland sequences look manufactured, something we really don't want for this magical land.

*Hook* culminates in a sword fight between Pan and Hook for the "parentage" of Peter's two children. Peter has regained his ability to fly, thanks to Tinkerbell's help and the "happy" thoughts of his kids, and they all ultimately return to London.

Steven Spielberg is brilliant at evoking the sensibility of childhood, that magical time when almost anything seems possible, and fantasy and reality whimsically change places almost at will. But the overwhelming logistical requirements of *Hook* seem to have distracted Spielberg and the others responsible for the film's faithfulness to the story. Yes, *Hook* works and is a meticulously professional achievement, but there is definitely something missing. Some of the Neverland scenes are a little boring, a genuine odd feeling while watching a Steven Spielberg film. Maybe the movie's too long? Maybe more time and effort was expended on the sets and costumes than on the development of the characters? Perhaps all of the above? The conclusion, however, is that *Hook* boasts a terrific performance by Robin Williams that, unfortunately, takes place in what must be described as an average, somewhat overlong film.

## Another Interesting Bit of Cinematic Synchronicity

In *Hook,* when Peter returns to London and gives the butler Toodles back his marbles (everyone had always said Toodles had lost his marbles!), allowing him to fly again, Toodles soars out the window, and cries, "Seize the day!" This maxim holds a special significance to Robin Williams's career. First, in 1986, Robin starred in *Seize the Day,* the adaptation of the Saul Bellow novel; second, the adage "seize the day" was the code of conduct for Robin's character, John Keating, in the 1989 film, *Dead Poets Society;* and now, in *Hook,* thanks to Peter Pan's efforts, Toodles can once again proclaim his own personal motto, "Seize the day!"

## What Robin Had to Say

"Steven [Spielberg was] amazing. At first you think, here's a guy who basically deals in visuals. But no, he knows every movie that's ever been made. He's seen every movie twice. So he knows if someone did something before. And from that, he can give you an idea that goes beyond that. The weird thing that I never expected from him was this humanistic, behavioral directing. I thought he would be more into special effects. Just the opposite. The special effects he likes, they're fun—but he'll suggest pulling back, or adding a little bit more, trying things to make the story have a reality base. If it works, it'll play because the human element works, because of the interrelationships of the characters, not because of all the effects. The effects will be like this wonderful icing. But if the cake sucks, the icing won't mean shit. (From *Playboy,* October 1992)

## What the Critics Had to Say

**Roger Ebert:** "The crucial failure in *Hook* is its inability to reimagine the material, to find something new, fresh or urgent to do with the Peter Pan myth. Lacking that, Spielberg should simply have remade the original story, straight, for this generation." (From his *Movie Home Companion*)

*The vivacious Julia Roberts in her "comeback" as Tinkerbell. (Photofest)*

**Leonard Maltin:** "If this is Peter Pan for the 90s, give us the 50s instead." (From his *Movie and Video Guide*)

**Videohound's Golden Movie Retriever:** "The sets and special effects are spectacular; the direction less so. Big-budget fantasy lacks the charm it needs to really fly. Still, kids seem to love it." (From the 1997 edition)

**Director:** Steven Spielberg
**Cast:** Robin Williams (Peter Banning and Peter Pan), Dustin Hoffman (Captain Hook), Julia Roberts (Tinkerbell), Bob Hoskins (Smee), Maggie Smith (Granny Wendy), Charlie Korsmo (Jack), Caroline Goodall (Moira), Amber Scott (Maggie); with Phil Collins, Arthur Malet, Dante Basco, Gwyneth Paltrow, David Crosby, Glenn Close
**Writer:** Nick Castle, based on the story by J. M. Barrie
**Music:** John Williams
Rated PG; 142 minutes

# FernGully: The Last Rainforest
## (1992)

*"Humans can't feel anything.*
*They're numb from the brain down."*
—Robin Williams's character, Batty Koda

Robin Williams's character of Batty Koda in the animated film *FernGully: The Last Rainforest* is the creative ancestor of Robin's Genie character in *Aladdin*. Both films came out in 1992 and in Batty, Robin hinted at the brilliant multicharacter persona he would take on in *Aladdin*.

Batty first appears about ten minutes into the film as an escapee from an animal testing laboratory where he was subjected to all manner of bizarre and painful experiments, including having electrodes implanted into his brain.

FernGully is an enchanted rainforest peopled by tree sprites, talking animals, and magical beings, both good and evil. Many, many years ago, the mystical forest spirit Magi Lune succeeded in imprisoning the evil demon Hexus in a giant tree, and since then he has been locked away forever, powerless and unable to do any more harm. Magi tries to teach the young tree fairy Crysta about the past and about the dangers of Hexus, but Crysta is young and carefree and thinks Magi worries needlessly.

But what the rainforest denizens don't know is that humans have begun invading FernGully, marking trees with big red Xs and then cutting them

*Robin's character Batty was just that, with much of his dialogue undoubtedly improvised. (Photofest)*

down with huge saws and a machine known as The Leveler.

Crysta, during an ill-advised trip to where the machines are cutting trees, rescues Zak, a young human worker, from a falling tree by magically transforming him into a tiny creature the same size as she. Zak and Crysta become friends and ultimately must save FernGully from destruction after Hexus's tree is cut down and his evil, noxious, pollution-loving spirit is freed.

Robin's character Batty helps the two young people save the forest, all the while throwing out some hilarious wisecracks and pop culture references (which he absorbed while being experimented on in the lab) that remind us very much of his portrayal of Genie. Batty recites Shakespeare, imitates Bette Davis and John Wayne, does Luke Skywalker, and speaks in California surfer lingo.

After summoning the magic powers of nature to defeat Hexus and The Leveler, Crysta, Magi, and the others watch as Zak plants a seed which instantly grows into a giant tree, a blossom which serves as the beginning of the rebirth of FernGully.

Robin Williams adds a lot to *FernGully* and

132

*Batty and the other denizens of the enchanted FernGully rainforest. (Photofest)*

his character is the cleverest and funniest in the film. It is clear that some of Batty's dialogue was improvised by Robin and he definitely makes the film more enjoyable and much less saccharine than it could have been without his irreverent wise-cracking from the sidelines.

This eco-fable is well worth renting, if only to experience an abridged version of *Aladdin*'s Genie character.

## What the Critics Had to Say

**Roger Ebert:** "Although the movie is not a masterpiece, it's pleasant to watch for its humor and sweetness. Kids may like it." (From his *Movie Home Companion*)

**Leonard Maltin:** "Lively and enjoyable, if not memorable, with plenty of laughs for grownups in the free-flowing dialogue of Batty Koda, a wacked-out bat voiced by Robin Williams." (From his *Movie and Video Guide*)

**Mick Martin and Marsha Porter:** "Robin Williams's inspired voice work elevates this environmental plea aimed at children." (From their *Video Movie Guide*)

**Videohound's Golden Movie Retriever:** "So-so script with politically pristine environmental message may grow tiresome for both adults and children, though decent animation and brilliant coloring enlivens the tale." (From the 1997 edition)

**Director:** Bill Kroyer
**Voices:** Robin Williams (Batty Koda), Samantha Mathis (Crysta), Christian Slater (Pips), Jonathan Ward (Zak), Grace Zabriskie (Magi Lune), Geoffrey Blake (Ralph), Robert Pastorelli (Tony), Cheech Marin (Stump), Tommy Chong (Root), Tone-Loc (The Goanna)
**Writer:** Screenplay by Jim Cox, based on the stories of "FernGully" by Diana Young
**Music:** Original score by Alan Silvestri, with songs written by Thomas Dolby, Jimmy Webb, Jimmy Buffett, and Elton John; performed by Johnny Clegg, Sheena Easton, Tone-Loc, Robin Williams, Raffi, Tim Curry, Ladysmith Black Mambazo, and Elton John
Rated G; 76 minutes

# *Shakes the Clown*
## (1992)

*"You're a clown, aren't you?"*

—Mime Jerry to Mime Chuck

Clowns hate mimes. Who knew?

*Shakes the Clown* is a very strange, oddly compelling, but ultimately disastrous movie that was written and directed by the deliberately psychotic, often screaming comedian Bobcat Goldthwait.

The whole movie takes place in Palookaville, a bizarre all-clown town where Shakes and his colleagues practice their craft at birthday parties and then drink themselves into oblivion (especially Shakes) at the town's all-clown bar, the Twisted Balloon. (There is apparently a regimented caste system in clown world. Rodeo clowns hate circus clowns. TV clowns look down on birthday party clowns. And all clowns hate mimes.)

Robin Williams appears uncredited as mime instructor Jerry in two brief scenes.

In the first scene, Shakes goes undercover as Mime Chuck and attends one of Jerry's classes. It appears as though much of this scene was improvised by Robin, since Mime Jerry does a few jokes Robin has used elsewhere. Robin has repeatedly used a joke about someone's pants being so tight you can tell what religion he is (a reference, of course, to the fact that Jews are always circumcised), and he uses this same gag in the mime class. [See the feature on this joke in the "All-Time Favorite Joke" section.]

He also uses a joke about Bobcat's penis being like "a roll of quarters," (where have we heard *that* before) as well as asking Bobcat if he's "on medication," a common riff from Robin's stand-up routines. (Jerry also mimes "puberty" in which he pretends he's got an erection the size of a broomstick. And we all know how much Robin loves "Mr. Happy" jokes, now don't we!!)

Robin's second scene is at the conclusion of the movie when he appears as a guest on Bobcat's new kid TV show and does the "trapped in a box" mime routine he had been trying to teach his motley crew of students during his mime class.

Robin's scenes are funny and he definitely adds to the movie, but he does not succeed in elevating this film above what it unquestionably is: a failed attempt at creating a dark, offbeat, cult

comedy like *The Rocky Horror Picture Show* (1975) or *Eating Raoul* (1982).

You may find yourself wondering why such a film was ever made. The idea of an all-clown town is a funny idea and it could have worked. But Goldthwait's script is lame and much of it is not funny.

An oddity in the filmography of Robin Williams, *Shakes the Clown* is nonetheless worth a rental just to see how Robin can take three minutes of screen time and hit a home run. (He's actually a pretty good mime, if you happen to like mimes, of course. If you're a clown, and you don't, we'll understand.) If you want to skip the rest of the movie, Robin appears about an hour into *Shakes* and then again at the very end.

You might also want to muddle through to the end of *Shakes* just because of LaWanda Page (TV's *Sanford and Son*'s Aunt Esther) who, believe it or not has almost all the funny lines in the movie and is the only character who will consistently make you laugh.

## What the Critics Had to Say

**Leonard Maltin:** "Excruciating would-be-comic mishmash. . . . Aimless, crude, and headache-inducing, not even salvaged by Williams's brief, unbilled appearance as a mime teacher." (From his *Movie and Video Guide*)

***Videohound's Golden Movie Retriever:*** "Meant as a satire of substance-abuse recovery programs and the supposed tragedies of a performer's life, the film is sometimes zany, but more often merely unpleasant and unamusing." (From the 1997 edition)

**Director:** Bobcat Goldthwait
**Cast:** Robin Williams (Mime Teacher), Bobcat Goldthwait (Shakes the Clown), Paul Dooley (Mr. Cheese), Julie Brown (Judy), Tim Kazurinsky (Binky); with Adam Sandler, Blake Clark, Tom Kenny, Sydney Lassick, Florence Henderson, LaWanda Page
**Writer:** Bobcat Goldthwait
**Music:** Tom Scott
Rated R; 83 minutes

*Robin serves up some zany laughs as Aladdin's free-form, fun-loving Genie. (Walt Disney Company)*

# *Aladdín*
## (1992)

*"You ain't never had a friend like me!"*

—Genie

Since *Aladdin* was first released in 1992, Robin Williams and the producers of the film have been deliberately coy about how much of Genie's "performance" in the film was spontaneous improvisation by Robin and how much was actually scripted by the film's writers. Noted film critic Roger Ebert, in his three-star review of the movie, said, "I would like to know which came first, the pictures or the words, because Williams sounds like he's improvising as he careens from one character to another."

Ebert is right: Genie is a manifestation of the ultimate Robin Williams riff; a free-form, stream-of-consciousness romp that is even more wonderful when Genie's eye-blink physical transformations are added to the experience.

Genie first appears about thirty-five minutes into the film and his first manifestation is as an old Jewish guy.

Here is a rundown of all fifty-two of the transformations that the ebullient and irrepressible Genie makes during the film:

1. An old Jewish guy

2. A Las Vegas emcee and comedian

3. A Scotsman

4. A dog

5. A jive street guy

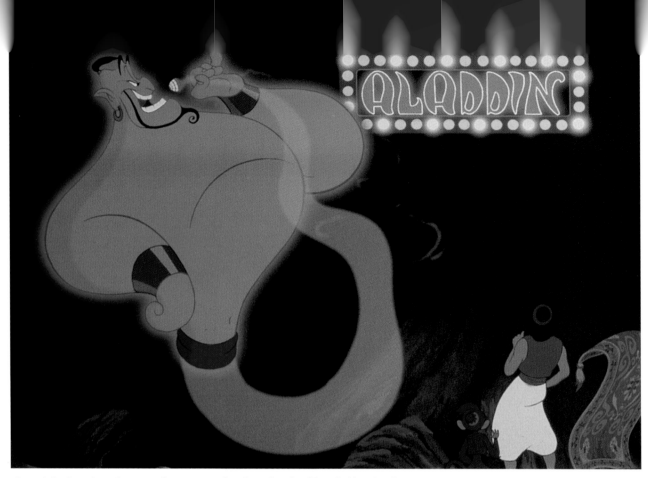

*One of the Genie's earliest transformations, when he is first freed by Aladdin. (Walt Disney Company)*

6. Arnold Schwarzenegger

7. A ventriloquist

8. Ed Sullivan

9. Groucho Marx

10. A maître'd

11. A snobby yuppie

12. A hick

13. A surfer dude

14. A song-and-dance man

15. A dragon

16. William F. Buckley

17. A Peter Lorre ghoul

18. Robert De Niro

19. A stewardess

20. Carol Channing as a stewardess

21. A Shakespearean character

22. A sheep

23. Pinocchio

24. A magician

25. Maurice Chevalier

26. A Roman centurion

27. Arsenio Hall

28. An effeminate tailor

29. A game-show host

30. A drum majorette

31. Peter Allen

32. Harry, a commentator at the Thanksgiving Day Parade

33. June, another commentator at the Thanksgiving Day Parade

34. A lion cub

35. A goat

36. A buxom dancing girl

37. Rodney Dangerfield

38. Jack Nicholson

39. A professor

40. A light bulb

41. A bumblebee

42. A submarine

43. A bandleader

44. A one-man band

45. A commercial announcer

46. A script continuity person

47. Another script continuity person

48. William F. Buckley (again!)

49. Cheerleaders

50. A baseball pitcher

51. A pinball machine ball

52. A tourist in a Hawaiian shirt and Goofy cap (final character)

This may look like just a laundry list of characterizations but if you read through them you will see that Robin's transformations in the film are quick, clever, and funny, and show the mercurial and amazing way his whirlwind mind actually works!

The more mainstream, run-of-the-mill transformations (the dog, the dragon, the light bulb, the submarine, etc.) were probably in the original script, but the remaining, over-the-top, pop culture characterizations (Arnold Schwarzenegger, Ed Sullivan, Groucho, Carol Channing, William F. Buckley, Arsenio Hall, Jack Nicholson, etc.) may have been improvised by Robin and then drawn by the animators to accompany his schtick.

The character of Genie gave the creators of *Aladdin* an opportunity to have some fun with the whole Disney gestalt. Number 23, Pinocchio, was the first reference to the Disney universe; followed by number 34, the lion cub (a possible hint of 1994's *The Lion King*); number 45, the commercial announcer; and the final character, number 52, the tourist in the "Goofy" cap.

The most blatant acknowledgment of the Disney corporate identity came with number 45, the commercial announcer. After Princess Jasmine

accepts Aladdin's marriage proposal, Genie says to him, "Aladdin, you've just won the heart of a princess! What are you gonna do next?", an obvious, in-your-face reference to Disney's ubiquitous Super Bowl commercials in which an announcer asks members of the winning team the same question and they respond enthusiastically, "I'm going to Disney World!" And to make the plug even more obvious, as Genie poses his question, "When You Wish Upon a Star" can be heard on the sound track. (They did stop short, however, of actually having Aladdin announce that he was, indeed, going to that most magical of all tourist traps!)

We all know the *Aladdin* fairy tale: The lovely young princess Jasmine is told that she must marry within three days and that her chosen betrothed must be a prince. Jasmine, an independent young lady who wants to marry for love, flees the palace and runs into Aladdin, a street urchin who survives by his wits and the quick fingers of his companion, Abu the monkey. The two hit it off, but ultimately realize they can never be together because of their disparate social status. They part. Aladdin later finds the magic lamp. He uses his first wish to become a prince, thereby assuring himself of Jasmine's hand in marriage—even though he must deceive her to get it.

Into all this romantic intrigue is factored the evil vizier, Jafar, who not only wants Jasmine but also plans on taking over as sultan after betraying her father.

Jasmine and Aladdin's story ends happily, after many frightening battles with Jafar and many exciting adventures with Genie and a magic carpet. *Aladdin* will win over even the most diehard "anti-animated films" moviegoers.

## What the Critics Had to Say

**Roger Ebert:** "Robin Williams and animation were born for one another, and in *Aladdin* they finally meet. Williams's speed of comic invention has always been too fast for flesh and blood; the way he flashes in and out of characters can be dizzying. In *Aladdin*, he's liberated at last, playing a genie who has complete freedom over his form—who can instantly be anybody or anything." (From his *Movie Home Companion*)

***Videohound's Golden Movie Retriever:*** "Superb animation triumphs over average songs and storyline by capitalizing on [Robin] Williams's talent for ad-lib with lightning speed Genie changes, lots of celebrity spoofs, and even a few pokes at Disney itself." (From the 1997 edition)

**Directors:** Ron Clements, John Musker
**Voices:** Robin Williams (Genie), Scott Weinger (Aladdin), Linda Larkin (Jasmine), Jonathan Freeman (Jafar), Frank Welker (Abu), Randy Cartwright (Carpet), Gilbert Gottfried (Iago); with Douglas Seale, Brad Kane, Lea Salonga
**Writers:** Ron Clements, John Musker, Ted Elliot, Terry Rossio
**Music:** Alan Menken, Howard Ashman, Tim Rice
Rated G; 90 minutes

# The Return of Jafar (1995)

Imagine being Dan Castellaneta.

Dan Castellaneta (*The Simpsons*—he "voices" Homer himself!) is the guy who was tapped to do the voice of Genie in this second installment of Disney's *Aladdin* series. (Robin boycotted continuing in the series because Disney used his voice and likeness to "cross-promote" *Aladdin* tie-in merchandise without his permission.)

Granted, the straight-to-video release *The Return of Jafar* was hugely successful, but how does it stack up when compared to the two Robin Williams installments of the series?

"Merely okay" is the unfortunate answer.

The animation is as superb as Disney animation always is, the story is engaging, and the songs, entertaining.

But let's face it: The character of Genie *makes* the *Aladdin* movies. And what happens when you replace the irreplaceable Robin Williams with someone else!

You get a pale imitation of greatness.

The writers, animators, and producers of *The Return of Jafar*, along with Castellaneta, tried very hard to duplicate the Robin Williams experience.

But since they did not have the talents of the man himself, they were forced to try and deduce what they *thought* Robin might do with the character, and then write the character and his tranformations accordingly.

It was a valiant attempt, but the Genie in *The Return of Jafar* comes off as lifeless and unimaginative, as compared to the truly inventive and mesmerizing Genie in Robin's two *Aladdin* movies.

Rent *The Return of Jafar* if you've got kids who love the stories and the characters.

But if you don't have little ones and you watch the *Aladdin* movies solely because you're a Robin Williams fan, then don't waste your time with *The Return of Jafar*.

# Toys (1992)

*"I like jokes."*

—Leslie Zevo

*"We originally sold* Toys *to Fox back in 1978, and it was going to be my first film as a director. But then Sherry Lansing joined the studio and she didn't think it was funny, and others agreed."*

—Barry Levinson

Barry Levinson uses the ethereal and haunting song "Ebudae" by Enya (which is sung in Gaelic and is about the spiritual role of women) on the *Toys* sound track but instead of enhancing a cinematic moment, it comes off as inappropriate and confusing. The song is used in a scene where Robin Williams's character, Leslie Zevo, and his sister Alsatia (played by Joan Cusack) are driving in their father's funeral procession. Leslie is driving a toy car similar to the kind used in the bumper car rides at carnivals and he keeps banging into the limousine in front of him. "Ebudae" is almost hymn-like, and when used effectively, can imbue a scene with a sacred feel that is most moving. But in *Toys*, the song is wasted.

And that is the overwhelming impression one gets when watching *Toys*: It is truly a waste of talent, set design, music, and, of course, money.

When an eccentric toymaker dies, he passes on his strange and colorful toy factory to his military-general brother rather than his son and daughter, even though his children are the two people who are truly kindred spirits and would continue on in the tradition of their offbeat dad. The uncle immediately implements security procedures and begins making war toys, much to the dismay of Leslie and Alsatia. The story revolves around Leslie and Alsatia's attempt (with the help of their cousin Patrick, the general's son) to regain control of the factory and to stop the manufacture of killer toys, which are really prototypes for new and deadly remote-controlled war weapons.

But *Toys* is not sure what it wants to be. Is it a comedy? A fantasy? A dark satire? In a sense, it is all three, and none.

It's a comedy thanks solely to the genius of Robin Williams. When he gets a chance to be *Robin*, he comes up with some truly funny (and seemingly improvised) lines, including a crack that has significance following Robin's legal problems with Disney over the use of his voice in *Aladdin*. In a scene where Robin's character Leslie is doing market tests for a pair of gigantic toy ears, he says, "These ears are so big, we're going to have a legal problem with Disney." He also has a funny moment when he arrives for a meeting wearing a jacket from which smoke is pouring from the pockets. It's a "smoking jacket," of course.

Is *Toys* a fantasy? Yes, because of the sets and the wholehearted commitment the cast and crew makes to the surrealistic fantasy world the toy factory exists in. In a 1992 interview with Roger Ebert, Robin described *Toys* as "Willy Wonka Meets Dr. Strangelove." He told another interviewer the movie was like "Fisher-Price Meets Fellini," or "Disneyland Designed by Dante." Robin also said the film was like "Dada Meets Magritte." Roger Ebert described the movie as "The 5,000 Fingers of Dr. T Meets L'Avventura." And indeed, visually, *Toys* is all of that and more. But the fantastic set designs and vibrant colors are not enough to carry the film.

Is *Toys* a dark satire? Yes, because it wants to be like *Dr. Strangelove* and make a statement about war, war toys, and military budgets. But the final confrontation between the new and deadly military toys of Leslie's uncle and the innocent windup toys that once belonged to Leslie and Alsatia comes off as too long, too overblown, and ultimately boring.

*Toys* is worth viewing if only for the visual effects and set designs: They are truly of Academy Award–caliber excellence (although the film's visual design was not nominated) and amazing to watch.

*Robin dressed, appropriately, as a wind-up toy in Barry Levinson's comedy,* Toys. *(Photofest)*

*Robin as Leslie Zevo, in the Magritte-inspired art for* Toys. *(Photofest)*

But as an engaging movie with a story that intrigues and entertains, *Toys*, unfortunately, just doesn't play.

## What Robin Had to Say

During an interview with Jay Leno on the *Tonight Show With Jay Leno* to promote *Jumanji*, Robin talked about being a father and setting an example for his kids. He acknowledged that sometimes it's hard to offer himself as a model: "[My] kids look at [me] and go, 'Hey, you made *Toys*.' "

## What the Critics Had to Say

*Videohound's Golden Movie Retriever:* "Disappointingly earnest comedy. . . . Flat characters; generally falls short by trying too hard to send a message to viewers about the folly of war." (From the 1997 edition)

**Tom Cunneff:** "This is unlike any film you've ever seen, a *Dr. Strangelove* meets *Willy Wonka and the Chocolate Factory*. Although the movie often misfires, it's heartening that something this bizarre can get made in Hollywood. . . . Although this seems like a perfect role for Williams, he is too subdued." (From a review in *People*, January 11, 1993)

**Director:** Barry Levinson
**Cast:** Robin Williams (Leslie Zevo), Joan Cusack (Alsatia Zevo), LL Cool J (Patrick), Michael Gambon (the General); with Robin Wright, Donald O'Connor, Debi Mazur, Jack Warden
**Writers:** Valerie Curtin and Barry Levinson
**Music:** Hans Zimmer, Trevor Horn
Rated PG-13; 121 minutes

# Mrs. Doubtfire
## (1993)

*"Could you make me a woman?"*
—Daniel to his brother Frank

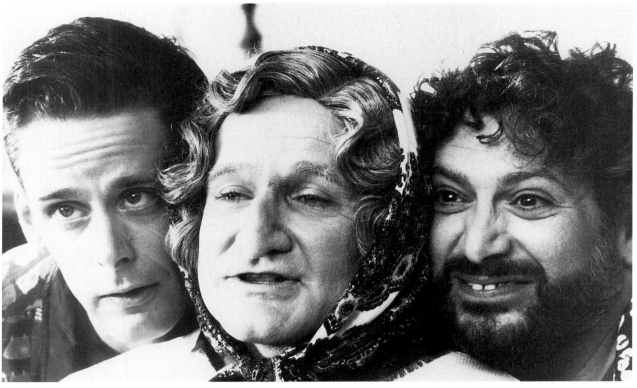

*Robin as Daniel Hillard, in one of his brother Frank's early tries at transforming him into "Mrs. Doubtfire." Harvey Fierstein (far right) played Frank and Scott Capurro (far left) played Frank's companion, "Aunt Jack." (Photofest)*

**M**rs. *Doubtfire*, like *Good Morning, Vietnam*, gave Robin Williams the opportunity to both act *and* perform, a creative context in which his greatest talents can blossom and be spotlighted.

*Mrs. Doubtfire* is a supreme achievement for Robin, as is his portrayal of the *character* Mrs. Doubtfire. He successfully creates two completely different personalities and makes them dance, both literally and figuratively.

*Mrs. Doubtfire* opens with an amazing scene of Robin's character, Daniel Hillard, plying his trade providing the voices for cartoon characters, in this case, a parakeet (Pudgy) and a cat that bear a striking similarity to Tweety Bird and Sylvester the Cat of Looney Tunes fame. Robin (as Daniel

playing Pudgy) sings a difficult aria from *The Marriage of Figaro* and does a flawless job with the Italian pronunciation.

Daniel quits, though, when the producers refuse to allow him to veer from the script and insert an antismoking message into the cartoon. When he surprises his kids by meeting them at school, we learn that Daniel losing a job is not that uncommon an occurrence and that he is actually a textbook definition of the word "irresponsible."

So what does Daniel do? Does he contritely call his wife Miranda (Sally Field), a successful and busy interior designer, tell her what happened, and then start looking for another job? No, instead he throws a wild birthday party for his son Chris, complete with animals from a petting zoo, kids hang-

*Robin as Mrs. Doubtfire in one of the most memorable scenes from the movie. (Photofest)*

makeup artists—a necessary plot device, of course, but one that works, thanks to the wonderful performance by Harvey Fierstein as Frank. (The way Harvey plays Frank, you completely believe he wouldn't want to be anything *but* a makeup genius.)

A court hearing grants Miranda temporary sole custody of the kids, and the judge gives Daniel ninety days to find a job and establish a stable residence in order for the ruling to be changed to joint custody.

Daniel then meets with his assigned court liaison, Mrs. Sellner, who innocently asks him what he used to do for a living. In a very funny scene Daniel does a series of characters for Mrs. Sellner, but she doesn't even crack a smile. In lightning-quick cuts, Robin as Daniel imitates a preacher, an alien, a man from India, a monster, Groucho Marx, Zeppo Marx, James Bond, a car salesman, Ronald Reagan, Walter Brennan, Humphrey Bogart, an opera singer, and even a hot dog (Robin straightens his spine, keeps his arms tightly by his sides, and reclines in the chair as though he were encased in a giant bun). Mrs. Sellner sits stone-faced through all this and then asks him if he thinks he's funny. "There was a time," a chastened Daniel responds, "when I found myself funny."

Daniel takes a job as a shipping clerk at a local TV station and rents a small apartment. One day, Miranda arrives an hour early to pick up the kids from a visit with Dad and Daniel notices she's carrying a classified ad. She is looking for a nanny, she tells him, and Daniel surreptitiously changes the phone numbers in the ad so that she won't get any calls. Daniel then calls Miranda as several different applicants for the job, each one of them a major loser.

In his calls, Daniel pretends that he's a singer with the punk band Severe Tire Damage; that he's Ilsa Immelman, a Swedish transsexual; that he's a hick (who apparently was keeping someone in a

ing from the chandeliers, and dancing on the dining room table. This is the insane scene Mom comes home to and it is the final insult; the straw that breaks Miranda's back. She tells Daniel she can't take it anymore and she wants a divorce. Daniel pleads with Miranda to go to therapy with him but she has had it with his immature and thoughtless antics and out he goes.

Daniel stays for awhile with his gay brother Frank and his companion Jack, both brilliant

cell); that he's a foreigner who can only say, "I am job"; and finally, that he is an elderly British woman named Euphegenia Doubtfire who had previously worked for many years with the Smythe family in England. (While talking on the phone to Miranda, Daniel spies a newspaper headline that says something like "authorities *doubt fire* was accidental," and improvises the name "Doubtfire.") After the nightmare calls Miranda has been receiving, Mrs. Doubtfire was clearly her dream nanny.

Daniel then enlists the services of Uncle Frank and Aunt Jack, who try several female personas on him, including a Gloria Swanson type, a Cuban with black hair, a Jewish grandmother type, and a Barbra Streisand type, before finally settling on the buxom, matronly version of Mrs. Doubtfire that prompts Frank to comment, "Any closer, you'd be Mom."

Mrs. Doubtfire starts working at the house after leaving his day job at the TV station, cooking, cleaning, watching the kids, and it isn't long before she becomes a beloved part of Miranda's household. Miranda, meanwhile, has begun dating a wealthy client of hers, Stu (Pierce Brosnan), and Daniel must stay in character as he watches this guy move in on his family.

Complications develop when Daniel must be present at a birthday dinner party for Miranda as Mrs. Doubtfire, *and* as Daniel at a dinner meeting with his boss to discuss the possibility of his doing a children's show at the TV station—both at the same restaurant at the same time.

Daniel has to do several quick changes in the women's bathroom during that fateful evening and Robin Williams does a terrific job with the physical humor required for these scenes.

Ultimately, Daniel's ruse is revealed and the court rules him unfit and says he can only see his kids in supervised situations. In the meantime, he gets the position at the TV station that he wanted, hosting a children's show as the kindly and knowledgeable Mrs. Doubtfire. One day Miranda visits the studio and tells him that the kids were happier when Mrs. Doubtfire was a part of their lives. She realizes Daniel has changed and she arranges things so that he can be with them for a few hours every day after school—unsupervised.

The performances in *Mrs. Doubtfire* are superior, from Sally Field as the beset-upon yet softhearted Miranda, to Harvey Fierstein's flamboyant portrayal of Frank. Pierce Brosnan plays the wealthy British entrepreneur Stu with a nice demeanor of confused dignity; and the kids are all quite believable, (especially Lisa Jakub as the oldest girl, Lydia—she has down pat the arrogant disdain that only teenage girls can wield like a chainsaw).

*Mrs. Doubtfire* is one of the most important movies Robin Williams has made to date and it is one of the few in his body of work that effectively utilizes almost *all* of his prodigious talents in the same movie.

## What the Critics Had to Say

**Roger Ebert:** "Everyone knows that [Robin] Williams is a mercurial talent who loves to dart in and out of many different characters and voices. But a little of that goes a long way, and already has. Any review of *Mrs. Doubtfire* must take into account Dustin Hoffman's transvestite comedy, *Tootsie*, which remains by far the better film: more believable, more intelligent and funnier. *Tootsie* grew out of real wit and insight; *Mrs. Doubtfire* has the values and depth of a sitcom. Hoffman as an actor was able to successfully play a woman. Williams, who is also a good actor, seems more to be playing himself playing a woman." (From his *Movie Home Companion*)

**Mick Martin and Marsha Porter:** "Robin Williams is a howl." (From their *Video Movie Guide*)

***Videohound's Golden Movie Retriever:*** "Williams schtick extraordinaire with more than a little sugary sentimentality." (From the 1997 edition)

**Director:** Chris Columbus
**Cast:** Robin Williams (Daniel Hillard and Mrs. Doubtfire), Sally Fields (Miranda Hillard), Pierce Brosnan (Stu), Harvey Fierstein (Frank Hillard), Robert Prosky (Mr. Lundy), Lisa Jakub (Lydia Hillard), Matthew Lawrence (Christopher Hillard), Mara Wilson (Natalie Hillard), Scott Capurro (Jack)
**Producers:** Marsha Garces Williams and Mark Radcliffe
**Writers:** Randi Mayem Singer and Leslie Dixon, based on the book *Alias Madame Doubtfire* by Anne Fine
**Music:** Howard Shore
Rated PG-13; 125 minutes

# The *Mrs. Doubtfire* Interview on *Donahue* (1993)

This was one of Phil Donahue's "single subject" shows and it featured four of the principal creators of Robin's blockbuster hit film, *Mrs. Doubtfire*.

The show guests were the movie's three male leads, Pierce Brosnan, Harvey Fierstein, and Robin Williams; and the film's director, Chris Columbus.

Phil started off by talking about the scene in which Harvey Fierstein (as Frank, the gay brother in the movie) transforms Robin (as Daniel) into Mrs. Doubtfire. Robin jumped on Phil's comments and cracked, "And if you give him the material, he'll make *you* into one, Phil!"

Phil moved on to Chris Columbus and remarked that he must really have a lot of money (since Columbus also directed the enormously successful films, *Home Alone* and *Home Alone 2*). Robin again ad-libbed with, "The wonderful world of points!" Phil then asked Robin if Chris was a good director. Robin answered Phil in a weird foreign accent, "Yes, he very good director . . . besides looking like he's twelve!"

Throughout the show, Phil took questions for the guests from the audience.

One woman asked Robin what part of his new anatomy took the most getting used to.

First of all, losing the *old* part of the *old* anatomy. [Scottish accent] You know what they say, tucking away the little soldier!

Robin mimed tucking away his "little soldier" and continued:

M. *Butterfly*, the home game! Lift and separate! Finally, for a brief moment, understanding how Mr. Bobbitt felt! Hey, it's on the freeway! Bobby! Bobby? Let the dogs out. They'll find it! [Mrs. Doubtfire voice] The best part is to have those incredible, what I like to call, my dirty pillows . . . my airbags of bliss! Those are fun. I would see grown men looking at me once I was dressed as Mrs. Doubtfire . . . or as the doctor said, "I just want to numb them—num, num, num, num, num!" [mimes nuzzling two big breasts]

A woman audience member then asked Robin if wearing all the Mrs. Doubtfire makeup was uncomfortable:

Yeah, it's like wearing the world's largest condom. It's very hot—it encases your face, plus the body suit, plus orthopedic socks, plus what we talked about earlier. . . . And when you have the wig on, the heat won't escape, so some days you felt like a Tennessee Williams play.

They then showed the scene where the character is transformed into Mrs. Doubtfire, followed by a scene from Robin's first appearance as Mork on the sitcom, *Happy Days*. (It must be noted that Robin looked aghast and horrified watching the *Happy Days* clip.)

An audience member then asked Robin if his family was funny, and he talked about his mother's sense of humor, illustrating the anecdote with a poem his mother used to recite to him:

I love you in blue,
I love you in red,
But most of all,
I love you in blue!

He said his mother was from the South and, at times, it was like living with a character from

---

## INTERESTING ASIDE

*In October of 1982, Robin spoke with* Playboy *about his mother's penchant for humorous poetry and other intriguing literary concoctions:*

Even when I was very young, [my mother'd] recite all these nasty poems to me. One of her best:

Spider crawling on the wall,
Ain't you got no sense at all?
Don't you know that wall's been plastered?
Get off that wall, you little spider.

She thought that was great. . . . Mom also had an inexhaustible supply of jokes and stories. The one I remember most was a book supposedly written by a nineteenth century English princess who was famous for throwing parties. The title of the book—Mom swears it's real—is Balls I Have Held.

"Tennessee Williams meets Neil Simon."

An audience member then asked Pierce Brosnan if Robin was a lunatic on the set, to which he replied:

> Sure. There's a performance going on the whole time with Robin and that's just so entertaining. I mean, you can *pay* to go to work. But, the concentration is there the whole time, [even while] Robin is going. It's like the Eveready [Duracell] battery: It just goes and goes and goes and goes!

Later, an audience member asked Robin how long it took to make the quick changes he did in the movie:

> Forty-five seconds . . . if you're not afraid to lose a layer of skin!

They then showed the scene from the movie in which Robin's character has to be both Daniel Hillard *and* Mrs. Doubtfire at the same time.

An audience member then asked Robin a serious question about whether or not he appreciated women any more now that he had actually played one. This led to a lengthy (and very funny) response from Mrs. Doubtfire's alter ego:

> I've always appreciated us women. I appreciate the self-imposed bondage you have to go through. . . . Heels to me are the most amazing thing . . . the first day I thought, these are just three-inch heels, I'm fine. By the end of the day, I'm like [Hunchback of Notre Dame voice]. "I need help! Chiropractor!" I [mentioned that] I was in makeup for four hours and [one woman] said, "Four hours? That's just the beginning, honey!" It's incredible, the attention to detail that you have to go through. That, combined with the happy pillows . . . you think about women getting breast implants, I'm going, noooooooooo. Next time he tells you to do that, tell him to get a scrotum implant! Get something in there, baby! He wants these bigger, you tell him make those bigger!

Later, Phil showed a retrospective of clips featuring men in drag, including Jonathan Winters, Milton Berle, Dustin Hoffman, and, of course, Phil

*Robin as Daniel Hillard in* Mrs. Doubtfire. *(Photofest)*

himself, in a scene from the infamous *Donahue* show when he wore a skirt.

As further evidence of Robin's quicksilver ability to ad-lib complete routines in a millisecond, after the clips, Robin immediately launched into a full-blown parody of those cheesy old "SUNDAY, SUNDAY, SUNDAY!!" racetrack TV commercials:

> "DRAG RACERS! THIS SUNDAY, SUNDAY, SUNDAY IN NEW JERSEY!! DRAG RACERS! INCREDIBLE FUEL-INJECTED BREASTS! SUNDAY!!"

An audience member asked Robin what his favorite impression was and Robin instantly executed a flawless impersonation of Ross Perot transforming into Walter Brennan on the old *The Real McCoys* series. Next came an impression of Phil. An audience member asked him if he got more money for playing two roles and he laughed, "No!"

Robin then discussed what it was like working with Sally Field, and how she took it upon herself to change her character from the book so that she was less a villain and instead, someone the audience could empathize with.

A tense moment followed this exchange

*Robin and his* Mrs. Doubtfire *costars (from left): Mara Wilson, Matthew Lawrence, and Lisa Jakub. (Photofest)*

when a guy in the audience stood up and asked Robin if his performance as Mrs. Doubtfire had been inspired by his marrying his own kids' babysitter. Robin is a consummate pro, however, and handled this rude and insensitive question the way he apparently handles most things in his life: with humor. "You must also believe that Bigfoot lives in my nose!" he fired back at the guy. He then gave a calm and reasoned explanation of the scandal *People* magazine caused by implying in a cover story that Robin's wife Marsha had broken up his previously happy marriage:

> The fact that my wife took care of my son at one point . . . here is where the great myth has been created by one magazine in particular. They made it seem like we were involved romantically when she took care of my son, which is bovine residue. [In Mrs. Doubtfire's voice] Let's set that straight so we can put your little mind back in order and you can stop wearing the dickeys!

The talk then moved to an old appearance of

Harvey on *Cheers*, only Phil mistakenly said it was Robin who had been the guest star. This blunder prompted a spirited rendition by Harvey and Robin of the theme from *The Patty Duke Show* (They walk alike, they talk alike . . .).

An audience member asked Robin if he could cook, to which he replied, "No, I can't even do cereal!"

A woman then told Robin that the sad emotions so obvious in the part of his character in the film seemed genuine and asked him about his own family history. Robin spoke briefly about finding, late in life, two half-brothers he had never known, and how he was now getting to know them both. He then talked about his childhood as an only child and used a line he has used many times (always successfully) in many of his interviews: "I only had myself to play with."

Overall, this *Donahue* show was just another stop on the press junket to promote *Mrs. Doubtfire*—but with one exception: *This* one featured an hour-long appearance by Robin Williams, a show business event of a caliber not usually seen on daytime talk shows.

# Being Human
## (1994)

*"This is the story of a story. Once upon a time, there was this story, and the story said to itself, 'How shall I begin?'"*

—Opening narration

Being Human is an important film, if not a total success, simply because of its far-reaching insights and unique and honest narrative voice. That said, there is no denying that *Being Human* is one strange little movie.

*Being Human* (which is narrated by actress Theresa Russell as the all-knowing "Storyteller") tackles enormous themes, including the true meaning of identity and the search for self; slavery and the master/slave paradigm; the concept of karma; the theory of reincarnation; the impact of fear on a person's code of conduct; and the impact of divorce on children in a modern, industrialized world.

Whew!

*Being Human* tackles colossal themes, and this ambitious scope is surely what must have attracted Robin Williams to the film and convinced him to participate. (Robin previously played a character who had a passionate interest in reincarnation and the paranormal. In 1991's *Dead Again*, Robin had a

*Hector and Lucinnius try to foretell the future by watching the actions of a chicken in* Being Human. *(Photofest)*

cameo as the disgraced and esoteric-minded psychiatrist, Dr. Cozy Carlisle.)

In *Being Human*, Robin plays five separate roles, all of whom are named Hector, and all of whom are reincarnations of the same soul. (In Greek legend, Hector was the eldest son of the Trojan King Priam and his wife Queen Hecuba. In Homer's *Illiad*, Hector is depicted as the perfect warrior and the principal defender of Troy.)

The wraparound story that begins and ends the film is about a divorced, ex-con father who is seeing his two children for the first time in years.

Robin plays this incarnation with sensitivity and is very effective at communicating the heartfelt pain and guilt his character is feeling about neglecting his children during the years they were growing up. Hector is literally overwhelmed by his teenage daughter, a pretty young girl who is so poised, so confident, and so smart, that Hector spends much of his time with her awed by her presence and wondering just where the hell she came from.

Hector's son, the youngest child, has not reached that state of ironic, contemptuous disdain towards his father that his sister has achieved, and still remembers back to when Hector used to hug him so hard he couldn't breathe.

The two kids and their dad reach an understanding on a moonlit beach one night and the movie ends with the soul that is Hector finally learning from his past and making an obvious breakthrough to a higher plane of consciousness.

Throughout *Being Human*, we learn that in each of Hector's incarnations he has been a slave.

The first Hector is a prehistoric man who lives in a mountain cave with his mate and their two young children. This Hector is a slave to many things. He is a slave to his environment, a harsh landscape from which he must glean enough food each day to feed his family. He is a slave to fear, because he never knows when his children may be killed by wild animals or his wife sickened by bad food or water. And he is a slave to the strangers who come one day in boats and simply take, for their own, his woman and his children. Hector, knowing he cannot fight all of these men with their bows and clubs, makes a halfhearted attempt at holding on to what is his by screaming "Mine!" at the departing boats, but it doesn't do any good. We see that Hector is either a coward or a pragmatist, and we ultimately realize the truth is that he is

equal parts of both.

Hector's next incarnation is as a slave in ancient Rome. Hector's master, Lucianus (John Turturro), has been ordered to die to settle a debt which he cannot pay. Lucianus has reluctantly agreed to this sentence and orders Hector to kill himself and accompany him into the next world. Hector is horrified by this command but agrees to help his master kill himself and then to commit suicide immediately after. Hector, who is in love with one of the household's slave girls, recants on his promise, however, and as soon as Lucianus is dead, takes his master's shoes and flees with his lover Thalia.

It seems that in this incarnation, Hector's soul has evolved somewhat and has found an inner source of bravery and a desire for self-preservation. As a Roman slave, Hector was bound to his master, but in the end, he is the one who achieves true freedom—not the faux freedom of death pathetically embraced by his former master, a man who obviously could not find the courage to fight for his own life.

Hector's next incarnation is as a nomad of the Middle Ages traveling by wagon and on foot across Europe. This segment, the narrator tells us, is a love story, and the object of Hector's affection is an Italian beauty named Beatrice. (Beatrice was the great love of Italian poet Dante Alighieri's life and the woman to whom he dedicated most of his poetry. In Dante's classic *The Divine Comedy*, Beatrice acts as his mediator in the *Inferno*, his quest as he travels through *Purgatorio*, and his guide through *Paradiso*.)

Hector and Beatrice break off from their fellow travelers and Hector accompanies Beatrice to her home, where it is obvious that he is welcome to remain as her lover and companion if he so desires.

Hector briefly revels in the comforts of a home and family, but ultimately leaves Beatrice and continues on with his travels, his sights set on his own home and family, still a great distance away. This Hector seems to have learned devotion and commitment and has acquired the moral strength to renounce temporary happiness for the more permanent and lasting joys of his own wife and family.

Hector's last, pre-modern reincarnation is as a shipwrecked New World voyager who is in love with Ursula, a woman who wants nothing to do with him. He and his fellow passengers are stranded

*Robin as the slave Hector with his master Lucinnius (John Turturro) in* Being Human. *(Photofest)*

on an island and must find food and water or perish. Hector's soul seems to have backslided a bit in this incarnation: He hoards food and wine from the others and tries to steal Ursula away from her lover. This segment concludes with Hector leaving for Lisbon and accepting that he will never possess Ursula.

*Being Human* then travels to New York in the present time and we once again meet up with the latest Hector. He has legal (and possibly criminal) problems with an apartment building he owns in which the floor collapsed. He frantically tries to tie things up so he can go pick up his kids for a very

important weekend in which he will reacquaint himself with his family. He borrows his girlfriend's flower delivery car and they all ultimately end up at the beach, where *this* Hector uses the lessons of the past to heal some old wounds and reestablish his relationship with his children.

*Being Human* is ambitious and well-conceived, but there are too many sluggish spots and, for today's short-attention-span audiences, not enough "in-your-face" explanation of the complex and layered themes running throughout the film.

Nevertheless, this movie must be counted as one of Robin Williams's most important films, simply because it *is* a daring and unexpected artistic choice from the guy who did *Good Morning, Vietnam* and *Popeye*.

Robin Williams deserves kudos for not falling into the trap of giving his fans and his audience (only) what they expect.

That willingness to take creative risks is the mark of the true *artist*, something Robin Williams unquestionably is.

Bill Forsyth's big-screen meditation on the plight of unexceptional men is neither funny (as were his earlier films) nor very dramatic." (From their *Video Movie Guide*)

**Director:** Bill Forsyth
**Cast:** Robin Williams (Hector), John Turturro (Lucianus), Anna Galiena (Beatrice), Vincent D'Onofrio (Priest), Hector Elizondo (Don Paulo),

*Robin as the nomad Hector with his lover Beatrice (Anna Galiena) in one of the segments from* Being Human. *(Photofest)*

## What the Critics Had to Say

*Videohound's Golden Movie Retriever:* "Ambitious comedy drama promises more than it delivers. . . . One of Williams's periodic chancy ventures away from his comedic roots occasionally strikes gold, but often seems overly restrained." (From the 1997 edition)

**Mick Martin and Marsha Porter:** "Writer-director

Lorraine Bracco (Anna), Lindsay Crouse (Janet), Kelly Hunter (Deirdre), William H. Macy (Boris), Jonathan Hyde (Francisco), Lizzy McInnerny (Ursula), Grace Mahlaba (Thalia), Theresa Russell (the Storyteller), Charles Miller (Tom), Helen Miller (Betsy)
**Writer:** Bill Forsyth
**Music:** Michael Gibbs
Rated PG-13; 122 minutes

*Robin as the New World explorer Hector in one of the*
*segments from Being Human. (Photofest)*

# To Wong Foo, Thanks for Everything, Julie Newmar (1995)

*"How Three Sisters! How Chekov!"*

—John Jacob Jinglheimer Schmitt (Robin)
upon hearing that the three drag queens
are driving to Hollywood together

Robin Williams has a funny, two-minute scene in *To Wong Foo*, appearing as a multilingual, slick-as-silk booking agent who gives Vida (Patrick Swayze), Chi Chi (John Leguizamo), and Noxeema (Wesley Snipes) cash for their two prize airline tickets and turns them on to a car dealership where, if they mention his name, any car on the lot is fifty bucks.

Robin appears at fourteen minutes into the movie wearing a sportjacket, a gigantic medallion, and an improbable blue-beaded hat with what looks like a satin brim.

He visits the restaurant where the three drag queens have just made a triumphant entrance and tells Vida (in Italian) she is beautiful and kisses her hand. Vida responds with "Enchante," to which Robin replies, "Oh, you spoke French! How *bi*!"

He then slides into their booth next to Chi Chi, calling her his "little piñata." After basking in their assembled drag queen glory, Robin gushes, "Look at you! I'm like a compass near north!"

The "ladies" then tell him that they're all going to Hollywood together and Robin says, "How *Three Sisters*! How Chekov! That's fabulous!"

After they all agree to drive cross-country, Robin gives them a card: "Crazy Elijah: My Cars Are My Children." Chi Chi tells him he's a lifesaver, to which Robin replies, "All day sucker!"

Robin then snaps his fingers and leaves.

Robin's character of John Jacob Jinglheimer Schmitt could justifiably be regarded as a distant cousin of his refined and elegant Armand Goldman character in *The Birdcage*. Here, though, he plays it a little over the top, but considering the rest of the cast, his is probably the most restrained performance in the film.

The remainder of the film tells the story of the three "girls'" trip to Hollywood. They get stranded in the small town of Snydersville where their infectious gaiety (sorry), flamboyant style, and no-nonsense attitudes transform the townsfolk from drab, bored, hopeless hicks into fashionable, hip, exuberant party animals.

*To Wong Foo* is entertaining and a lot of fun. The three leads—Swayze, Leguizamo, and Snipes—are brilliant.

## What the Critics Had to Say

**Roger Ebert:** "I cannot be quite certain, but I believe [this] is the first movie about drag queens to be rated PG-13. And it earns that PG-13 rating by being so relentlessly upbeat, wholesome, and asexual that you walk out of the theater thinking of the queens as role models; every small town should be as lucky as Snydersville, and have its values transformed by them. . . . It's amazing how entertaining it is in places, considering how amateurish the screenplay is and how awkwardly the elements of the story are cobbled together. I feel like recommending the performances, and suggesting they be ported over to another film. The actors emerge with glory, for attempting something very hard, and succeeding remarkably well. They deserve to be in a better movie. (From his *Movie Home Companion*)

***Videohound's Golden Movie Retriever:*** "Hot on the high heels of *The Adventures of Priscilla, Queen of the Desert*, comes the sanitized for your protection Yankee version. And it's all about hanging on to your dreams, and how we're all the same inside, with politically correct gay drag queens doing the sermonizing. . . . One-dimensional characters, flat direction, and inconsistent script undercut exceptional performances by Swayze and Leguizamo." (From the 1997 edition)

**Director:** Beeban Kidron
**Cast:** Robin Williams (John Jacob Jingleheimer Schmitt), Wesley Snipes (Noxeema Jackson), Patrick Swayze (Miss Vida Boheme), John Leguizamo (Chi Chi Rodriguez), Stockard Channing (Carol Ann),
Blythe Danner (Beatrice), Arliss Howard (Virgil), Jason London (Bobby Ray), Alice Drummond (Clara), Chris Penn (Sheriff Dollard); with RuPaul, Julie Newmar, Naomi Campbell, Quentin Crisp
**Writer:** Douglas Carter Beane
**Music:** Rachel Portman
Rated PG-13; 109 minutes

# *Jumanji*
# (1995)

*"A game for those who seek to find a way to leave their world behind. You roll the dice to move your token; doubles get another turn. The first player to reach the end wins."*

—The "Jumanji" instructions

Beginning with a forest scene that visually alludes to the opening sequence of *ET: The Extraterrestrial*, Robin Williams's 1995 fantasy adventure film *Jumanji* is a thrilling story of horrible, impossible creatures sent to our earthly realm by a supernatural game with a distinctly nasty personality and a vicious sense of humor.

*Jumanji* is, at the same time, a touching and emotional tale of childhood and lost innocence.

*Jumanji* begins in Brantford, New Hampshire in 1869 with two young boys burying the Jumanji game. They are obviously terrified of the game and glad to be rid of it.

The scene then shifts to Brantford one hundred years later. It is now 1969 and Alan Parrish, the timid young son of a successful shoe manufacturer, hears the drum sounds that the game sends out (but that only certain people can hear). He pulls the game out of the ground at a construction site near his father's factory.

When he opens the game, the pieces fly into place by themselves. He begins playing the game with Sarah (Bonnie Hunt), a girl from his school who has just brought his bike back after it was taken by her bully boyfriend. The two find that the game presents them with a riddle—the words swirling into sight (reminding older viewers of the ubiquitous Magic 8-Ball toy from times past)—after each roll of the dice.

The first riddle reads "At night they fly, you better run, these winged things are not much fun." This is immediately followed by high-pitched squeaking sounds coming from the fireplace. The clock chimes and a frightened Alan accidentally drops his dice, causing the next riddle to appear: "In the jungle you must wait, until the dice reads five or eight." To Sarah's horror, Alan is then "melted" alive and sucked into the center of the game. Sarah is then attacked by swarms of vicious bats and she flees the house in terror.

*Jumanji* then jumps ahead twenty-six years.

Judy (Kirsten Dunst) and Peter (Bradley Pierce), two sweet kids who have recently lost their parents in a skiing accident, are moving into the Parrish house with their new guardian, Aunt Nora (Bebe Neuwirth). Healthy these kids are not: Judy is a compulsive liar, and Peter hasn't spoken a word since the death of their parents. The kids are soon told something unsettling by the exterminator brought in to get rid of the bats (uh, oh) in the attic. He tells them that the rumor around town is that Alan Parrish was murdered by his father in this very house and his body was cut up into pieces and hidden in the walls.

155

Following this alarming and frightening news, it isn't long before Judy and Peter hear the ominous Jumanji drums and find the old game hidden away in the attic. As soon as they open the game, the pieces (Sarah and Alan's from the past, remember) again fly to their proper place. Peter adds two new game pieces (the ones on the board cannot be budged), and Judy rolls a six and is presented with the riddle, "A tiny bite can make you itch, Make you sneeze, Make you twitch."

Judy and Peter are then attacked by giant mosquitoes which Judy fights off with a tennis racket. Peter rolls a two and is told, "This will not be an easy mission, monkeys slow the expedition." The two astonished siblings are then immediately attacked by hordes of vicious monkeys that trash the kitchen and hurl knives at them. Peter rolls again ("doubles get another turn") and throws the all-important five. His riddle reads, "Its fangs are sharp. He likes your taste. Your party better move posthaste." A giant lion appears and chases them, but out of nowhere, a bearded jungle man clad in leaves and skins appears and fends off the lion.

This jungle man is none other than the long-lost and now adult Alan Parrish (Robin Williams) who has been "waiting" in the jungle for the past twenty-six years. Alan's roll of a five rescues him from his Jumanji-caused imprisonment.

Alan is ecstatic to be back, but at first does not realize that his parents are dead and that he did not return to the time that he left. He runs through the town and finds the place a poor, rundown shadow of the bright and friendly hamlet he left as a kid. Robin Williams is very good in these scenes and we can feel his sorrow as he realizes that everything and everyone he knew and loved is gone. Alan's family's shoe factory is abandoned and now serves as a refuge for the homeless. He learns that his father exhausted his entire fortune trying to find him after he disappeared in 1969.

A dejected Alan returns to his old family home and cleans himself up (while singing the theme from *Gilligan's Island*). Judy and Peter try to persuade him to finish the game, and he eventually consents, but then realizes that they are all playing the same game that he and Sarah started back in 1969, and in order to complete it, Sarah has to resume playing as well. The three of them go visit the emotionally scarred Sarah (now making a living as a psychic named Madame Serena) and persuade her that the only way to be free from the terror of the past is to finish the game they started those many years ago.

Sarah finally gives in and the rest of the movie recounts the adventures the four of them have to survive (not an easy task) in order to finish the game and be free of its hold.

Here is a rundown of the game's final riddles—as well as a look at their accompanying terrors:

"They grow much faster than bamboo.
Take care or they'll come after you."

Giant sentient vines invade the house, tear it asunder, and turn it into a dark and deadly jungle.

"A hunter from the darkest wild
Makes you feel just like a child."

A mean and heartless jungle hunter named Van Pelt (complete with pith helmet, elephant gun, and jungle fatigues) appears with only one thing on his mind: killing Alan Parrish. Van Pelt pursues Alan throughout the remainder of the story, tracking him through town, into a department store, and back to the vine-entwined house.

"Don't be fooled, it isn't thunder.
Staying put would be a blunder."

This riddle summons a full-blown jungle stampede (consisting of elephants, rhinos, and all other manner of jungle wildlife) that tears through the Parrish house and then storms the town, destroying buildings, cars, and everything else in its path. The stampede scenes of *Jumanji* are the most visually amazing and, thus, it makes sense that the clip that was shown during Robin Williams's promotional appearances for the film was of the animals bursting through a library wall, rampaging through the house, and then raging through the town.

"A law of Jumanji has been broken,
You'll set back even more than your token."

This is the riddle that transforms Peter into a miniature Wolf Boy, complete with a hairy face and hands and a tail.

"Every month at the quarter moon,
There'll be a monsoon in your lagoon."

This riddle brought a flooding rainstorm to the inside of the Parrish house, complete with man-eating crocodiles that Alan had to fight underwater.

*Robin as the grownup Alan Parrish in Jumanji. (Photofest)*

"Beware the ground on which you stand,
The floor is quicker than the sand."

This one changes the attic floor to quicksand, trapping Sarah and Alan.

"There is a lesson you will learn:
Sometimes you must go back a turn."

This riddle hardens the quicksand attic floor and leaves Alan suspended *in* the ceiling of the room below.

"Need a hand? Well, you just wait.
We'll help you out, we each have eight."

What else? This brings a giant spider attack.

"You're almost there with much at stake,
Now the ground begins to quake."

An enormous earthquake splits the house in two.

After this last riddle, Alan rolls a three, gets to the center of the board, and says "Jumanji," ending the game and reversing all its terrible effects. Alan and Sarah are sent back to 1969, just moments after they started playing the original game.

Time again flows for them at a normal rate, except that Alan and Sarah can remember what happened because of the game. They get married, and the movie concludes in 1995, with Sarah pregnant with their first child. In the concluding scenes of the film, we learn that Alan's father has hired Peter's dad to work at the shoe factory and an overwhelmed Alan and Sarah finally meet Judy and Peter, only now the kids do not, of course, because the game changed the future, remember anything of their great adventure.

Sarah and Alan prevent Peter and Judy's parents from going on their fateful ski trip and everyone lives happily ever after. Except, that is, for two kids who, after hearing the sound of drums, find the Jumanji game washed up on a beach in France.

*Jumanji* is one of Robin Williams's most enjoyable films and, again, his *Good Morning, Vietnam* and Genie identity are nowhere to be found, proving, once again, Robin's facility at creating realistic characters that are clearly independent of his stand-up persona. (Okay, so the film's animals are somewhat less realistic looking than the dinos in *Jurassic Park*. Nonetheless, *Jumanji* moves right along and is definitely worthwhile entertainment.)

### Robin on the Making of *Jumanji*

"You basically run down the hall and things start breaking apart and . . . there's a Teamster with a little 'X' going, 'I'm the rhino.'" (During a 1995 promotional interview for

*Alan Parrish (Robin) is trapped in the quicksand floor in one of the special effects shot from* Jumanji. *(Photofest)*

*Robin and his* Jumanji *costars cower in fear (from left): Bonnie Hunt, Bradley Pierce, and Kirsten Dunst. (Photofest)*

Jumanji on *The Tonight Show with Jay Leno*)

"There's a scene in the movie where [I] wrestle a crocodile. And there's things in the movie—part of them are computer effects and the rest are animatronics, which means they're like Muppets on steroids. I was wrestling this crocodile and I pounded it on the head and all of a sudden from inside I hear, 'Hey!' There was this guy in there going, 'Hey, man, it's me, it's Jim! Cut the overacting, man! It's hot in here! I just had a burrito!

Don't do that!' " (From *The Tonight Show*)

## What Robin Had to Say

"I hope to show it to my kids. I mean, my four-year-old enjoyed *Pulp Fiction*." (From *The Tonight Show*)

## What the Critics Had to Say

**Roger Ebert:** "The underlying structure of the film seems inspired by—or limited by—interactive video

*Elephants rampage through town thanks to the game with a mind of its own,* Jumanji. *(Photofest)*

games. There is little attempt to construct a coherent story. Instead, the characters face one threat after another, as new and grotesque dangers jump at them. The ultimate level for young viewers will be being able to sit all the way through the movie." (From his *Movie Home Companion*)

***Videohound's Golden Movie Retriever:*** "[R]elies too heavily on cutting-edge special effects to make up for a thin story. Many of the creatures and effects are utterly too bizarre and unsettling for younger audiences." (From the 1997 edition)

**Director:** Joe Johnston
**Cast:** Robin Williams (Alan Parrish), Jonathan Hyde (Van Pelt and Sam Parrish), Kirsten Dunst (Judy), Bradley Pierce (Peter), Bonnie Hunt (Sarah), Bebe Neuwirth (Nora), David Alan Grier (Bentley)
**Writers:** Jonathan Hensleigh, Greg Taylor and William Teitler, based on the book, *Jumanji*, by Chris Van Allsburg
**Music:** James Horner
Rated PG; 103 minutes

# The Birdcage
## (1996)

*"I'm the only guy in my fraternity who doesn't come from a broken home."*

—Armand's son, Val

*"It looks like young men playing leapfrog."*

—Conservative Senator Keeley's wife Louise, upon seeing Armand and Albert's "decadent" china pattern

There is precisely one scene in *The Birdcage* when Robin Williams gets to go nuts: Exactly once do we experience the full force of the comedic genius who can, in an instant, transform himself into everyone (and everything) from Jack Nicholson to an unsuccessful sperm cell battling an unyielding diaphragm.

Robin's character, Armand, is directing his lover, Albert, in the rehearsal of a new song he has just written (actually a song by Stephen Sondheim) for their very successful and extremely popular drag show in Armand's south Florida club, The Birdcage.

The (not too bright) young man who is playing Albert's love interest in the staged scene is confused about the meaning of the song and asks if he should "feel" anything. Armand (Robin) tells the dancer that he can go right ahead and "feel" . . . Bob Fosse, Martha Graham, Twyla Tharp, Michael

*Armand tries to persuade the always histrionic Albert to come home in a scene from* The Birdcage. *(Photofest)*

Kidd, and Madonna—and Armand explains his artistic suggestions by bounding all over the stage and performing mini-versions of these brilliant choreographers' dance styles, complete with flawless reconstructions of their trademark leg and arm routines. Armand concludes his direction by telling the young man to feel all of this *inside*, however. This is a hilarious scene, and the one that the producers wisely chose to use in all the TV commercials for the movie—even though it does mislead somewhat by suggesting that Robin is as wacky as this throughout the entire movie, something he is most assuredly *not*.

*The Birdcage* (a remake of the very popular and successful 1978 French farce *La Cage Aux Folles*) opens with an amazing camera shot that begins out over the water, speeds onto the beach, and then glides right into Armand's drag club, The Birdcage, where his "We Are Family" production number is being performed. (Using the song "We Are Family" as the movie's opening and closing theme, was this director Mike Nichols's and screenwriter Elaine May's slap at the right-wing conservative "family values" platform? Just wondering.)

The first time we see Robin Williams as Armand, he is strolling through his club, resplendent in silk and gold, kissing favored patrons and checking in on the kitchen help. The

*Robin with his* Birdcage *costar Nathan Lane. (Photofest)*

next number coming up features the club's headliner, Starina, a flamboyant female raconteur and vocalist who is played by Armand's lover, Albert (Nathan Lane, in a role everyone assumed would be played by the oft-flamboyant Robin Williams). But Starina, Armand learns, refuses to perform. "She" is throwing a tantrum. Armand must placate her and convince her to go on, which she eventually does.

While Starina is performing, Armand meets with his twenty-year-old son, Val (Dan Futterman), who was raised by him and Albert. Val gives his

father some earthshaking news: He is getting married, and his fiancée's father just so happens to be Senator Keeley (Gene Hackman), a right-wing conservative who is the cofounder of the Coalition for Moral Order—a man who believes that the Pope is too controversial and that Billy Graham and Bob Dole are too liberal.

Val wants his father to meet his future in-laws, but he does not want them to know the truth about Armand's lifestyle, and he *especially* does not want them to know about "Auntie Albert." Val and his fiancée, Barbara (Calista Flockhart), have told

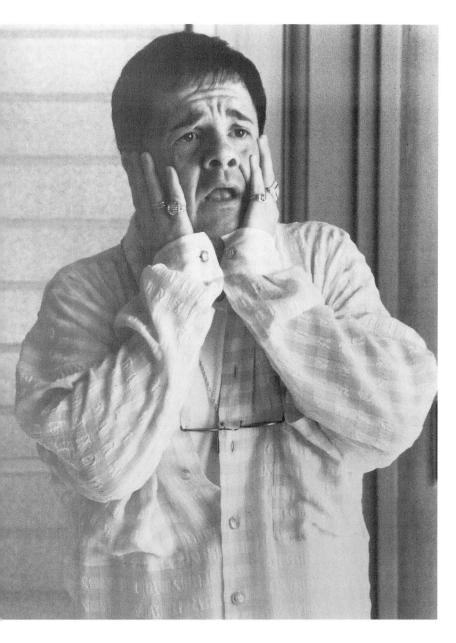

off as Val's "Uncle Albert."

In the meantime, Armand and Val also decide to enlist the help of Val's mother (Christine Baranski), a successful businesswoman who has not seen her son in twenty years.

The last half hour or so of the movie is the dinner party at Armand's apartment, a comedy of confusion and errors during which Albert appears in drag as Val's mother (looking very "Mrs. Doubtfire"-ish!); Val's real mother arrives; and Armand and Albert's gay Guatemalan house servant Agador (played brilliantly by Hank Azaria) serves them some strange soup that he just "made up" after revealing to Armand that he has not prepared an entrée.

There is also a subplot in the film involving Senator Keeley's coalition cofounder Senator Jackson, who is found dead in the bed of an underaged black hooker. When interviewed about the Senator's death on a "CNN"-like station, the young lady says, "Well, he looked kind of funny, but he was smiling so I didn't worry," which, of course, becomes the definitive sound bite for the scandal. This development sets the media on the trail of Keeley and his family and acts as the catalyst for the final sequence in which (1) Val and Barbara reveal the truth to her parents; (2) the media is camped outside The Birdcage waiting for the Senator to emerge; and (3) Albert and Armand facilitate the Senator's escape by dressing him in drag and turning him into what one woman described as "the ugliest woman I have ever seen in my life."

her parents that Val's dad is a Cultural Attaché to Greece, and that Val's mother is a housewife.)

At first, Armand angrily resists his son's request to act straight and tone down the apartment, but ultimately he consents to the charade and agrees to send Albert away for a few days while the Senator and his wife (Dianne Weist) are in town.

Upon hearing of the plan to send him away, Albert goes into histrionics and tells Armand that his heart is breaking over this terrible rejection. Armand relents and decides to try and pass Albert

Robin Williams's performance in *The Birdcage* is one of the finest of his career. He plays this "middle-aged fag" (which is the way he describes himself to his son in the movie) with a dignity and *gravitas* that perfectly complements the incredibly outrageous *tour de force* performance of Nathan Lane. And aside from the scene described earlier in which he wildly imitates the choreographers (something one might not expect the usually very subdued Armand to do), there isn't a moment when

*Robin as the always dapper Armand Goldman in The Birdcage. (Photofest)*

his portrayal of fifty-year-old gay Armand does not ring true.

The remainder of the cast is, likewise, superb. Nathan Lane plays Albert like a swishy, flaming queen. Some have suggested that his performance validates a stereotype but, let's face it, there *are* incredibly effeminate gay drag queens in the homosexual community and Nathan acknowledges their mannerisms and predilections with his performance, but never demeans or degrades them for a moment.

It is clear that Lane—and the entire cast and crew for that matter—approached this project with respect, good humor, and affection for the people they were playing, and this regard shows in every scene of the movie. We come away from *The Birdcage* liking these people—*a lot.* Surely some previously intolerant people may have left this film surprised at themselves for thinking that the gay people portrayed might be a lot of fun to know and be friends with—no matter what they do in their private lives or for a living.

It is not an exaggeration to state that *The Birdcage* is one of the funniest comedies of all time. The writing is sharp; the directing, inventive; the performances, Oscar caliber. And it was a mainstream hit at the box office as well. A movie about gay drag queens turning into one of the most successful movies of all time: Who'd've figured?

## What Robin Had to Say

On his spontaneous "explosion" of dancing during Albert's rehearsal: "It just came about. Armand's this choreographer. It came out in rehearsal one day. . . . It wasn't difficult because Mike [Nichols] always let us try things. Nathan and I would go off and do strange and wonderful things. . . . When you improvise something, it all comes into place. . . . Always great to do that Martha Graham. Twyla is great because you can fling your head around. You get that lovely whiplash." (From the *New York Times,* March 31, 1996).

## What the Critics Had to Say

**Roger Ebert:** "The first time Mike Nichols and Elaine May, who helped define improvisational comedy in the 1950s, have worked together on a movie. What mostly sparkles from their work here is the dialogue, as when the Senator's daughter, trying to cast the situation in the best possible light, explains that South Beach is 'about two minutes from Fisher Island, where Jed Bush lives.'" (From his *Movie Home Companion*)

*Videohound's Golden Movie Retriever:* "Somewhat overlong but well-played remake." (From the 1997 edition)

**Director:** Mike Nichols
**Cast:** Robin Williams (Armand Goldman), Nathan Lane (Starina-Albert), Gene Hackman (Senator Keeley), Dianne Weist (Louise Keeley), Hank Azaria (Agador), Dan Futterman (Val Goldman), Calista Flockhart (Barbara Keeley), Christine Baranski (Katharine)
**Writer:** Elaine May
**Music:** Arranged and adapted by Jonathan Tunick
Rated R; 118 minutes

# Jack
## (1996)

*"I just want to be a* regular *star."*

—Jack

Despite scathing critical reviews, *Jack* was the number one film its opening weekend of August 9, 1996, proving two things: that fans don't always pay attention to critics, and that Robin Williams can unquestionably "open" a film. Reuter's News Service spelled it out the following week:

> Once again movie audiences defied the critics and flocked to see a film that received a lukewarm reception from the experts. The Francis Ford Coppola–

*Jack, a ten-year-old trapped in a forty-year-old body. (Photofest)*

(and others) gave *Jack*.

*Jack* tells the story of a boy who is born with a rare disease that causes him to age physically at four times the normal rate. He is born after only ten weeks in the womb and by the time he is ten years old, he looks like a forty-year-old man.

For his entire first decade, Jack's overprotective mother (Francis Ford Coppola fave Diane Lane) and resigned father (Brian Kerwin) keep him at home and have him tutored by Mr. Woodruff (Bill Cosby), a kindly and intuitive man who provides the voice of reason that finally convinces them that Jack needs to go to school with other kids. (Some of the funny moments in these "housebound" scenes include Jack throwing a gooey eyeball at the taunting neighborhood kids and Jack snoring while sleeping between his parents.)

From here, the film moves on to Jack's first days at school, his acceptance by a group of his classmates after they realize he's tall enough to be a terrific basketball center, and his immediate infatuation with his teacher, Miss Marquez (Jennifer Lopez). Okay, there are two (exactly one too many) tipping desk gags where a too-big Robin squeezes into a tiny desk, tips over, and ends up on the floor.

directed Robin Williams movie *Jack* opened at the top of the box-office chart this weekend. It earned an estimated $11.3 million. A *Variety* poll of critics in major cities showed that nine liked *Jack*, twenty did not and seventeen were mixed.

Some of the reviews were so negative they bordered on the ludicrous. One especially hysterical review was by *Today*'s curmudgeonly film critic Gene Shalit, who was apoplectic and personally offended by *Jack*. Shalit's overreaction and verbal histrionics (often unnecessarily hyperbolic) diminished him. Shalit hated *Jack* so much that if he employed a rating system for his reviews (which he does not), he would have given it zero stars out of four.

*Puh-leeeeze.*

Granted, *Jack* has its problems. But the film is also heads above some of the other dreck that is released each year to better reviews than Shalit

*Robin with Jennifer Lopez, who played Miss Marquez, the teacher he falls in love with in* Jack. *(Photofest)*

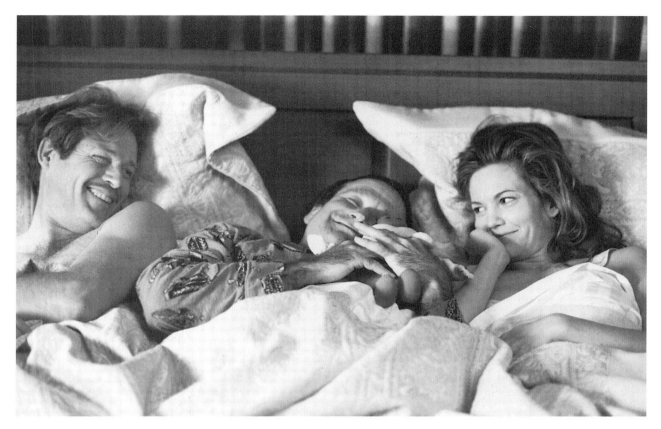

*Not-so-little Jack in bed with his parents, played by Brian Kerwin and Diane Lane. (Photofest)*

But it must be acknowledged that Robin Williams's talent is such that he immediately transmutes his physical appearance with his performance, completely convincing us that there is, indeed, a ten-year-old boy living inside a hairy forty-year-old body.

Ten-year-old minds working the way they work, it isn't long before one of Jack's new friends persuades him to impersonate the principal when his mother comes to visit the school because of his own misbehavior. Jack pretends he's the school principal and is convincing enough that the boy's mother, Dolores Durante (Fran Drescher) actually makes a pass at him and slips him her phone number. This is a very funny scene, especially when Jack sticks his hands under his jersey and makes fake breasts while gawking at Dolores's cleavage in the kind of juvenile way only boys that age can get away with.

There follows a few gross farting and eating scenes and a lame collapsing tree house sequence that the film could have done without but these don't really detract from the main story, which is Jack's increasing realization that his time is limited

and that he may not live to see twenty. This new awareness is effectively and poignantly illustrated in a scene where Jack and his classmates are instructed to write an essay about what they want to be when they grow up. As one little girl talks about her dreams, we see Jack multiplying twenty-eight times four and circling the result: one hundred and twelve.

Jack withdraws from school after an angina attack caused by this sudden profound understanding of his lot in life, and it is weeks before he can be convinced (with a great deal of help from Mr. Woodruff and Jack's entire class) to come back.

There are a few noticeable "Robin Williams" moments in *Jack*. One is when he does a goatee joke and says, sheeplike, "That would be baaaad!" a line he's often used in his comedy; and a Dr. Kevorkian joke that is too adult for it to have genuinely come from a ten-year-old.

Also unsettling is the scene in which Jack goes to the bar where Dolores hangs out and he gets drunk. The scenes in which Jack talks about impotence and divorce with Michael McKean do not work, and the eventual bar fight that ends with

from everybody else. I would come home and there were no brothers or sisters. It was lonely. It was stimulating in the sense that I had a lot of toys, or whatever. But there is that need for contact, the good and the bad of it." (From an interview in the *Boston Globe*, August 9, 1996)

"This is the last one. This is the ultimate one. This is the metaphor gone beyond the hyperbole into simile. I can't do it anymore after this. I'm 45. This is way beyond the Peter Pan syndrome." (From *TV Guide*, August 3, 1996)

## What the Critics Had to Say

**Roger Ebert:** "Williams works hard at seeming to be a kid inside a grownup's body, and some of his

Jack in jail derail the pace of the film and detract from its gentler tone.

There are also a couple of noticeable plot holes, one of which is, if everyone in town knows about Jack and his condition, why doesn't Dolores?

The film ends with an epilogue that takes place seven years later at Jack's high school graduation. Jack is now physically sixty-eight years old and he gives a mawkish valedictorian address that concludes with him riding off for a night of partying with his seventeen-and eighteen-year-old friends.

*Jack* is yet another example of Robin Williams stretching as an actor and for the most part, he gives a touchingly effective and moving performance.

## What Robin Had to Say

"I could relate to Jack's desire to be with other children because I also lived in a big house on a lot of land, but way away

*Robin as Jack, with Bill Cosby as his tutor Mr. Woodruff. (Photofest)*

*Jack with his fifth grade class. (Photofest)*

inspirations work well. But he has been ill-served by a screenplay that isn't curious about what his life would *really* be like." (From his *Movie Home Companion*)

**Tom Gliatto:** "Williams moves through the film very lightly, never overdoing the physical comedy of a giant squeezing in among other schoolchildren, not milking the pathos of a boy who has to touch up his graying, thinning hair. Williams himself seems to have grown up into an unexpectedly soulful actor." (From a review in *People*, August 12, 1996)

**Richard Schickel:** "One is left wondering why Williams has granted early retirement to his inner anarchist, what dark need compels a great clown to become a sad, fuzzy one in movies only Bob Dole—

faking it—could love." (From a review in *Time*, August 12, 1996)

**Director:** Francis Ford Coppola
**Cast:** Robin Williams (Jack Powell), Diane Lane (Karen Powell), Jennifer Lopez (Miss Marquez), Brian Kerwin (Brian Powell), Fran Drescher (Dolores Durante), Bill Cosby (Lawrence Woodruff), Michael McKean (Paulie), Don Novello (Bartender), Allan Rich (Dr. Benfante), Adam Zolotin (Louis Durante), Todd Bosley (Edward), Seth Smith (John-John), Mario Yedidia (George), Jeremy Lelliott (Johnny Duffer), Rickey D'Shon Collins (Eric), Hugo Hernandez (Victor)
**Writers:** James DeMonaco, Gary Nadeau
**Music:** Michael Kamen
Rated PG-13; 113 minutes

# Aladdin and the King of Thieves
## (1996)

*"I was having an out-of-movie experience."*

—Genie, during his transformation into Pumba
the warthog from *The Lion King*

s previously mentioned, Robin Williams did not perform the role of Genie in the second film of the *Aladdin* series, the straight-to-video *The Return of Jafar*, because of contract problems with Disney.

He returned for this third installment, however, and, once again, scored enormously with his free-wheeling, free-associating portrayal of the always-blue Genie.

This third chapter of Aladdin and Jasmine's story features the much-anticipated wedding of the two young lovers. It also tells the story of Aladdin's dangerous and exciting search for his long-lost father, a quest that leads him right into the deadly hidden den of the foreboding King of Thieves.

But it is Genie who interests us as Robin Williams fans and here is a rundown of the close to ninety character transformations Genie makes during the film. (He'd out done himself this time!)

1. An entire caravan entering Agrabah

2. A Princess

3. A pixie

4. A tuxedoed emcee

5. A bride in a wedding gown

6. An Italian manicurist

7. A white-haired evangelist

8. An earring

9. Ethel Merman

10. A French painter

11. Fred Astaire

12. A rabbi

13. A giant exploding pig

14. Rocky (as played by Sylvester Stallone)

15. Groucho Marx

16. A street kid with his hat on backwards

17. A truck filled with flowers

18. A surfer dude parking valet

19. A woman

20. A maître'd

21. A harem girl bursting out of a cake

22. Woody Allen

23. A pair of talking bunny slippers

24. A radio talk show host

25. A clock

26. A tailor

27. A cameraman

28. An entire choir

29. James Brown

30. A reporter for *Lifestyles of the Rich and Magical*

31. Jack Nicholson

32. The rabbit from *Alice's Adventures in Wonderland*

33. A beefeater-type guard

34. A cowboy

35. An entire army of samurai warriors

36. Forrest Gump

37. A pot-bellied construction worker

38. Rain Man (as played by Dustin Hoffman)

39. Mrs. Doubtfire (as played by . . . well, you know)

40. Harpo Marx

*The big blue guy once again stands behind his pal, Aladdin. (Walt Disney Company)*

41. Zeppo Marx
42. Groucho Marx
43. An effeminate wedding planner
44. Elvis (or an Elvis impersonator, depending on your interpretation)
45. A fashion show emcee
46. Several yuppie marketing guys
47. Bing Crosby
48. Bob Hope
49. RoboCop
50. An entire armed SWAT Team
51. A troupe of Scottish bagpipers
52. A cavalry
53. A team of paratroopers
54. Pocahontas

55. A waiter
56. A fortuneteller
57. Several constellations
58. A necktie
59. A fisherman riding on the back of a fish
60. Louis Armstrong
61. A football referee
62. Albert Einstein
63. The planet Saturn
64. A Jetson
65. A tree
66. A grumpy old Grandpa
67. Triplets
68. A basketball

*With Robin returning, zanier than ever, the spotlight was once again returned to the Genie. (Walt Disney Company)*

69. Shaquille O'Neal

70. A pair of bumper cars

71. A stewardess

72. Don Vito Corleone, the Godfather (as played by Marlon Brando)

73. Pumba the warthog from *The Lion King*

74. A dog

75. Sénor Wences

76. A prisoner

77. The Oracle

78. A Southern lawyer

79. A paratrooper with a machine gun

80. A swami

81. A hick farmer

82. A professional wrestler

83. A sportscaster

84. Ozzie Nelson

85. All of the bridesmaids at Aladdin and Jasmine's wedding

As we saw in the *Aladdin* list of characters, Robin is capable of instantly changing from one wacky incarnation to another and he proves this again in *Aladdin and the King of Thieves*—only this time he adds even more strange denizens to the Agrabah population!

## Robin on the Genie, Part 1

"I went into a room and started improvising, and these guys just kept throwing ideas at me. It just got wild. They let me play. That's why I loved it—it was like carte blanche to go nuts. Of course, there were times when I'd go tasteless, when I knew the mouse was not going to approve: 'Oh, come on, boy. Rub the lamp, the big spout. Don't be afraid!' " (From *TV Guide*, August 3, 1996)

## Robin on the Genie, Part 2

In the September 1996 issue of the kids' magazine, *Disney Adventures*, Robin Williams was interviewed and had some interesting things to say about his most recent roles. Here are a few of his comments about playing Genie:

DISNEY ADVENTURES: What's the best thing and worst thing about being Genie?

ROBIN WILLIAMS: The best thing is I've got phenomenal powers. The worst part? My *leeettle* tiny living space.

DA: Who would be your ultimate master?

RW: *Hmm,* who would be the kindest and the best? Well, Gandhi wouldn't ask for much—the wishes would be kept to a minimum: Peace in India, world peace. I'd say, "Oh, that's easy, boss! Come on, get serious." Mother Teresa, just because she would have me do good things. I don't think all of a sudden she would say, "I want my own fragrance!"

DA: Since Genie has been stuck in a bottle for 10,000 years, how does he know all the pop culture icons that he morphs into and portrays?

RW: It's not like he doesn't get cable! He can travel forward and backward in time. He's traveling at the speed of life. He knows many things from other times. That's why I love the gig: Morphin' Mindy.

Robin also revealed during the interview that the one thing he would change about Genie if he could would be to give him a little more hair.

## Robin on The Genie, Part 3

In the Fall 1996 issue of *Disney Magazine*, Robin talked about what was on his mind while working on the sequel to *Aladdin*: "The Genie," he reveals,

"comes closest to my own stand-up performances."

He described the animators who tried to keep up with him as "all traveling at the same speed of light." Ted Stones, the director and producer of *Aladdin and the King of Thieves* noted, "It's a good thing we lay the vocal tracks first; it gives us enough time to draw all the characters Robin comes up with."

When asked how he came up with his stream-of-consciousness creations, Robin joked, "I do a good take, they give me food."

"Something happens," he continued. "It's almost uncontrollable." He also admits to censoring himself: "It can get too bizarre or too blue, and I certainly don't want to scare children or drag them through puberty in five seconds."

**Director:** Ted Stones
**Voices:** Robin Williams (Genie), Scott Weinger (Aladdin), Linda Larkin (Princess Jasmine), Gilbert Gottfried (Iago), Jerry Orbach (Sa'luk), John Rhys-Davies (Cassim, the King of Thieves); with Jim Cummings, Frank Walker, CCH Pounder
**Writer:** Mark McCorkle, Robert Schooley
**Music:** Mark Watters and Carl Johnson; Songs by David Friedman; Randy Petersen and Kevin Quinn
Rated G; 80 minutes

# The Aladdin and the King of Thieves Interview on The Today Show (1996)

In early August of 1996, Robin appeared in a taped segment with Al Roker on *The Today Show* for an interview to promote both *Jack* and the upcoming video release of *Aladdin and the King of Thieves*.

Robin is absolutely amazing when he does these brief five- or six-minute interviews and this appearance was no exception. He kept Al Roker laughing almost the entire time they were talking.

Roker introduced the taped interview by talking about Disney's 1994 apology to Robin for using his Genie voice without permission in *Aladdin* merchandise, and his first question to Robin was about the reconciliation:

Yeah, I'm back working for the Mouse! It just took one big stuffed plush toy . . . it was a Pamela Sue Anderson doll!

Al Roker then asked Robin why he liked playing the Genie:

Just because he can be anybody. Because, you know, he can switch. [Walter Cronkite voice] I can be Walter Cronkite for a minute and then [Carol Channing voice] become Carol Channing! I didn't know that's possible! [in his own voice] It's just a total freedom.

They then showed a clip from the original 1992 *Aladdin* movie as Robin commented on his Genie character:

Because he's magical, anything's possible . . . there's no time reference . . . he's not bound by any particular thing. He can bring in any different character from any time . . . be any person at any given moment.

The talk then turned to Robin's mega-hit from earlier in the year, *The Birdcage*. Roker asked Robin if he had had any idea when he was working on *The Birdcage* that the movie would be the enormous hit it became. "I just knew that it was funny," Robin replied. "And I knew that if it was that funny, people would go. That it would kick like that? I had no idea that it would do that well." Robin also said that because the movie had so many funny moments, he had hoped that people would see it more than once to "pick up what they missed the first time."

After a funny scene from *The Birdcage*, Robin was asked, "Is that the point of the exercise now, to do things that are maybe a little bit different?"

Robin explained that he tried to keep expanding his body of work by trying different aspects of acting that allowed him to "explore other human behavior." He then remarked, "And for me, that's why I want to just play characters," which led to a clip of the schoolyard scene from *Jack*.

After the clip, the talk turned yet again to Robin's penchant for taking on "man-boy" roles. Al Roker asked him if *Jack* was his last "man-child" movie, to which Robin replied, "I've done enough man-boy parts. After *Hook* and *Jumanji*, they said, 'Here's another man-boy part.' I went, 'Get real!

I'm having sex with my wife! Come on, I'm not a boy! I'm forty-four! Look at me! I'm furrier than the gorilla in *Congo!*' "

This naturally led the conversation to a discussion of Robin's amazing hairiness. Al Roker queried him about why his hirsute appearance was made fun of so much in *Jack*.

I've actually gone to the zoo and had monkeys come up to the cage and go, "What am *I* doing in here?" . . . They've actually tried to groom me. . . . They thin it out occasionally for movies now just so it doesn't distract. They just take a weed-whacker . . . two guys from Seattle . . . "I'm sorry, Robin, we just can't get through that damn thunder-brush on your thighs! And I'm not going *near* your butt!" I've actually seen bugs get trapped in it going, "Kill me! Kill me!"

This hilarious interview came to a close with one of the funniest bits Robin has ever done. He starts off talking about the newly-released movie *Independence Day*, telling Al Roker (who had not seen it yet) that an earthling (Jeff Goldblum) was able to crash the alien mothership by downloading a virus into the ship's computer:

And I thought, my God, how can that work? And I realized, it's Windows 95! And there's Bill Gates going, [as Bill Gates] "See, it even hits an alien mothership and crashes *that* system! Hi, I'm Bill Gates, and if you enjoyed Windows 95, what about Doors 96? [as a demon] It allows me access to your soul! Don't be afraid! WORSHIP ME!"

Roker, laughing uproariously, shook Robin's hand and thanked him for the interview, and when they returned to *The Today Show* studio live, Al had but one thing to say: "Wow."

Well put.

# William Shakespeare's Hamlet
## (1997)

*"A hit, a very palpable hit."*

—Osric during the sword fight between
Hamlet and Laertes

Perhaps I have too contemporary a sensibility, or maybe I'm just shallow, but I found sitting through Kenneth Branagh's four hour, full-text version of William Shakespeare's *Hamlet* something of a chore.

It's not that I don't like Shakespeare. I do. One of my most enjoyable evenings ever at the theater was seeing Fred Gwynne (remember Herman Munster?) perform in *Macbeth* at the Shakespeare Theater in Stratford, Connecticut.

And there's no dismissing the brilliance of Shakespeare's writing: It's always a thrill to recognize an incredibly well-known and oft-used line or phrase from Shakespeare and hear it in its original use and in context. *Hamlet* is a veritable cornucopia of such linguistic concoctions. To wit:

- "This above all: to thine own self be true."
- "Something is rotten in the state of Denmark."
- "Murder most foul."
- "Brevity is the soul of wit."
- "Though this be madness, yet there is method in't."
- "There is nothing either good or bad, but thinking makes it so."
- "What a piece of work is a man!"
- "The play's the thing."
- "To be, or not to be: that is the question."
- "To sleep: perchance to dream."
- "What dreams may come."
- "Get thee to a nunnery."
- "The lady doth protest too much, methinks."
- "I must be cruel only to be kind."

- "Alas, poor Yorick."
- "Sweets to the sweet."
- "Good-night, sweet prince."

No, the problem I had with Branagh's colossal production was the way Shakespeare's words were actually *spoken*.

Shakespearean language is syntactically complex and relentlessly imagistic and poetic. It takes time (at least it does for me) for the words to sink in and reveal their full brilliance. Branagh and company spoke with such rapid-fire cadence (shooting for, I'm sure, a true conversational rhythm), I found it a daunting task to keep up with them. Since I am not as intimately familiar with *Hamlet* as Branagh and company obviously are, their explosive diction, combined with the fact that the cast all had thick English accents, made at least half of the dialogue completely unintelligible to me. Branagh, in particular, as Hamlet, had the lion's share of the lines in the play and often spoke so quickly and with such a breathless delivery that at times his words sounded like a foreign language.

That said, there is no denying that Branagh's *Hamlet* is a masterpiece. It is the first film shot in glorious 70 millimeter since Ron Howard's 1992 epic, *Far and Away*, and it is the only full-text version of the play *ever* filmed. (It also reunited Branagh with Robin—they had worked together in 1991 in *Dead Again*.)

The story is familiar: When the play opens, young Hamlet, Prince of Denmark, is shocked to learn that his mother Gertrude has married his father's brother, Claudius, less than a month after the King's untimely death. Hamlet's father appears to him as a ghost and tells him that he was murdered by Claudius and enjoins him to avenge his death. Hamlet's inner torment over whether or not to actually kill his uncle is the emotional engine that drives the play to its tragic and bloody conclusion.

The visuals in *Hamlet* are extraordinary and Alex Thomson's cinematography makes stunning use of the full capabilities of the wider film. The scene that concludes Part 1 (most theaters showed *Hamlet* with a fifteen-minute intermission about two and half hours into the film) is particularly notable. It is the last scene in Act 4, in which Hamlet, after a brief conversation with the traitor Rosencrantz, gives a lengthy speech that begins,

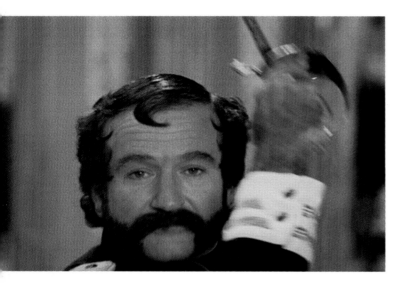

*As Osric, the "referee" at the duel between Hamlet and Laertes. (Photofest)*

"How all occasions do inform against me and spur my dull revenge! What is a man, if his chief good and market of his time be but to sleep and feed?" Hamlet, dressed completely in black from head to toe (he is, after all, still in mourning for his father), delivers this soliloquy on a huge, glaringly white, snow-covered field. As the Prince's words become more impassioned and his anger more intense, the camera pulls back ever so slowly, widening the shot until, at the powerful conclusion of the speech—"O, from this time forth, my thoughts be bloody, or be nothing worth!"—Hamlet is but a black speck in the center of a giant white landscape. Truly a breathtaking moment.

But the reason *Hamlet* is included in this book is, of course, because of Robin Williams's participation in the film.

Robin plays a minor role, that of Osric, a royal courtier who serves as a referee in the fatal sword fight between Hamlet and Laertes. (Robin's Comic Relief cohort, Billy Crystal, also appears in

*Hamlet,* likewise in a minor role. Crystal plays the gravedigger who digs up the skull of Hamlet's jester, Yorick, prompting Hamlet's famous "Alas, poor Yorick" speech.)

Robin first appears about a half hour before the end of the film. (This is the second scene of Act 5 in the text.) He is dressed in a uniform and carries a sword. He has a beard, but no hair on his chin, and his hair is styled in spit curls that drape over his forehead. Robin does not have many lines in this scene (most of which he delivers in a watered-down English accent) and his only other task in the film is to referee the aforementioned deadly duel. Osric is ultimately stabbed in the stomach during the duel and he dies as the English army invades the castle.

Robin gives a good performance, his handful of lines notwithstanding. He does one little bit of physical comedy when he bows to Hamlet and hits a table with his sword, but overall, he plays Osric straight.

Regarding the company of actors in *Hamlet*, it's fair to speculate on whether or not the inclusion of Robin, Billy Crystal, Gerard Depardieu, and Jack Lemmon was "stunt casting" by Branagh.

Admittedly, such high-profile, mostly comedic actors are a bit of an anachronistic distraction, but is that Robin and company's fault?

For many reasons, most of the cast members do not surprise us when we hear them recite Shakespeare's words. But in the case of these other albeit talented, yet somewhat "unexpected" actors, Shakespeare's language sounds strange issuing from their lips. Billy Crystal's performance, in particular, is noticeably jarring: One almost expects Billy to lapse into a bit of comedic schtick as he recites some of the odd dialogue his character speaks.

As for Robin, people laughed out loud when he first made his entrance, even though Osric's lines or actions were not even remotely funny. People laughed at the mere *sight* of Robin Williams. This kind of knee-jerk reaction on the part of an audience to the mere sight of an actor cannot, in the end, be good for the film.

Was Robin (and the others mentioned) miscast? Probably. Perhaps Branagh wanted to attract an audience not normally familiar with Shakespeare. As the excerpt below from the review by critic Roger Ebert notes, though, others felt the same shock upon seeing "non-Shakespearean" actors reciting Shakespeare.

If you are not a Shakespeare fan and are considering seeing *Hamlet* just to see Robin, you might want to rethink that idea and skip it. Robin's tiny role in the flick may not warrant a four-hour (plus intermission) commitment. If you *are* an aficionado of Shakespeare, then you will probably greatly enjoy this elaborate, yet lengthy, *complete* version of what some consider one of Shakespeare's greatest works and what has often been regarded as *Entertainment Weekly* critic Owen Gleiberman described it, "the pivotal text in all of English literature."

## What the Critics Had to Say

**Roger Ebert:** "[Branagh's] *Hamlet* is long but not slow, deep but not difficult, and it vibrates with the relief of actors who have great things to say and the right ways to say them. Robin Williams, Jack Lemmon and Gerard Depardieu are distractions, their performances not overcoming our shocks of recognition." (from his syndicated column, *On Film*).

**Owen Gleiberman:** "Branagh's *Hamlet* is . . . reminiscent of a horror film, but a very different one: It's like an Elizabethan version of *The Shining*. Shot on huge, bold, dazzlingly well-lit sets, it too is about a man led to dementia—and murder—by a ghost preying on his demons. It doesn't help that the performances of Billy Crystal, and Robin Williams are corny and flat-footed." (from *Entertainment Weekly*, January 24, 1997).

**Director:** Kenneth Branagh
**Cast:** Robin Williams (Osric), Kenneth Branagh (Hamlet), Derek Jacobi (Claudius), Julie Christie (Gertrude), Kate Winslet (Ophelia), Richard Briers (Polonius), Charlton Heston (Player King), Nicholas Farrell (Horatio), Michael Maloney (Laertes), Timothy Spall (Rosencrantz), Reece Dinsdale (Guildenstern), Billy Crystal (First Gravedigger), Gerard Depardieu (Reynaldo), Richard Attenborough (English Ambassador), John Gielgud (Priam), Rosemary Harris (Player Queen), Judi Dench (Hecuba), Jack Lemmon (Marcellus), Brian Blessed (Ghost), John Mills (Old Norway)
**Writer:** Adapted by Kenneth Branagh from the play by William Shakespeare
**Music:** Patrick Doyle
Rated PG-13; 238 minutes (plus additional time for intermission)

*Was Robin miscast in* Hamlet*? Decide for yourself, after you watch the nearly four-hour spectacle! (Photofest)*

# Three Unusual Robin Williams Video Appearances

*"This will be one of the strangest documentaries ever made—full of scientific information and the occasional fart joke."*

—*Dolphins* narrator Robin Williams

## In the Wild: Dolphins With Robin Williams

This fascinating, one-hour 1995 documentary was a PBS Home Video production that featured Robin Williams and several dolphin friends of his with whom he chatted, swam, played, and learned from.

*Dolphins* is part of PBS's acclaimed *In the Wild* nature documentary series that takes noted actors into the wild and introduces them to individual animals while filming their reactions and interaction, providing comprehensive information about the species covered in the individual episodes. Other titles in the series include *Gray Whales With Christopher Reeve* and *Pandas With Debra Winger*. Future titles include *Elephants With Goldie Hawn; Tigers With Bob Hoskins; Lions With Anthony Hopkins;* and *Wolves With Timothy Dalton*.

Robin Williams was probably the perfect choice for a documentary about those intelligent, playful creatures called dolphins. Early in the hour, Robin admits to a lifelong fascination with these unique and beautiful sea mammals:

Why am I so fascinated by dolphins? Ever since I was a child I've always wanted to meet one—even though I lived thousands of miles away from an ocean.

*Dolphins* begins with Robin Williams as the host and narrator—on a beach, with Robin winging an introduction:

You know, it's incredibly dangerous work making a documentary. That's why I'm standing here on a glorious beach in the Caribbean, my feet lapped by lukewarm water, with a dog named Flipper. Ironic, isn't it? Today I'm gonna swim with a dolphin, one that's trained to swim with humans for fish. God knows what'll happen. All I know is I'm here and the dolphin's out there, working for scale. I don't know what I'm gonna meet today—possibly, maybe, the dolphin that worked with George C. Scott?

Robin then takes out a windup toy dolphin that he said he brought for his dolphin "date," and immediately transforms the toy into an "urban" dolphin who angrily tells Robin, "Man, that's for the *aquarium* dolphins. The white man has transformed those dolphins into aquarium dolphins working for fish!"

Robin continues musing about dolphins: "I don't know what they're like, except they're smooth, fast, bright, playful. Sounds like Sharon Stone, doesn't it?"

Robin then does a Jack Nicholson dolphin and a Marlon Brando dolphin (specifically the "Brando as Kurtz" character from *Apocalypse Now*), which he concludes with a yuppie dolphin: "Gosh, Tom, you've got to come over here. This salmon is *fabulous!*"

Robin then wades into the ocean up to his waist and two beautiful dolphins playfully swim around him. At one point, Robin touches one of the dolphins in a place he does not want to be touched, and ends up getting rammed in the stomach and nipped. Robin remarks as he walks up onto the beach, "I guess I'm one of the only human beings on the planet who can piss off a dolphin."

The documentary then travels to Hawaii where Robin meets Dr. Ken Martin, a scientist who has been studying bottle-nosed dolphins for years. Martin, who gamely assumes the role of Robin's straight man, lets him speak to the dolphins via an underwater speaker system and, in a very funny segment, Robin does dog, elephant, and sheep noises; a Sammy Davis, Jr. dolphin; a Scottish racing announcer; and Forrest Gump. When he is told that dolphins converse with each other at ten times the speed of human speech, Robin speeds up his words until they are completely unintelligible.

We then move on to an island east of Cuba where Robin meets a dolphin named Jo-Jo who, for years, has deliberately sought out human companionship and actually enjoys our company. (Go figure.)

Robin swims with Jo-Jo and then, with a live cow as a prop, gives an informative mini-lecture on the beach, explaining that dolphins are the distant cousins of cows, but that it has taken 60 million years for evolution to split them into two species.

And then, in one of the most impressive displays of intelligence by the dolphins shown during the documentary, Robin interacts with Elly, a female dolphin who mimics his actions so precisely it's uncanny. We also learn that dolphins are one of the few mammals that have a sense of self-awareness and can recognize images on a TV screen or in pictures.

During the remainder of the documentary, Robin swims with a group of spotted dolphins forty miles out in the ocean, and bonds with an older male named Stubby. While out on the research ship, he also improvises a very funny routine as he's cooking in the kitchen that alone is worth the price of the video. (When he can't open a can of beans with an electric can opener, he cracks up the crew by telling them there's one other way of opening a can: "Erosion.")

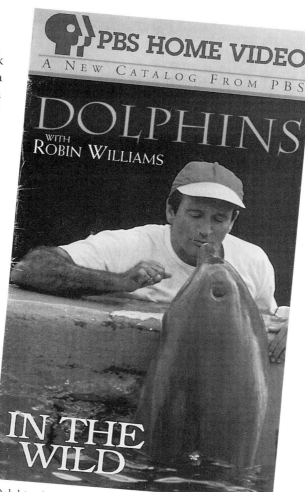

[Dolphins brochure cover] The cover of a recent PBS video catalog advertising Robin's documentary, Dolphins. (PBS)

*Dolphins* is an informative documentary that is also truly entertaining thanks to the talents of Robin Williams. During the hour, he tells us that 250,000 dolphins a year are drowned in tuna drift nets—and we immediately understand that that is 250,000 dolphins too many. Just coming away from this documentary knowing that horrifying statistic makes *Dolphins* worth your while, and a project Robin Williams should be commended for.

**Narrator and Presenter:** Robin Williams
**Director:** Nigel Cole
**Music:** Bruce Smith and Seamus Beaghen
60 minutes

## Can I Do It . . . 'Til I Need Glasses?

**"Question:** *What role or movie of yours would you most like to forget?*

**Robin Williams:** *A movie I did years ago called* Can I Do It . . . 'Til I Need Glasses?"

—Robin Williams, from a live interview on America Online on Monday, August 5, 1996

As the epigraph above indicates, this 1977 film bears the notoriety of being a project Robin Williams obviously wishes he had never done.

So how bad is it? And what exactly does Robin Williams do in *Can I Do It...'Til I Need Glasses?* that he's now so ashamed of?

179

Not much, really.

*Can I Do It . . . 'Til I Need Glasses?* is a vaude-villian-style revue of skits that are nothing more than the acting out (with sets and props) of raunchy sex jokes that have been around forever. You know the type: A woman in a robe comes out of the bathroom with a ragged old bra in her hands and asks her husband if she can have ten dollars so she can go buy a new one. The husband then sarcastically asks, "What do you need a new bra for? You haven't got anything to put in it," to which the wife replies, "You wear a jockstrap, don't you?"

Ba-dum-bump.

*Can I Do It . . . 'Til I Need Glasses?* has loads of nudity, including a few full frontal female nude shots that were probably quite scandalous back in the seventies. (The sensibility of filmgoers today is quite different, of course, and the nudity in *Can I Do It?*—pubic regions notwithstanding—would actually be viewed as rather tame by today's standards.)

*Can I Do It?* was a sequel to the film, *If You Don't Stop It . . . You'll Go Blind* (which some of the characters in *Can I Do It?* go see at a theater), that also consisted of a series of juvenile, risqué sex skits. The title, *Can I Do It . . . 'Til I Need Glasses?*, is the punchline to an old joke about masturbation: A father bursts in on his son, a horny young man who is energetically flogging his baloney. Dad warns him that if he keeps that up, he'll go blind. The son stops in mid-stroke and asks his father if it would be all right, then, if he did it until he needed glasses.

The first skit Robin appears in takes place about thirty-five minutes into the film and is set in a courtroom. Robin is a Los Angeles prosecutor in a divorce case. He is asked to question a woman named Lucretia Frisby, "whose lurid sexual escapades have shocked the nation." After Mrs. Frisby is sworn in, Robin steps up to the witness stand. He has slicked-down hair, tiny round glasses, and a black bowtie. He asks his first and only question:

## PROSECUTOR

Is it true, Mrs. Frisby, that last summer you had sexual intercourse with a red-headed midget during a thunderstorm, while riding nude in the sidecar of a Kawasaki motorcycle, performing an unnatural act on a Polish plumbing contractor, going sixty miles an hour up and down the steps of the Washington Monument, on the night of July fourteenth?

Is that true, Mrs. Frisby? Is that true?

## MRS. FRISBY

Could you repeat that date again, please?

Robin then turns and looks right into the camera with a bemused look of exasperation on his face. That ends this first skit, which runs less than one-and-a-half minutes.

Robin's second appearance in *Can I Do It?* (about fifty minutes into the film) is in a thirty-second skit that takes place in the hallway of an office building. Robin plays a rural hick who is visiting the big city and unluckily comes down with a toothache. He needs a dentist desperately, which we can tell because he has his head and jaw wrapped in a red bandanna. The suspendered country boy waits outside a doctor's office which has a giant tooth hanging over its door. When Dr. Fisher finally arrives, Robin says to him, "Oh, thank goodness you're here, doc. I'm new in this town and this tooth is *killing* me!"

"Your tooth?" the doctor replies. "I'm afraid you've made a mistake, young man. I'm not a dentist, I'm a gynecologist."

The naive hick is surprised and says, "A gynecologist? Whatcha got that big tooth outside your office for?" The impatient doctor testily responds, "Schmuck, what'd you *expect* me to hang up there?!"

A couple of sources consulted for information about this movie revealed that Robin was not in the original film and that his two brief appearances were added when his TV series, *Mork and Mindy*, became a huge hit. This is probably true, since Robin's name appears nowhere in the opening or closing credits and the only way he is acknowledged is after the credits when they flash his picture with the words, "And of course . . . Robin Williams."

Robin probably regrets his appearance in *Can I Do It?* because this movie is technically his feature film debut, and, after suffering through it for over an hour, one can easily understand why he wouldn't want *that* fact on his resume. It is a unique milestone in his career, though, and if you're a real Robin Williams fan, the film is worth a rental just to see what all the hubbub, bub, is about.

**Director:** I. Robert Levy
**Cast:** Robin Williams, Roger Behr, Debra Klose,

Moose Carlson, Walter Olkewicz
**Writers:** Mike Callie and Mike Price
**Music:** Bob Jung
Rated R; 72 minutes

# Dear America: Letters Home From Vietnam

*"Dear Bill,*

*Today is February 13, 1984. I came to this black wall again to see and touch your name, William R. Stocks, and as I do I wonder if anyone ever stops to realize that next to your name, on this black wall, is your mother's heart."*

—An excerpt from a mother's letter to her dead son, read by Ellen Burstyn, in *Dear America.*

This acclaimed 1987 documentary featured film footage and photographs of the Vietname War accompanied by voice-over readings of actual soldiers' letters home from Vietnam. The letters were read by many Hollywood celebrities, including Robin Williams.

This moving and powerful film was originally produced for HBO and is now available on video. It also enjoyed a short theatrical release before it came out on video.

In addition to Robin Williams, *Dear America* boasts a veritable "Who's Who" of big-time stars, including Robert De Niro, Michael J. Fox, Ellen Burstyn, Kathleen Turner, Sean Penn, Tom Berenger, Brian Dennehy, Martin Sheen, Charlie Sheen, Matt Dillon, Kevin Dillon, and Howard Rollins, Jr.

The film also has a kick-ass sound track, ranging from 1960s classics (The Beach Boys, Motown favorites, etc.) to Bruce Springsteen's "Born in the USA," (which comes across as a heartwrenching lament when it is heard at the end of the film over footage of the long black Vietnam War Memorial in Washington).

*Dear America: Letters Home From Vietnam* was based on the book by the same name by Bernard Edelman and is one of those genuinely unique collaborative artistic mélanges that informs, educates, and enlightens while also hitting the viewer at an emotional level that puts an entire subject into stark perspective.

*Dear America* was first aired on HBO back in 1987 and was poignant and gripping. Director Bill Couturie and his team culled through close to four hundred *miles* of news footage to find just the right snippets of film to accompany each letter, lending a fidelity to the portrayal of what happened in Vietnam that is startling and palpable.

Couturie and company actually watched all of the 926 hours of film shot in Vietnam by NBC-TV in the years 1967 through 1969. He was granted unprecedented access to previously classified Department of Defense footage. In addition to these news and government sources, Couturie reviewed hours and hours of "home movie" footage shot by the Vietnam soldiers themselves.

Robin Williams is just one of many Hollywood luminaries who participated in this project, one of many he's done over the past twenty years; but, in the end, *Dear America* could be one of the most important films he has ever made.

## What the Critics Had to Say

**Roger Ebert:** "Choose any film as the best movie ever made about Vietnam, and this is the other half of the same double feature. Francois Truffaut once wrote that it was impossible to make an 'anti-war film,' because any war film, no matter what its message, was sure to be exhilarating. He did not live to see this film." (From his *Movie Home Companion*, 1991 edition)

**Director:** Bill Couturie
**Writer:** Richard Dewhurst and Bill Couturie
**Music:** Todd Boekelheide
Rated PG-13; 86 minutes

*The three stars and guiding lights of Comic Relief, seen backstage at the 1991 show (clockwise): Billy Crystal, Robin Williams, and Whoopi Goldberg. (Photofest)*

# Chapter 5
# *Comic Relief*

*"It's no joke. 1-800-528-1000."*

R obin Williams is one of the most philanthropic artists working today and nowhere is this more evident than in his unstinting support for and involvement in Comic Relief.

This feature looks at the first decade of Comic Relief's existence and highlights the HBO 10th Anniversary Special, and the Comic Relief book.

This section also provides a behind-the-scenes look at Robin during his preparation for a skit on one of the fund-raisers. (A hint: Look for the dick joke.)

## Ten Years and $35 Million: Robin, Whoopi, and Billy Help the Homeless

*"The boys have sort of nurtured me along, and now, I've finally come into my own with them. They're a tough duo. They are so fast. It took me until three or four years ago to just bust in. They were always really good to me, encouraging me, going, Pow! you're on. I always considered myself the Vanna White of Comic Relief, because I do all the serious stuff—the information, the phone numbers. I finally busted loose with them. Now we run wild. These boys are always talking about their genitalia, and I finally said, "Look. Explain this to me. What is it about your dick? Why are we talking about it, yet again?"*

—Whoopi Goldberg, talking about what it's like to work with Robin Williams and Billy Crystal on Comic Relief (*Playboy*, January 1997)

C omic Relief began in 1986 as a way for comedians en masse to help the homeless. The luminaries of show business immediately rallied around this cause and over its first ten years, more than $35 million was raised and distributed to a number of homeless relief causes.

The three "anchors" of every one of the seven

HBO Comic Relief benefit shows have been Robin Williams, Whoopi Goldberg, and Billy Crystal.

These three mega-stars do the introductions during the shows, plus perform both individually and as a team. Some of the funniest moments on the Comic Relief shows have been when these three stars would just stand on stage and talk to the audience at home and in the theater. Sure, they each had a script to follow but, as you can imagine, it wouldn't take long before Robin or Billy would go off and improvise an entire comic routine, while Whoopi, as the epigraph to this chapter reveals, would try hard to keep up with those two lightning-fast comic geniuses.

In one routine Robin and Billy did (it was repeated on the Comic Relief 10th Anniversary Special), Robin got behind Billy and thrust one arm through his legs and made a fist, making Billy look like he was sporting the biggest—and ugliest!—erection anyone could imagine.

The list of the 235 entertainment luminaries who participated in Comic Relief over the ten years of the fund-raiser reads like a "Who's Who of Show Business," including sports figures (Kareem Abdul-Jabbar); politicians (David Dinkins); singers (Natalie Cole); dancers (The Rockettes); music

acts (Heavy D & the Boyz); cartoon characters (The Simpsons); as well as dozens of comedians and actors, and also the unclassifiable (Larry "Bud" Melman).

By 1996, there had been seven Comic Relief fund-raisers. Here is a rundown of the totals raised at each:

| 1986 | Comic Relief I | $2.5 million |
| 1987 | Comic Relief II | $2.5 million |
| 1989 | Comic Relief III | $5 million |
| 1990 | Comic Relief IV | $7 million |
| 1992 | Comic Relief V | $6.7 million |
| 1994 | Comic Relief VI | $7.8 million |
| 1995 | Comic Relief VII | $5 million |

The phone number for pledges to Comic Relief is 1-800-528-1000. It's no joke.

# A Look at the *Comic Relief* Book and 10th Anniversary HBO Special

*"Compared to the problem, [Comic Relief] is a flea fart in a hurricane."*
—Robin Williams

Comic Relief celebrated ten years of helping the homeless in two ways—with a book and a TV special.

The $22 hardcover book, titled simply *Comic Relief*, was edited by Todd Gold and published by Avon.

The HBO TV special was a one-hour clip-filled extravaganza hosted by Robin, Whoopi Goldberg, and Billy Crystal.

Here is a look at each.

## Comic Relief

This 238-page hardcover was subtitled "The Best of Comedy for the Best of Causes" and consisted of transcripts of performances from ten years of Comic Relief broadcasts. Scattered throughout were stories of the homeless who have been helped by the project, as well as some background on the problem of homelessness in the United States.

In addition to Robin, Billy, and Whoopi, the cast of comedic luminaries who participated in the book reads like a contemporary Who's Who of Yuks:

- Gary Shandling
- Elayne Boosler
- Louie Anderson
- Paula Poundstone
- Bill Maher
- Bob Saget
- Steven Wright
- Paul Rodriquez
- Jake Johannsen
- Rita Rudner
- Dennis Miller

- Richard Jeni
- Richard Belzer & "Weird" Al Yankovich
- Caroline Rhea
- Bob "Bobcat" Goldthwait
- Judy Gold
- Richard Lewis
- Sinbad

Each comedian had a chapter in the book and the excerpts chosen included some *very* funny routines, jokes, one-liners, and stories.

A joke from Robin's routine went: "What's so offensive about a movie like *The Last Temptation of Christ?* Nothing to me. Except that Jesus is always played by a guy who looks like Ted Nugent."

The *Comic Relief* book is available in bookstores and a portion of the proceeds goes to Comic Relief.

## The *Comic Relief* 10th Anniversary Special on HBO

This one-hour special was hosted by Robin, Billy, and Whoopi and consisted of clips from the seven Comic Relief shows as well as backstage footage of the stars who have participated in the fund-raiser over the years. In the tradition of Comic Relief, the hilarity in this special would occasionally be put on pause while a film clip about the homeless problem was shown.

The special began with clips of the openings from all seven Comic Relief programs. On Comic Relief I, Robin, Billy, and Whoopi wore red sweatshirts emblazoned with the Comic Relief logo; on II, they did a skit in which the homeless burst into song; on III, they were dressed in black tie and sang a song which included the lyrics, "Don't be a greedy bastard/Those yuppies days are over and gone"; on IV, they danced with the Rockettes; on V, they were rappers; on VI, they opened the show with an old-fashioned, roof-raising revival meeting; and on VII, the most recent Comic Relief, they performed a song-and-dance number that looked like it came straight out of one of those 1940s war musicals.

Robin, Billy, and Whoopi, sitting in director chairs, then introduced the show. Robin cracked a small joke about how they were all twelve years old

when they started doing Comic Relief ten years ago, and then the clipfest began.

Of the impressive list of luminaries who have participated in Comic Relief over the past decade, young and old were equally represented, and included Jon Lovitz; Carl Reiner and his son, Rob Reiner; Paul Reiser; Arsenio Hall; Michael Keaton; Jerry Lewis; Harry Anderson; Garry Shandling; Dennis Miller; Jim Carrey; Pee Wee Herman; Don Rickles; Robert Klein; Joan Rivers; Faye Dunaway; Sharon Stone; Roseanne; Tom Arnold; Chris Rock; Elayne Boosler; Richard Lewis; Gilda Radner; Brett Butler; Bob Saget; Howie Mandel; Steven Wright; Kathy Bates; Jay Leno; the casts of *Your Show of Shows, The Dick Van Dyke Show, Golden Girls, The Honeymooners,* and *The Steve Allen Show*; Dana Carvey; Louie Anderson; George Foreman; Bobcat Goldthwait; Sinbad; Martin Short; Harold Ramis; Catherine O'Hara; John Candy; Eugene Levy; George Carlin; and Paula Poundstone.

The show included clips of performances and skits, and the funniest were: Bobcat Goldthwait actually juicing a squid and drinking it; Chris Rock doing his "Colin Powell/Isn't he well-spoken?" bit; and Dana Carvey doing his "Chopping Broccoli" ballad at the piano.

HBO also showed a funny clip of Robin and Billy doing their gay dance routine from the *Betty and Her Boys* skit, sans Betty.

The show concluded with Robin, Billy, and Whoopi back in their directors chairs, reminiscing about the past ten years. It ended on a funny note when Robin started singing "Try To Remember"— but couldn't remember the words.

Comic Relief is a wonderful cause that does a lot of good for a lot of people. Robin Williams has been an integral part of the program since its genesis and deserves kudos for his unconditional support.

Call 1-800-528-1000 and make a pledge. It'll do your heart good.

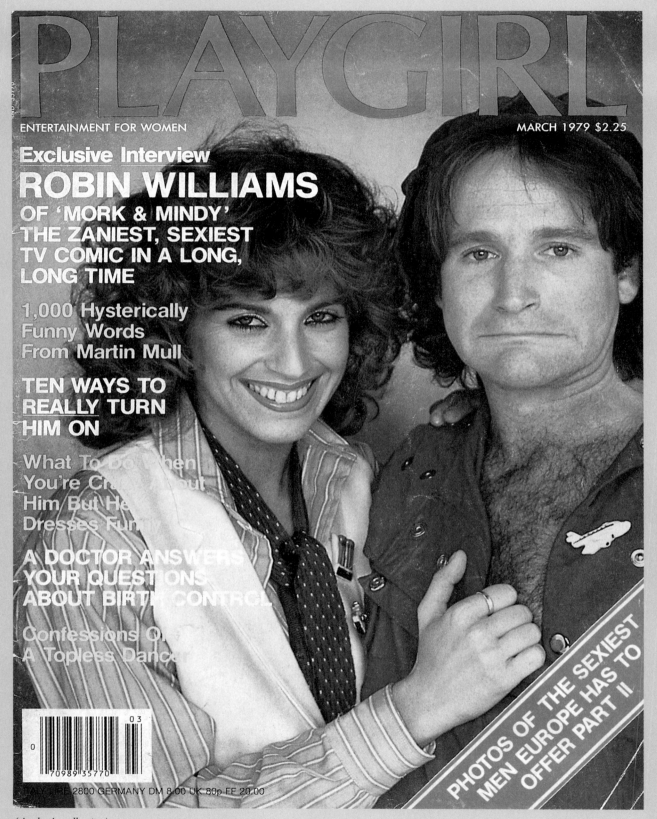

# PLAYGIRL

ENTERTAINMENT FOR WOMEN

MARCH 1979 $2.25

**Exclusive Interview**
## ROBIN WILLIAMS
OF 'MORK & MINDY'
THE ZANIEST, SEXIEST
TV COMIC IN A LONG,
LONG TIME

**1,000 Hysterically
Funny Words
From Martin Mull**

**TEN WAYS TO
REALLY TURN
HIM ON**

What To Do When
You're Crazy About
Him But He
Dresses Funny

**A DOCTOR ANSWERS
YOUR QUESTIONS
ABOUT BIRTH CONTROL**

Confessions Of
A Topless Dancer

PHOTOS OF THE SEXIEST
MEN EUROPE HAS TO
OFFER PART II

0 70989 35770    03

ITALY LIRE 2800 GERMANY DM 8.00 UK 80p FF 20.00

(Author's collection)

# Chapter 6
## Robin Speaks

*"It's like two lepers doing a tango"*

—Robin's Philosophy of the Interview

This section looks at a couple of Robin's more unusual interviews.

Appropriately (for a guy who loves dick jokes more than life itself) the first talk took place in that homage to Mr. Happy himself, *Playgirl* magazine, back when Robin was still married to Valerie Velardi and *Mork and Mindy* was a huge hit.

The second interview is at the other end of his career—as well as being at the other end of the publishing spectrum: Robin's live interactive chat on America Online.

The AOL talk is notable for the fact that Robin was thrown one of the questions he claims he is asked most often, "Did you ever do Pam Dawber?" The undeniably gallant Mr. Williams ignored the question and wisely moved on.

## Robin Williams's 1979 *Playgirl* Interview

*"I love to see him work. I think it's a gift, and so does he. If I knew what it was, I'd package it."*

—Robin's first wife, Valerie Velardi, talking about her husband in 1979

The March 1979 *Playgirl* interview ran at a time when Robin was one of the hottest stars on television, but still had not made the crossover into feature films.

The cover headline read:

Exclusive Interview
ROBIN WILLIAMS
OF *MORK AND MINDY*
THE ZANIEST, SEXIEST
TV COMIC IN A LONG, LONG TIME

The cover of the magazine featured a photograph of Robin and his then-wife, dancer Valerie Velardi. Robin's profile was sandwiched between articles like "I Was a Topless Dancer . . . and I Loved It!" and photo spreads of completely nude men proudly displaying their own Mr. Happys. Inside this issue, the subtitle of this *Playgirl* profile was as flattering to Robin as the cover blurb: "Comedy's Great WASP Hope is a bratty imp of a sex symbol known to millions as space alien Mork from Ork."

Writer Richard J. Pietschmann spent time with Robin and Valerie on the *Mork and Mindy* set at Paramount Studios and concentrated on filling in the blanks on Robin's upbringing and start in show business. In addition to a full-page photo of Robin and Valerie that led off the piece, there were four color photos accompanying the profile. In one Robin and Valerie were dancing; in another, Valerie is opening her jacket (she's not wearing anything underneath) and flashing a wide-eyed, gape-jawed Robin her left breast; and in the other two, Robin is, appropriately, playing with his crotch.

The profile begins, "Comedy's newest star is like a kid in a toy shop." There is quite a bit of interesting information in this look at TV's latest (at the time) phenomenon, and here is a sampling of highlights from this entertaining interview:

- Robin was twenty-six at the time of this interview and was just beginning to formulate the *Legend of Robin* that would become the standard biographical rendering of his early life. The profile tells us that "As a child, he was surrounded by thousand of miniature soldiers and other toys and equipped with a vivid imagination." Almost two decades later, Robin would still be talking about those miniature soldiers in interviews, most recently on the Donahue show plugging *Mrs. Doubtfire*. He also expounded on this diminutive army of his in a 1982 interview with *Playboy*:

PLAYBOY: Growing up alone in a 30-room house sounds as if it must have made for a very lonely childhood. Did it?

ROBIN WILLIAMS: Yes, but I got started kind of early in finding stuff to do. . . . Pretty early on, I banished myself to the attic, where I had a huge army of toy soldiers. I must have had about 10,000 of them, and I had them separated by periods in boxes. I'd have time-machine battles, with Confederate soldiers fighting GIs with automatic weapons and knights fighting Nazis.

PB: That doesn't seem quite fair to the knights.

RW: We didn't care about fair; we needed a warm-water port. I'd throw all those soldiers into battle and build castles in the attic, and I always made Carl, my turtle, the king. Unfortunately, one day I flushed Carl down the toilet, because I wanted him to be free. I told Mother, "I let Carl go. He's happy now." Yeah, it was real lonely after Carl left.

- Robin attributes his family's move to San Francisco when he was a teen as the pivotal event that shaped his comedy: "It all came out when we moved to California; that kind of let it all out. It was just an incredibly loose time at the end of 1969. Everyone was going [buzzer sound], 'Let's go, Tommy, let's drop acid and go to history class.'"

- Robin liked working on *Mork and Mindy* because of the improvisational freedom he was given: "I just love to improvise and play, that's why *Mork and Mindy* is so much fun," he said. "It's infectious. If you're having a good time playing, then everybody will enjoy themselves."

- Amazingly, Robin made a habit of repeatedly grabbing women's butts and squeezing their breasts on the set, and not one word was ever said about sexual harassment. Instead, the women would often cuddle the irrepressible sex maniac.

- Robin described his "sexual awakening" as looking down at his crotch one day and asking, "Hey! What's that?"

- After a health scare that Valerie nursed him through, Robin turned to vitamins, health shakes, and a chiropractor.

- Robin described himself as a "performance junkie." He talked about his penchant for dropping in at comedy clubs and doing a set unannounced. "I'm always looking for a club to go to, and in some strange way performing at the clubs is relaxing. Our honeymoon was the only time I didn't perform, and then I was looking for microphones and making them out of coconuts."

- While attending Julliard, Robin would often perform mime in front of the Metropolitan Museum of Art as a way of helping support himself. In this interview, he revealed that during a 1979 trip to New York, he was astonished to see a young mime doing exactly the same thing in exactly the same place as he had done years earlier. Robin spontaneously jumped in and did a forty-five-minute comic improvisation with the guy. Eventually there was a crowd of four hundred delighted people watching this hilarious, *free* performance.

▨ Robin took up comedy in 1975. Prior to that, he wanted to be an actor. "I love films, I've always loved going to them, and I want to be in them real bad," he said.

▨ Robin admitted that he had made it in show business fairly quickly ("I've paid *some* dues, but maybe I didn't suffer too heavily") and described his ambition as "boundless."

▨ Robin told Pietschmann that his dream someday was to make "a fine comedy film, a classic." He cited Woody Allen's work as the type of movie he was talking about but admitted that Jonathan Winters was his comic idol, describing Winters as "the Buddha of comedy." Now, almost twenty years and thirty films later, it seems that Robin achieved his goal of making not just one, but several comedy classics.

▨ During this period, one of Robin's best lines about growing up in white middle-class suburbia was, "I didn't have my first Porsche until I was sixteen."

▨ Regarding his instantaneous success on television, Robin told Pietschmann, "I can't believe it. I can't imagine thirty million people watching me every week."

The interview ended when Valerie bounded into Robin's trailer and saw him collapsed in exhaustion on the sofa. "Look at you!" she scolded. "Your adrenal glands are fucked!"

# Robin in Cyberspace: The America Online Interview

Robin Williams did a live online interview on America Online on Monday, August 5, 1996 from 3:00 to 4:00 P.M. EST to promote the theatrical release of *Jack* and the video release of *Aladdin and the King of Thieves*.

For those of you who have never participated in an online chat, essentially the "guest" sits in a room with the "host," who types the guest's answers to submitted questions from people who are logged on to the service and participating in the interview in realtime. Hundreds of questions are sent to the host's computer and the host is responsible for picking and choosing what to ask the guest.

Robin's interview consisted of twenty-four selected questions and was typical of the kind of participation these interviews generate. Some of the questions were reasonable and intelligent (Which role of yours has brought about the greatest personal growth in you?—*Awakenings*), while some were rude, crude, and lewd (Did you ever do Pam Dawber?—no answer).

Here is a rundown of what Robin revealed in this cyberspace chat:

▨ He had been in comedy since birth and he needed it to breast-feed.

▨ He was trying to find something in which he and Jonathan Winters could work together.

▨ He revealed that the worst part of being famous is doing interviews.

▨ There is absolutely no chance of a *Mork and Mindy* reunion movie. By the way, Robin has been fairly consistent on his feelings about this. Here's what he said in a 1982 interview with *Playboy* about resurrecting Mork:

PLAYBOY: What happens to Mork now? Will we ever see him again?

ROBIN WILLIAMS: No, I don't think so. It was wonderful while it lasted, but I wouldn't want to bring the character back. When something like that ends, you just say thank you and put it away. In Mork's case, he ended with a kind of "videonasia." I carefully lowered the volume on my TV set, let loose the vertical hold, put down the rabbit ears and let him go gently into that last good night.

▨ He would not reveal a favorite actor or actress

because "The list is too long to start."

- When asked if he liked Woody Allen's work, he didn't respond, which is odd, considering that Robin subsequently worked with Woody in *Deconstructing Harry*, and in 1979, cited the brilliance of Woody's work as something he himself aspired to. (Could have been a transmission problem.)

- Robin admitted that he would love to play a villain in a *Star Trek* movie—"Some sort of lizard creature named Art Gecko."

- He said that kids responded to him mostly as either Mrs. Doubtfire, the Genie, or Peter Pan.

- He has no plans to ever do another TV sitcom.

- His favorite club to perform in is the Other Cafe in San Francisco.

Robin wound up the interview using a joke he would also use on *The Today Show:* That the virus that crashed the alien mothership in *Independence Day* was Windows 95—even though Jeff Goldblum's computer was a Mac!

The interview ended with this final risqué gag: "Remember why the typing is not so good in the adult chat rooms: Because it is very difficult to type with one hand!"

# Chapter 7

# The Robin Williams Movie Titles Word Search Puzzle

Find the titles of Robin's movies in this puzzle. Words can be found forwards, backwards, or diagonally. First, fill in the blanks in the following clues and then find the words in the puzzle.

Robin played the Genie in _____
Robin played a bearded doctor in _____
The Adventures of _____ Munchausen
Robin played a gay nightclub owner in The _____
Robin was a car salesman in _____ Man
_____ Paradise
Robin played a homeless visionary in The _____ King
The World According to _____
Robin was Peter Pan in _____
Robin played five different characters in Being _____
Robin was a ten-year-old forty-year-old in _____
Robin was trapped in a jungle in _____
_____ on the Hudson
_____ Months
Dead _____ Society
Robin was _____, the Sailor Man
Robin played a mime in _____ the Clown
Robin costarred with Walter Matthau in The _____
Robin was a toy designer in _____
Good Morning, _____

Answers on page 196.

```
C P P F A P J W G B Q P D D H
A I O O I W A S A L H Z D U H
D X J E P S A L L S E V M J C
I A U T T E H K J G N A S L H
L Y M O H S Y E E E N U U O B
L I A Y T C A E R N R B O W V
A Y N S H A T C N V I K A U P
C W J U I A G I I B M N U G X
N N I R E R N V I O B P G X N
A I O C U E O R S S D A R S M
N D C F P R D C E B Z K R A O
E D D I S C O K M T E H C O G
T A S V A W A X H G O H X A N
H L J G X H Z Q Z Q O L I G J
A A E A S V I E T N A M C Q O
```

## Robin Williams Movies, TV Appearances, and Concerts Available on Video

*The Adventures of Baron Munchausen* (1989) Columbia Tristar Home Video: VHS, Beta, LV, 8 mm.

*Alladin* (1992) Walt Disney Home Video: VHS, Beta, LV.

*Aladdin and the King of Thieves* (1996) Walt Disney Home Video: VHS, Beta, LV.

*Awakenings* (1990) Columbia Tristar Home Video: VHS, Beta, LV, 8 mm.

*Being Human* (1994) Warner Home Video: VHS, LV.

*The Best of Comic Relief* (1986) HBO Home Video: VHS, Beta.

*The Best of Times* (1986) New Line Home Video: VHS, Beta, LV, 8 mm.

*The Birdcage* (1995) MGM/UA Home Entertainment: VHS.

*Cadillac Man* (1990) Orion Home Video: VHS, Beta, LV.

*Can I Do It . . . 'Til I Need Glasses?* (1977) Media Home Entertainment: VHS, Beta.

*Club Paradise* (1986) Warner Home Video: VHS, Beta, LV.

*Dead Again* (1991) Paramount Home Video: VHS, LV.

*Dead Poets Society* (1989) Buena Vista Home Video: VHS, Beta, LV, 8 mm.

*Dear America: Letters Home From Vietnam* (1988) HBO Home Video: VHS, Beta.

*Dolphins With Robin Williams: In the Wild* (1995) Turner Home Entertainment/PBS Home Video: VHS.

*An Evening With Robin Williams* (1983) Paramount Home Video: VHS, Beta, LV.

*FernGully: The Last Rainforest* (1992) FoxVideo: VHS.

*The Fisher King* (1991) Columbia Tristar Home Video: VHS, Beta, LV, 8 mm.

*Good Morning, Vietnam* (1987) Buena Vista Home Video: VHS, Beta, LV, 8 mm.

*Hook* (1991) Columbia Tristar Home Video: VHS, Beta, LV, 8 mm.

*Jack* (1996) Buena Vista Home Video: VHS, LV.

*Jumanji* (1995) Columbia Tristar Home Video: VHS, LV.

*Mork and Mindy* (1978–1982, selected episodes) Paramount Home Video: VHS.

*Moscow on the Hudson* (1984) Columbia Tristar Home Video: VHS, Beta, LV, 8 mm.

*Mrs. Doubtfire* (1993) FoxVideo: VHS, LV.

*Nine Months* (1995) 20th Century Fox: VHS, LV.

*Popeye* (1980) Paramount Home Video: VHS, Beta, LV.

*Seize the Day* (1986) Monterey Home Video: VHS, Beta, LV.

*Shakes the Clown* (1992) Columbia Tristar Home Video: VHS, LV.

*The Survivors* (1983) Columbia Tristar Home Video: VHS, Beta, LV.

*The Tale of the Frog Prince* (1983) FoxVideo: VHS, Beta, LV.

*To Wong Foo, Thanks for Everything, Julie Newmar* (1995) MCA/Universal Home Video: VHS, LV.

*Toys* (1992) FoxVideo: VHS.

*The World According to Garp* (1982) Warner Home Video: VHS, Beta, LV.

# Appendix B

## Robin on the Net

For all you Robin Williams fans with Internet access, there are Web sites and Internet newsgroups out there that might interest you.

■ Check out http://zimmer.csufresno.edu/~robb/Robin.html for Robin Williams info and graphics.

■ Also, you will find a Web page for virtually every movie Robin has ever made. Just use Yahoo, Alta Vista, Hot Bot, Excite, or some other search engine and search for the movies by name.

■ In addition to the Web, there are also several celebrity-themed newsgroups on the Internet that often include postings containing information about Robin and his films.

■ Since the newsgroup universe is constantly changing (and groups start up, disband, and change their names frequently) we suggest you try searching the newsgroups for any groups with the words "showbiz," "celebrity," "movies," or "comedy" in their titles. Subscribe to some of these, browse their postings a few times a week and you will likely find facts and features about Robin and his movies that will interest you.

■ So far there is no *Mork and Mindy* newsgroup or Web site, although there *are* several TV show newsgroups that often include stuff about sixties and seventies sitcoms.

Happy surfing!

# Word Search
## Solution

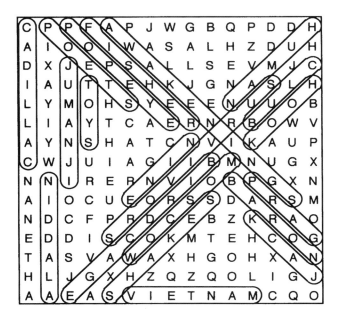

| ALADDIN | GARP | POETS |
|---------|------|-------|
| AWAKENINGS | HOOK | POPEYE |
| BARON | HUMAN | SHAKES |
| BIRDCAGE | JACK | SURVIVORS |
| CADILLAC | JUMANJI | TOYS |
| CLUB | MOSCOW | VIETNAM |
| FISHER | NINE | |

# About the Author

STEPHEN J. SPIGNESI specializes in popular culture subjects, including television, film, contemporary fiction, and historical biography.

He has written several authorized entertainment books and has worked with Stephen King, Turner Entertainment, the Margaret Mitchell Estate, Andy Griffith, Viacom, and other entertainment industry personalities and entities on a wide range of projects. Mr. Spignesi has also contributed essays, chapters, articles, and introductions to a wide range of books.

In addition to writing, Mr. Spignesi also lectures on a variety of popular culture subjects; has taught courses on writing and publishing; and is the founder and Editor-in-Chief of the small press publishing company, The Stephen John Press. He is a graduate of the University of New Haven, and lives in New Haven with his wife, Pam.